SIMPLY FRENCH

JAMIN

JOEL ROBUCHON

ALSO BY

JOËL ROBUCHON

· · · · · · · · · · · · · · · · ·

Ma Cuisine Pour Vous (1986)

ALSO BY

PATRICIA WELLS

· · · · · · · · · · · · · · · · ·

The Food Lover's Guide to Paris (1984, 1988)
The Food Lover's Guide to France (1987)
Bistro Cooking (1989)

SIMPLY FRENCH

PATRICIA WELLS

....

presents the cuisine of

....

JOËL ROBUCHON

Photographs by Steven Rothfeld
Jacket photographs by Robert Fréson

William Morrow and Company, Inc.
New York

Library of Congress Cataloging-in-Publication Data

Wells, Patricia.
    Simply French: Patricia Wells presents the cuisine of Jöel Robuchon
    p.   cm.
    ISBN 0-688-14356-3
    1. Cookery, French. I. Title.
TX719.W43 1991
641.5944—dc20   91-463
CIP

Printed in the United States of America

First Paperback Edition

3 4 5 6 7 8 9 10

Book design by Barbara M. Bachman

Once more, for Walter.
You just keep on making our mutual dreams come true.

ACKNOWLEDGMENTS

. . . .

There are many people who will be relieved to see this book finally reach its destination, among them the staff at Jamin. For years they kept inquiring, "Is the book done yet?" I wasn't sure whether the question was asked out of curiosity or sheer desire to have us out from underfoot! The kitchen and dining room staff deserve a group medal for their remarkable patience. I am particularly grateful to chefs Benoit Guichard and Philippe Gobet, who allowed me to stand at their sides in the kitchen for hours on end as I pestered them with questions and begged them to pause, again and again, for step-by-step photographs. Thank you, Guy and Monique Ducrust, for honoring the French translation with such meticulous care, and additional thanks to Antoine Hernandez, Jamin's sommelier, for expertly pairing wines with each recipe. I am particularly appreciative of the dining room staff, especially Jean-Jacques Caimant, Gonzagues Charpentier, and André Wawrzyniak. They were always smiling, ever cooperative, particularly on the days photographer Steven Rothfeld and I stretched their patience to the limit, and beyond.

Outside the boundaries of the restaurant, I want to thank Laura Washburn, who spent endless hours translating, juggling computer files, style and conversion sheets, who helped decipher recipes, then talked some sense into them in the kitchen. And, thank you, Laura, for your conscientious copyediting. Thanks to Sylvie Girard for her impeccable translations, as well as attentive editing.

The book could not exist in its present form without the help of colleagues, friends, and family, who enthusiastically tested each and every recipe, in France and in the United States: Thank you to Judy Jones, Susan Herrmann Loomis, Betsy Bernardaud, and Lydie Marshall. I also want to acknowledge my good friend Maggie Shapiro, who cheerfully edited the manuscript and asked all the right questions. Thanks as well to Michel Bernardaud from Limoges for allowing us to "go shopping" for china props in his Paris boutique.

I am particularly grateful to Janine Robuchon for her companionship and unselfish understanding throughout the years we worked on the book. And for Steven Rothfeld a big hug for transforming each photo session into a musical day filled with special friendship. Thank you, Mister Stevens, for your beautiful photographs.

In New York, I want to thank my agent, Susan Lescher, for her empathy, nurturing, and understanding during difficult times. I am eternally grateful to my editor, Maria Guarnaschelli, for her unbounded enthusiasm, professionalism, and support for the project from the very beginning. And thank you, Maria, for letting me have my way on the design.

So many people improved this book by their very presence, and I want to acknowledge Robert Freson for his jacket photograph, Barbara M. Bachman for her elegant design, Deborah Weiss Geline and Katherine Ness for their attentive and constructive copyediting, and Karen Lumley for a smooth journey through the production line.

Of course, the person who made it all happen from the start is Joël Robuchon: He taught me invaluable lessons in life that will sustain me far beyond the confines of the kitchen.

There is one man who, even during the most mercurial of moments, inspired a cool and steady course. That's my dear and wonderful partner in life, Walter Newton Wells, to whom there is no equal. I couldn't have done it without you.

Patricia Wells
PARIS, FRANCE

CONTENTS

THE CUISINE OF JOËL ROBUCHON

. . . .

S everal times every day, food offers each of us the promise of short-term happiness. As a source of satisfaction, joy, discovery, and renewal, few daily rituals have such extraordinary potential as the act of preparing and sharing a good meal.

The key word, of course, is "good"—and good cooking is no accident. But neither is it impossibly difficult. That realization has been reinforced in a very special way over the past few years as I worked on this book with Joël Robuchon, the best chef working in France today.

I am not sure how and when the idea for this collaboration came about. It seemed to grow naturally, out of mutual professional respect and a vision of food that I shared with Robuchon, chef and owner of the Parisian restaurant Jamin.

Late at night, after all the other clients had left the restaurant, Robuchon and I would sit and talk, often about the memorable dishes he and his staff had just prepared, or simply about the pleasures that fresh, natural ingredients can provide. Always there was talk of the celebratory nature of food, the realization that cooking is in fact one of the purest human acts of generosity and love.

Joël Robuchon in the Jamin kitchen, preparing Ivory Turbans of Shrimp and Pasta

In the beginning, I embraced the project out of selfishness: Who would not want to study with such a master? I also saw it as the ultimate challenge for someone who is both a food journalist and a dedicated home cook. As a result of our collaboration, I now divide my life as a cook into two distinct periods: Before Robuchon and After

Longtime friends and colleagues, Charles Barrier of Tours and Chef Robuchon share a meal.

Robuchon. For this chef—modest and self-effacing, reflective, intuitive, and driven—has changed forever the way I approach even the most basic tasks in my kitchen.

We worked together for nearly four years, a few hours or a few days here and there. We worked most often in the kitchens at Jamin. But sometimes with our spouses we would enjoy weekend gatherings at my country house in Provence. Joël is playful and a natural tease; not a large man, he seems at times almost pixie-like and elfin. The weekends spent with him and Janine were memorable for their celebration of all that is

simple, natural, and spontaneous about good times spent cooking with friends. We also traveled to Brittany and the Auvergne, to Robuchon's wine cellars in the Paris suburb of Bougival, and to his favored native region of the Poitou, sharing that mutual excitement about food and its wonders.

My original goal was simply to "translate" his magical Michelin three-star cuisine, bringing it within reach of the home cook who works without benefit of a brigade of sous-chefs. I had already spent enough time in his kitchens to know that Robuchon was obsessed with perfection. I also knew that he was a maniac for detail, and insisted that all around him share a devotion for the smallest of things. I secretly hoped those traits would rub off and that my cooking would take on new dimensions. Little did I know.

Although I assumed the project would expand my culinary repertoire and probably refine some of my cooking-class methods and self-taught techniques, I never anticipated how thoroughly the experience would affect me as a cook—the way I shop and the way I season food, the way I bake and roast, the rhythm of a menu, the way I cut and dice and chop, the way I approach a new recipe, my orderliness in the kitchen and my attention to detail.

From learning exactly when to season roast poultry or meat (immediately before cooking and again immediately afterward) to understanding that very finely minced ingredients release more flavors than coarsely chopped ones, working with Robuchon has been an adventure in culinary revelation.

Much of Robuchon's success as a chef can be credited to his ability to distill the very essence of an ingredient, creating a personalized style of cuisine marked by flavors that are intense, pure, and distinctive.

Robuchon taught me that the greatness of a cook can be measured by one's ability to work magic with the simplest of ingredients. He is, after all, the man who won the

Photograph above: Joël Robuchon at the dramatic oceanside harbor in Le Point du Raz in Brittany

hearts and palates of a gastronomically demanding nation with a memorable tossed green salad and bowls of heavenly mashed potatoes.

Robuchon's teachings drive home the point that although perfection may be unattainable, that's no excuse for not seeking it in the kitchen. Following his recipe for a green salad will take more time than just rinsing off a head of lettuce and breaking it into bite-size pieces, but it will also reward you with a burst of garden-fresh flavors.

In the beginning, I resisted details I felt added needless complexity. Could straining that sauce a second time really make a big difference? Who would know if I cooked the asparagus and the peas in the same water, instead of separate pots? How could that extra tablespoon of butter at the end really make a discernible difference?

Then little by little, as I followed his instructions to the letter, I began to see the connecting threads. Details began to count. I became more demanding of myself and more critical of my results. Recipes that at first seemed complex and daunting became clear and obvious. I realized that simplicity was not simple—but neither was it impossible.

Instinctively, I began to make things happen in the kitchen, so that green beans tasted more like green beans than ever before. I saw that the simple addition of a touch of lemon juice enhanced the true flavor of my freshly sautéed mushrooms and made them taste even more "mushroomy." When I properly seasoned my chicken after roasting, and let it rest tail in the air, the resulting flavors were a triumph of simplicity. When I took the time to blanch the vegetables separately for a sauté of spring vegetables, each retained its own specific flavor and the result was a magical symphony, not just a lot of pretty noise.

Before long, knowing when to season (and when not to) became second nature. My food tasted different (and better) and more of itself. I learned to nudge complex flavors out of the simplest combination of ingredients.

I no longer add or fuss or alter for the sake of change, a practice that generally passes for creativity. Now I stop and think about how that extra ingredient or substitution might change the character of the dish, and question whether it will really enhance.

All along the way, I listened to what Robuchon had to say about respect for raw ingredients, and I realized that most of us—home cooks and chefs alike—use the word "fresh" in a rather fuzzy, broad sense.

Photograph above: A handful of potatoes with their colorful blossoms, on Jean-Pierre Clot's farm in Villegagnon, just east of Paris

No matter where we live today, city or country, America or France, England or Australia, we all have fresh quality ingredients at our disposal. They may not be the same in variety, quality, quantity, or value, but they are out there. Caring about food is a matter of choice, but if you choose to care deeply about what you put on your table at home, there's no excuse for not seeking out the freshest and most flavorful ingredients, whether you're grilling a hamburger, tossing a salad, or creating a complex and extravagant meal.

That said, I'm well aware that we are not born knowing how to select the best-looking lobster, the finest cut of salmon, and we don't have divining rods for judging the freshness of an artichoke, the excellence of one chicken over another. That comes with experience, attention to detail, desire for excellence. To my mind, knowing how to select ingredients should be the number-one goal of a cook.

I also realized that once those fine ingredients have been gathered, many cooks spend more time embellishing or "improving" than working to make asparagus taste like asparagus, salmon like salmon. And we ignore or fail to utilize so many jewels (like the juices from roast or pan-fried meats, fish, or poultry) that are there for the taking.

Simply French is not necessarily "simple" French. But that does not mean that the recipes included here require exhaustive culinary proficiency. What they do demand is attention to detail, a certain degree of discipline, patience, neatness, and organization,

as well as an insistence upon top-quality ingredients.

In the end, I hope that you will view this book as more than simply a collection of recipes from a master chef. As you proceed, recipe by recipe, I hope you will be inspired to accept Chef Robuchon's intelligent approach to food, embracing a philosophy that will serve you a lifetime.

It's an approach that teaches you that a whisper of chervil and thyme is not just a garnish, but actually completes the character of the dish. It's knowing that parsley leaves snipped with scissors will have more flavor than the same herb chopped with a knife or machine. And those extra moments spent straining a sauce, waiting for dough to chill, scraping the seeds from a vanilla bean, patiently peeling a pepper, or garnishing a tart are not a waste of time at all. Rather, they're simply wise investments that pay you back with the very first bite.

Joël Robuchon shopping for fruits and vegetables in his native town of Poitiers

Patricia Wells and Joël Robuchon in the dining room at Jamin

AN INTERVIEW

WITH JOËL ROBUCHON

. . . .

Q: What gives you the greatest pleasure and satisfaction in the kitchen?

A: My dream is to create a dish, from beginning to end, without a single interruption. Today I've organized my kitchen so that when a dish demands it, I have the freedom to go to the stove and personally work on that dish.

No matter how proficient your staff is, there are certain cooking principles that cannot be explained, in words or in actions. And one of those is the fixing, or stabilizing, of flavors.

For example, when I cook a ragout of truffles, there's a moment—you can tell by the aroma—when the full flavor of the truffle is being released, and it's at that point I have to intervene. And I have to know what to do: Cover the pot. Or add broth. Or adjust the heat. If I don't jump in at precisely the right moment, the flavors disappear, lost to thin air. If I intervene at the perfect moment, the flavors are fixed forever. If you love cooking, the principle can be learned, but only by experience, by trial and error.

I've said it many times, but as a cook, you have an obligation to respect the flavor, the essence, the authenticity, of ingredients. You don't have the right to alter them. A mushroom grows, doesn't it? So when you cook a mushroom you don't have the right to make it taste like anything other than a mushroom. If it ends up tasting like straw, or like grit, you've not respected the nature of the mushroom.

The same goes for knowing when a dish is finished and when it's not. I like to give the example of a pot of tea. When you brew tea, there is an instant when it is underbrewed, an instant when it is prefectly brewed, an instant when it is overbrewed. It's not a principle that's easy to explain in simple words, but if you care about food, you'll make the effort to prepare that perfectly brewed pot of tea.

Q: In this century, French cuisine has gone from traditional to nouvelle and now beyond. Does modern-day cooking, such as yours, have a title? And where is contemporary cooking headed?

A: Today no one wants to use the words *nouvelle cuisine* because the movement was so abused. But it had a positive influence, in that it allowed French cooking to emerge from a state of lethargy. Look at the cuisine of forty or fifty years ago. If you study it carefully, you see that it evolved as a cuisine designed for people who couldn't chew. By the time people of my grandfather's generation were young adults, they had bad teeth or no teeth. That's why traditional French cooking was made up of so much soft food, so many purées, so many meats that were overcooked.

But traditional French cuisine—which is really regional French cuisine—is what earned French cooking its great reputation. And while it's a fine cuisine, often one had no idea what one was eating, for flavors were masked or destroyed.

Today's cuisine might be called a *cuisine actuelle,* a cooking in which we rediscover the savors, flavors, tastes, of an ingredient. If you're eating lobster, it should taste like lobster. If you're eating mushrooms, they should taste like mushrooms. As cooks, we have the right to enhance or heighten flavors, but we do not have the right to destroy them.

Q: What advice do you have for the home cook?
A: 1. Work in a clean environment. You can't create good food in a disorderly kitchen. I often look around in my own kitchen, at my staff. The cook who is clean, who has a clean work area, has a chance of succeeding. The cook who is messy, who works in a disorderly environment, has no chance at all of ever creating good food.

2. When you cook, of course you have the right to modify recipes. But only if you understand the sense of the recipe. Following a recipe is not like following instructions

on how to operate a television set or tape player, where you read the instructions—one, two, three—as you go.

A recipe must be read two, three times in advance, so that you understand clearly the sense of what you are after. Then, if you like, modify and change.

3. Don't let yourself get flustered in the kitchen. Work slowly and patiently.

4. Select the best ingredients your money can buy. When you cook with good ingredients, with care and with love, you can't turn out bad food. It's not possible. Even if it's botched or bungled, the dish is a success. That's what good cooking is all about. Recipes are secondary.

Q: Number one, number one! There's universal agreement that you are the top chef working in France today, perhaps in the world. Does this weigh heavily on you?

A: First, it is simply part of my character, and has been from childhood, to always do the best I can. When you do your best, it's not that difficult to be better than the others. In school I always tried to be number one, and in cooking I just followed through.

But much of the time it is really a competition with yourself, to do better today than you did yesterday or the day before. But I am always sad when I don't do as well as I know I might have.

Q: What regrets, if any, do you have about your profession and your career?

A: Today in restaurants, everything must be done with such speed. There is never enough time. Good cooking requires time. For cooking to be pleasurable, you must have time. And the pressures of today allow room for neither time nor pleasure.

Q: In a non-restaurant situation, when someone else is cooking, are there mistakes that bother you, that stop you from enjoying a meal?

A: Never. When I am invited into someone's home, the simple fact that I am there means I have respect for them. I'm not there to judge or to analyze. Yes, sometimes people do try too hard, but I'm not there as a critic, but to enjoy, to share friendship. Home cooking is not a competition.

Q: What are your thoughts on the future of restaurants in France. And, along with that, your image of the ideal restaurant?

A: I cannot predict the future of restaurants in France, but I know that it is going to be harder and harder to continue to offer the type of grand restaurants we have today. Currently I have forty employees for forty-five diners. In the future we are simply not going to be able to find that many qualified employees, and it will be economically impossible to employ such numbers.

What I would love to see in the future is the kind of restaurant that I feel can offer the finest cooking possible: It would be a small restaurant, serving no more than fifteen or twenty diners. There would be one, maybe two, people in the kitchen. It would be a spontaneous style of cooking, based on what the chef finds in the market each day. There would be no menu, just one or two first courses, one or two main courses.

When you invite people into your home for dinner, you cook what you are in the mood to prepare, don't you? That is the ideal restaurant as well—a chef cooking what he has the desire to prepare that day, with products fresh that day. Everyone eating the same dish. That's my dream. I don't know if it's feasible.

Restaurant menus are a constraint. A bad constraint. You have to serve a dish because it is on the menu, whether or not you can find the best ingredients, whether or not you are in the mood to prepare that food that day. Under those conditions, it is very difficult for every dish to be perfect.

There are days when you simply have a burning desire to prepare a certain dish. And that's when good cooking begins.

Q: What is your idea of the perfect meal?

A: The perfect meal does not exist. It could well be a slice of toasted bread and some melted cheese, or fondue, shared with a friend. You cannot organize or anticipate good times or ideal meals. It's a question of simplicity, spontaneity, good times with friends. Most often, it's only later, long after you've experienced a great meal, that you realize, in retrospect, how wonderful and how perfect it really was.

Q: Who or what has been the greatest influence on your cooking?

A: As a child, as a young seminarian in Poitiers, I often worked in the kitchen with the nuns. I remember those moments—making butter, peeling vegetables, the pots on the stove—with great pleasure. At the age of fifteen, because of a difficult family situation, I was obliged to go to work. I chose cooking because it seemed to be one trade that would offer some satisfaction in life. It is the only profession—I think we do have the right to call cooking an art—that uses all the five senses.

As an apprentice I was most influenced by the first chef for whom I worked, for with a few carrots and some water, he could create a bouillon full of rich flavors. He taught me a lesson I never forgot: You don't need expensive or exotic ingredients to create a great cuisine.

ABOUT JOËL ROBUCHON

. . . .

There are many paths to the top. Joël Robuchon's route has been straight and direct, without detours. Modest, reflective, and always driven, Robuchon has been at the stove since the age of fifteen. Here are some details:

Joël Robuchon was born on April 7, 1945, in Poitiers, a historic city in central France, roughly halfway between Paris and Bordeaux. His father was a mason and his mother a housewife.

At the age of twelve he entered the seminary to study for the priesthood. At fifteen, family problems required he seek employment. The seminarian had also dreamed of being an architect, but such schooling was now obviously out of the question. During his seminary years, his quietest, most rewarding, and most relaxing moments had been spent helping the nuns in the seminary's kitchens. Thus in 1960 Joël Robuchon became an apprentice at the hotel-restaurant Relais de Poitiers, where he remained for three years. The experience helped form the classic culinary education he relies on to this day.

As an apprentice Robuchon peeled vegetables and prepared stocks, but he also mopped floors and spent hours scrubbing pots—an experience that was not lost on him. "Once you've washed pots and polished copper for someone else, you'll never treat pots the same, even once someone else is cleaning them for you," he explains. Today he is a maniac for neatness and cleanliness, and his restaurant kitchen is thoroughly cleaned (including exhaust filters and oven hoods) twice daily.

In 1963 Robuchon became a Compagnon du Tour de France, beginning an invaluable traveling apprenticeship that allowed him to work with chefs all over France, not only to be exposed to a variety of points of view but also to work directly at the source of the products that make up the country's incredible culinary wealth.

The experience taught him not only technique but values, and what he calls "respect for work well done and for goals accomplished." Throughout France, *compagnons* in every trade from stonemason to cabinetmaker work toward the same high goals of manual, moral, and physical perfection. Robuchon's "trademark" image of the little man with top hat and cane is an artistic rendering of that itinerant worker, or *compagnon*.

"As a *compagnon*, I learned that no matter how well we think we do something, we can still do better. And that there is no greater personal satisfaction than in giving the very best of yourself each day," says Robuchon.

He also drew upon the *compagnon* philosophy when he was awarded the top culinary accolade in France, a third Michelin star. He said at that time: "The third star does not mean that I merit three stars. It only means that now I have the right to merit them."

From 1963 to 1973 Robuchon worked at various restaurants in Paris and in the provinces. During those years, he also concentrated his energies on numerous French culinary competitions, gathering bronze, silver, and gold medals at contest after contest.

In early 1974, at the age of twenty-eight, he was named chef of the newly constructed Hotel Concorde Lafayette in Paris, charged with the direction of a brigade of ninety chefs, serving three thousand diners per meal. The chef was continuing his own training in the broadest sense, testing his managerial skills and his culinary exactitude in a major hotel.

Two years later he achieved the greatest accolade a worker in any trade can aspire to in France: He competed for, and won, the title of Meilleur Ouvrier de France.

Robuchon was asked to take over the direction of kitchens at the Hotel Nikko in Paris in 1978, and in December 1981 he was ready to go off on his own, becoming chef and owner of restaurant Jamin, on Paris's Rue de Longchamp.

Within three years Robuchon had three Michelin stars, the fastest rise in the history of the Michelin guide. He is rarely seen in the dining room at Jamin, preferring to follow a simple philosophy: "Express yourself with the quality of your work, not simply with words."

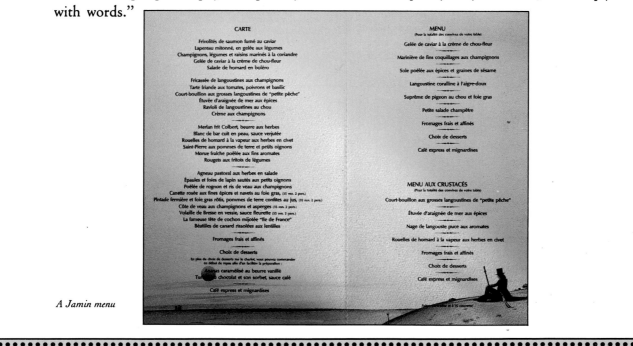

A Jamin menu

TRANSLATING THREE-STAR CONCEPTS TO THE HOME

. . . .

I wanted the recipes in this book to be accessible to all cooks and have attempted to limit the amount of hard-to-find ingredients and equipment. In cooking no element, no ingredient, can be too minor. The following are important thoughts on ingredients, techniques, procedures, that I hope you will keep in mind while working to improve the flavors and qualities of your food. This is not a teaching book, but I would be surprised if you did not continue to learn every step along the way. I know I did.

SALT AND PEPPER. I can't argue enough for the use of top-quality sea salt (not kosher salt) and freshly ground white or black pepper in the kitchen. They are minute elements that yield extraordinary results. Common table salt tastes like a mouthful of chemicals and masks the flavors of food. Sea salt has a clean, distinct flavor that helps draw out and intensify flavors. Measure for measure, I have found that one needs less sea salt to properly season a dish.

Preground pepper can quickly turn stale, adding a harsh, acrid flavor. Freshly ground pepper, when used judiciously, adds an extra layer of flavor and a "finished" sense of seasoning.

TASTE AS YOU GO. I've spent a good deal of time in professional kitchens, but never have I seen chefs taste, taste, taste, as they do in the Jamin kitchens. It seems like an obvious habit, but it's one I know many cooks and chefs fail to follow. You will never regret getting in the practice of tasting every step along the way—sauces, a filling, even a batter—to ensure well-measured flavoring and seasoning.

ON THE VIRTUES OF FRESH HERBS. Intentionally, the recipes here contain no dried herbs. Most often dried herbs have as much taste as dust and can in fact damage a dish, turning a sauce bitter or masking natural flavors. Today fresh herbs are readily available at garden shops and food markets, and there is no excuse for not making them everyday ingredients in your kitchen. Growing herbs at home is no more difficult than caring for the average houseplant. On my narrow balconies in Paris, I tend to a year-round herb garden, and these pots, window boxes, and mini-greenhouses not only offer me daily joy and satisfaction but make certain that I have at hand all the fresh chives, basil, mint, rosemary, thyme, bay leaf, summer savory, parsley, sage, and nasturtium leaves and blossoms that one could desire.

WHY RECIPES FAIL. If a well-written recipe fails, it's usually for one of two reasons: The cook failed to read the recipe carefully, or he chose to carelessly substitute ingredients, a not so mild form of cheating.

I've often heard people say "I prepared your rabbit with tarragon recipe, except I substituted chicken for the rabbit, and used nonfat yogurt instead of cream, and couldn't find tarragon so I used dried thyme. . . ." With that approach to cooking, the dish could not possibly resemble the original, so why bother with a recipe from the beginning?

If you don't want to eat butter, then select another recipe that doesn't require butter. But don't substitute margarine. And please don't carelessly substitute chicken for rabbit, fish fillets for whole fish, a frozen rock lobster tail for fresh live lobster, light cream for heavy cream, anything frozen or dried for anything fresh.

Recipes can fail, through no one's fault, because of the variations in oven temperatures. Always use an oven thermometer, keep a careful eye on the oven (that means don't answer the phone or leave the room), and learn to cook instinctively, by smell.

Remember, too, that cooking is a somewhat subjective activity. There are days when I am so harried and exhausted that I intentionally don't cook, or don't cook anything complex, for I know I won't have the patience, clarity of mind, or attention span necessary to succeed.

THE CONSIDERED GESTURE. Watching Chef Robuchon in the kitchen, I began to call his movements "considered gestures," for when he works with food he moves slowly, almost reflectively. Every move seems to be studied, measured, analyzed. In handling pastry, for instance, his motions are so deliberate that he never makes a move that cannot be repaired. If needed, every step along the way can be retraced. Before he slices an apple or carves a roast or chops an onion, he pauses momentarily, almost respectfully, as if he's looking into the soul of the ingredient to decide how to bring out its most positive traits.

GET IT RIGHT FROM THE START. No diner at Jamin could imagine the attention that is paid to what we would think of as a simple bowl of mashed potatoes. Almost daily, Robuchon would reject, for one reason or another, the potato purée placed before him for approval. Often he did not indicate what was wrong, leaving it to his young chef to find out for himself. Once the potatoes went back with this admonition: "Do it right from the beginning, and there's never a problem." Advice we all might well follow.

SIMPLY FRENCH

APPETIZERS AND SOUPS

....

Amuse-Gueules, Crèmes, Potages, et Soupes

TINY CHEESE PUFFS

Gougères

. . . .

These tiny cheese puffs are ideal appetizers. In Burgundy they're often served at wine tastings, generally warm from the oven. They melt in your mouth, with a delightfully crisp outer crust and an airy, moist interior. The puffs are best served fresh from the oven, but they can be prepared in advance, stored in an airtight container, and crisped in a preheated 300°F oven at the last minute.

Unsalted butter, softened, and all-
  purpose flour, for the baking sheets
8 tablespoons unsalted butter, chilled,
  cut into small pieces
Pinch of sea salt
1 cup water

1 cup minus 1 tablespoon all-purpose
  flour, sifted
4 large eggs, lightly beaten
¾ cup freshly grated imported Gruyère
  cheese

1. Preheat the oven to 400°F.

2. Lightly butter and flour 2 baking sheets; set aside.

3. In a medium-size heavy-bottomed saucepan, combine the butter, salt, and water over high heat. Bring to a boil, whisking occasionally. As soon as the mixture boils, remove the pan from the heat. Add the flour all at once, and beat vigorously with a wooden spoon until the mixture comes away from the sides of the pan. Return the pan to low heat and continue beating for 1 minute, to dry out the dough.

4. Quickly transfer the dough to the bowl of a heavy-duty electric mixer fitted with a flat paddle. Gradually add the eggs and ½ cup of the cheese, mixing at moderately high speed to incorporate the maximum amount of air. The dough should have the consistency of a very thick mayonnaise.

5. Transfer the dough to a pastry bag fitted with a plain ½-inch tip. (Depending upon the size of your pastry bag, this may have to be done in two batches.) Pipe into round 2-inch mounds, spacing them about 2 inches apart. (If you do not have a pastry bag, carefully spoon the dough onto the baking sheets with a tablespoon.)

6. Sprinkle the tops with the remaining ¼ cup cheese. Place in the center of the oven and bake until the puffs are an even golden brown, 20 to 25 minutes. Avoid

opening the oven door during this time, for humidity will escape and the pastry will dry out.

7. To test for doneness, remove one well-browned cheese puff from the oven. Split it apart: It should be moist and steamy in the center. Transfer the puffs to a rack to cool. Serve warm or at room temperature.

Yield: 30 TO 36 CHEESE PUFFS

Wine Suggestion: AN APERITIF CHAMPAGNE, SUCH AS A *BLANC DE BLANCS*

BROCHETTES OF BAY SCALLOPS
Bâtonnets aux Pétoncles

. . . .

Pétoncles are tiny French scallops, most often found in the market with their bright red coral attached. One cold wintry morning just before lunchtime, I watched as Chef Robuchon toyed around in the kitchen with new ideas for appetizers to serve in the restaurant. He carefully combined bright and fragrantly fresh scallops (without their coral) with just a touch of oil and butter, soy sauce and red wine vinegar, salt, pepper, and the freshest of thyme leaves. He arranged the *pétoncles,* one by one on a skewer, interlacing them with little "tiddlywinks" of fresh wild mushrooms that had been fried in oil. This simpler variation (omitting the wild mushrooms) is a terrific, quick appetizer that will wow your guests with its freshness. For this recipe, as with all those that list coarsely ground pepper, grind the whole peppercorns in a spice grinder—they'll have more bite and freshness than ready-ground pepper.

EQUIPMENT: Eight bamboo skewers

8 ounces fresh tiny bay scallops
1 tablespoon extra-virgin olive oil
2 tablespoons unsalted butter
Sea salt and freshly ground white
    pepper to taste
2 teaspoons best-quality soy sauce

2 teaspoons best-quality red wine
    vinegar
Coarse sea salt, for garnish
Freshly ground coarse white pepper, for
    garnish
1 teaspoon fresh thyme leaves, for
    garnish

1. If the scallops are large, trim them to form ³⁄₄-inch cubes. Thread 4 to 5 scallop pieces on each skewer. You should have about 8 brochettes.

2. In a large nonstick skillet, combine the oil and 1 tablespoon of the butter over moderately high heat. When hot but not smoking, add the brochettes in a single layer and cook just until browned on one side, 1½ to 2 minutes. Season, then turn over and cook until browned, 1½ to 2 minutes more. With the scallops still in the pan, deglaze

with the soy sauce, the remaining 1 tablespoon butter, and the vinegar. Shake the pan and gently roll the brochettes in the sauce.

3. Roll the brochettes one last time in the sauce, then drain, and transfer 2 brochettes to each of 4 warmed salad plates. There should be just a few drops of sauce on the plate. Carefully sprinkle each brochette with salt, pepper, and thyme, and serve immediately.

Yield: 4 APPETIZER SERVINGS

Wine Suggestion: AN APERITIF CHAMPAGNE, SUCH AS A *BLANC DE BLANCS*

FRESH SHRIMP SAUTÉED IN BUTTER

Crevettes Sautées au Beurre

. . . .

Few appetizers are as simple and satisfying as a quick sauté of fresh shrimp. Serve this with slices of rye bread spread with lightly salted butter, and a glass of chilled white wine. Chef Robuchon uses tiny shrimp from Brittany, but medium shrimp in the shell are equally delicious.

1 pound small or medium raw shrimp in the shell	Sea salt and freshly ground white pepper to taste
5 tablespoons unsalted butter	Few drops of Cognac

1. Rinse the shrimp under cold water and drain thoroughly.

2. In a large skillet, heat the butter over moderately high heat. Cook until the butter begins to brown and gives off a nutty aroma, 2 to 3 minutes. (Do not let the butter burn.) Add the shrimp and cook—shaking the pan to evenly toss the shrimp—until they turn pink and begin to curl, 2 to 3 minutes for small shrimp, 4 to 5 minutes for medium.

3. Add a pinch of salt, and season generously with pepper. Add a few drops of Cognac, and cook for 1 minute more.

4. Transfer to a warmed serving bowl and serve immediately. To best enjoy small shrimp in the shell, simply pull off the head and pop the tiny shrimp, shell and all, into your mouth. For medium shrimp, remove the shells before serving.

Yield: 4 SERVINGS

Wine Suggestion: A WELL-CHILLED MUSCADET OR A DRY WHITE GRAVES

CURRIED CHICKEN BROCHETTES

Brochettes de Poulet au Curry

. . . .

A supremely adaptable recipe, this combination of chicken, leeks, and curry sauce may be transformed into many guises to be used in a variety of ways. At Jamin, the bite-size brochettes, as described here, are often served as an appetizer, designed to stimulate the appetite and wake up the palate. One could also prepare larger brochettes by alternating chunks of chicken breast with chunks of leek or onion, sprinkling them with curry powder, and grilling them over hot coals. Serve the large brochettes with basmati rice and pass the warm curry sauce.

EQUIPMENT: Eight toothpicks or bamboo skewers

About 15 baby leeks or fresh scallions, trimmed and cleaned
3 boned chicken breasts
Generous pinch of curry powder

Several teaspoons soy sauce
2 tablespoons unsalted butter
About 1 cup curry sauce (page 324), heated

1. Prepare the leeks or scallions: Cut them into 2-inch pieces. Bring a large pot of water to a boil. Salt the water and add the leeks or scallions; cook for 2 minutes. Transfer to a colander and rinse under cold running water. Drain and set aside.

2. Prepare the brochettes: Cut the chicken meat into nuggets about 2 inches in diameter. Thread a toothpick or skewer with a nugget of chicken, a slice of leek (or scallion), a nugget of chicken, another slice of leek, and a final nugget of chicken. Repeat, using all the leek and chicken pieces, to make 8 brochettes. To finish, sprinkle each brochette with curry powder and a few drops of soy sauce. Marinate for 5 minutes. (A longer marinade could make the chicken too salty.)

3. In a large nonstick skillet, melt the butter over moderate heat. Add the brochettes and cook on all sides until nicely browned, about 2 minutes. Place 2 brochettes on each small salad plate, spoon the curry sauce all over, and serve immediately.

Yield: 4 APPETIZER SERVINGS

Wine Suggestion: AN APERITIF CHAMPAGNE, SUCH AS A *BLANC DE BLANCS*

FREDY GIRARDET'S GRILLED CHEESE SANDWICHES

Croûtes au Fromage "Fredy Girardet"

....

G reat bread, great cheese, and you have a meal in the making. I can just picture the scene: Two of the world's greatest chefs, Joël Robuchon and Fredy Girardet, take a long walk with their families in the Swiss mountains. They return to the Girardet family chalet, famished. There's not much to eat, but there are bread, cheese, white wine, potatoes, and the standard kitchen staples. This is the delightful postprandial "snack" the two chefs prepare, a traditional Swiss specialty designed to offer instant satisfaction. It's so much more than just grilled cheese on toast. Rather, anticipate a symphony of flavors, where bread and cheese play the lead and garlic, wine, and pepper chime in with their own impressive notes. There are many variations on this dish: Some like to rub the bread with garlic; others layer it with finely chopped onions; some sprinkle it at the end with a touch of paprika. For a copious snack, layer the bread first with paper-thin slices of country ham or with *viande des grisons,* the delicate air-dried Swiss beef. One can even top this off with an egg, fried separately in a skillet. For a more substantial meal, accompany the sandwiches with a green salad tossed with freshly cracked walnut halves, or serve with tiny potatoes cooked in their skins, cornichons, and a jar of hot mustard. Add a bottle of Swiss Fendant and you have an instant winter mountain feast, what the French call a dinner *sans façon.* Do take care to slice the cheese as thin as possible: It will make all the difference between a sandwich that's refined and elegant and one that's, well, a sandwich.

8 ounces best-quality imported Swiss
   cheese, preferably Fribourg
8 thick slices country bread, preferably
   homemade
3 tablespoons unsalted butter, softened

1 plump fresh garlic clove, halved
   (optional)
2 teaspoons dry white wine, preferably
   a Swiss Fendant
Freshly ground white pepper to taste

ACCOMPANIMENTS (OPTIONAL)
1 pound small potatoes, cooked in their
skins

Imported Dijon mustard
Cornichons or other small pickles

1. Preheat the oven to 400°F.

2. With a sharp knife, or a cheese or meat slicer, cut the cheese into very thin slices. Set aside.

3. Lightly brush both sides of the bread with the softened butter. Arrange the slices side by side on a baking sheet, place in the center of the oven, and bake until browned but still soft in the center, about 5 minutes. Remove from the oven and scrub each piece of bread with garlic, if desired. Very lightly sprinkle each piece of bread with a few drops of wine.

4. Overlap the cheese slices—about 1 ounce of cheese per slice of bread—on top of the bread. Return the baking sheet to the oven and cook until the cheese is bubbly and melted, about 5 minutes. Remove from the oven and season generously with pepper. Serve immediately—and pass the boiled potatoes, cornichons, and mustard, if desired.

Yield: 4 SERVINGS

BROWNING VS.

BROILING

. . . .

For bread that's warmed and soft, but neither fully toasted nor firm, brown buttered bread in a hot oven rather than toasting it beneath a broiler. You gain all the benefits of toast but end up with a softer, more pliable bread that's great for preparing open-face sandwiches.

SATINY PUMPKIN SOUP

Crème au Potiron

. . . .

Pumpkin soup has been a favorite of mine since childhood. But I must admit that Chef Robuchon's soothing, elegant version, with its pure, unmasked pumpkin flavor, takes me miles away from those days in the Midwest. This recipe is in fact a simple formula for any variety of creamy soups: Instead of pumpkin, substitute the same amount of cauliflower, asparagus, or even fresh fava beans. It's the final emulsion that gives the soup its creamy unctuousness.

EQUIPMENT: An immersion mixer (optional; see box, page 39)

2 pounds trimmed fresh pumpkin,
   cubed
1 quart chicken stock (page 334)
2 teaspoons sugar
2 tablespoons cornstarch
3 tablespoons water

1¼ cups heavy cream
6 tablespoons unsalted butter, chilled
   and cut into pieces
Sea salt and freshly ground white
   pepper to taste
Croutons, for garnish (optional)

1. In a stockpot, combine the pumpkin, chicken stock, and sugar. Cover, bring to a boil, and counting from the time the liquid begins to boil, simmer for 18 minutes. (Pumpkin should cook quickly to avoid any bitterness.) Once the pumpkin is cooked, purée the mixture in a food processor or blender. Then strain it through a coarse sieve back into the stockpot.

2. In a small bowl, dissolve the cornstarch in the water.

3. Return the soup to a boil, and skim off any scum that rises to the surface. Remove the pot from the heat and quickly whisk in the cornstarch. Stir in the cream and bring back to a boil. Purée again in the food processor or blender, or with an immersion mixer, incorporating the butter. The soup should have a velvety, creamy consistency.

4. Return the soup to the stockpot over moderate heat, and taste for seasoning. (Do not salt the soup during cooking, for the chicken stock should season it sufficiently.) Serve immediately. If desired, sprinkle with tiny croutons fried in clarified butter.

Yield: 6 TO 8 SERVINGS

MORE THAN JUST
ANOTHER GADGET

. . . .

A wandlike hand blender or immersion mixer is a useful tool that should be part of any cook's collection of kitchen equipment. The mixer—which resembles an electric hand mixer with a long, thin wand and a rotary blade at the end—is handy for whipping, blending, puréeing, and liquifying. Available in both electric and battery-operated models, immersion mixers are also sometimes sold as an attachment to hand-held mixers. I use mine regularly to obtain smooth soups and sauces: The mixer is plunged directly into the pot, which means there is no need to transfer liquids to a blender, then back to the pot. It's a neat, almost magical tool, for chunky soups are turned into smooth purées in seconds, without splashing or making a mess.

CREAMY LEEK AND POTATO SOUP

Potage Poireaux-Pommes de Terre

. . . .

This is a blueprint for a simple puréed soup, the most popular of which is a combination of leeks and potatoes. The same soup could be made with any combination of winter vegetables, including carrots and turnips, or with spring vegetables such as peas. As ever, the addition of a touch of butter at the very end makes for a rich, delicious soup. The soup tastes remarkably creamy, even though it is enriched with just a single tablespoon of cream.

EQUIPMENT: An immersion mixer (optional; see box, page 39)

1½ pounds small boiling potatoes, such
   as Red Bliss
2 leeks, white and tender green parts
3 tablespoons unsalted butter
1½ quarts water
Sea salt to taste

1 tablespoon heavy cream
Handful of fresh chervil leaves or fresh
   flat-leaf parsley leaves, snipped with
   a scissors
Freshly ground white pepper, for
   garnish

1. Peel, quarter, rinse, and drain the potatoes. Set aside.

2. Prepare the leeks: Trim the leeks at the root. Split them lengthwise for easier cleaning. Rinse well under cold running water, and then transfer to a bowl of cold water to soak for about 5 minutes. When all the grit has settled to the bottom of the bowl, remove the leeks and dry thoroughly. Chop coarsely and set aside.

3. In a medium-size stockpot, melt 2 tablespoons of the butter over low heat. Add the leeks and cook, stirring often, until tender but not browned, about 3 minutes. Add the water. Salt the water, and add the potatoes. Cover, and simmer gently for 35 minutes.

4. With a food processor, blender, or immersion mixer, process the soup until smooth. Return the soup to the pot, increase the heat to high, and bring to a boil. Skim

any impurities that may rise to the surface. Add the cream, and after a few seconds, add the remaining 1 tablespoon butter.

5. To serve, ladle the soup into warmed soup bowls and sprinkle with the herbs. Serve immediately, allowing guests to season with pepper to taste.

Yield: 4 TO 6 SERVINGS

THOUGHTS ON CREAM

AND BUTTER

· · · · · · · · · · · · · · · · ·

We've all become so afraid of fats—especially butter—that we forget the simplest trick of all: Adding a touch of cream and butter just before serving makes for a soup that tastes rich without being indulgent.

SPRING GARDEN SOUP

Potage Cultivateur

. . . .

The elegance of this simple soup belies its modest title. Many of the vegetables are cut into almost transparent triangles, making for a very flavorful, delicate soup. Serve it on a spring day, and sprinkle it with freshly grated cheese. Be sure to serve plenty of crusty homemade bread alongside.

2 ounces slab bacon or salt pork, rind
   removed
2 leeks, white and tender green parts
3 ounces green cabbage
1 cup fresh green beans
3 small boiling potatoes, peeled
1 celery rib
2 medium carrots, peeled
2 small turnips, peeled

3 tablespoons unsalted butter
Sea salt to taste
5²/₃ cups water
Freshly grated Parmesan cheese
   (optional)
Handful of fresh chervil leaves or fresh
   flat-leaf parsley leaves
Freshly ground black pepper, for
   garnish

1. Fill a medium-size saucepan with water and bring to a boil. Place the bacon in a fine-mesh sieve, and submerge it in the boiling water for 10 seconds. Set aside to drain.

2. Prepare the leeks: Trim the leeks at the root. Split them lengthwise for easier cleaning. Rinse well under cold running water, and then transfer to a bowl of cold water to soak for about 5 minutes. When all the grit has settled to the bottom of the bowl, remove the leeks and dry thoroughly. Chop finely and set aside.

3. Prepare the remaining vegetables: Slice the cabbage into thin strips, and chop finely. Cut the green beans into ³/₄-inch pieces. For the potatoes, celery, carrots, and turnips: Cut in half lengthwise, cut each half in thirds lengthwise, and then slice into thin, almost transparent, triangular pieces. (This method of slicing the vegetables is important to the taste and consistency of the soup.) Keep the potatoes separate: Place them in a bowl, cover with cold water, and set aside.

4. In a large stockpot, melt 2 tablespoons of the butter over moderately low heat. Add the leeks, celery, carrots, and turnips. Cook, stirring constantly, until softened, 4 to 5 minutes. Season with salt (this will help the vegetables to release their flavorful liquid). Add the water and bring to a boil.

5. Add the bacon and cabbage. Taste for seasoning. Cover (to keep the steam in and to prevent the soup from reducing). Simmer gently for 40 minutes.

6. Meanwhile, cook the green beans: Prepare a large bowl of ice water and set aside. Bring a large pot of water to a boil. Salt the water, add the beans, and cook until crisp-tender, about 4 minutes. Drain the beans and plunge them into the ice water, so they cool down as quickly as possible. This will help them retain their crispness and bright green color. Drain the beans and set aside.

7. After 40 minutes, the vegetables should be cooked but still somewhat crisp. Remove the bacon and reserve. Add the potatoes. Cover, and increase the heat. Dice the bacon and return it to the soup. Continue cooking for 15 to 20 minutes. Add the green beans, reduce the heat, and simmer 5 minutes more. Taste for seasoning.

8. To serve, ladle the soup into warmed soup bowls. Divide the remaining 1 tablespoon butter among the bowls. Sprinkle with cheese (if desired) and herbs. Serve immediately, allowing guests to season with pepper to taste.

Yield: 4 TO 6 SERVINGS

SMALL IS FLAVORFUL

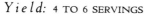

Soups containing finely chopped vegetables have several advantages: When the vegetables are cut into small, uniform pieces, they cook more quickly and evenly, and also release a good deal more flavor, than large irregular cuts. And when you eat the soup, you also manage to combine many of the vegetables and some of the broth in a single spoonful, making for more complexity of flavor.

SPICY TOMATO SOUP WITH PEPPERS AND CUCUMBERS

Gaspacho

,,,,,,,,,,,,,,,,,,

Benoît Guichard, Chef Robuchon's assistant, prepared this easy and elegant *gaspacho* for lunch one day when we were in the midst of a photo session. Served as a first course on a warm summer's day, it really hits the spot. Unlike other versions of this ever-popular cold soup, this *gaspacho* contains no garlic or raw onions, which some people find difficult to digest. I like to make a big batch in the morning, so there's no fuss at lunchtime.

2 pounds vine-ripened tomatoes, cored, peeled, seeded, and chopped

1 cup water

¼ cup best-quality sherry wine vinegar

¼ cup tomato paste

Sea salt to taste

Tabasco sauce to taste

1 red bell pepper, cored, seeded, and minced

1 European or hothouse cucumber, peeled, seeded, and minced

Small handful fresh basil leaves, snipped with a scissors

1. In a food processor, process the tomatoes until smooth. Add the water, vinegar, tomato paste, salt, and Tabasco, and process just until blended. Taste for seasoning. (The recipe may be prepared to this point 4 hours in advance. Cover securely and refrigerate.)

2. To serve, spoon the soup into chilled shallow soup bowls. Add the peppers and cucumber, and sprinkle with the basil. Serve immediately.

Yield: 4 SERVINGS

A TOUCH OF HOME

. . . .

An assortment of varied raw salads, or crudités, *is a welcoming starter any time of year, offering a nice homey touch. One of my favorite dishes to prepare is guinea hen roasted on a bed of potatoes, a dish that calls out for a good red Bordeaux. For dessert, serve a thin apple tart and a young Sauternes.*

. . . .

GRATED CARROT SALAD WITH LEMON
CAROTTES RÂPÉES AU CITRON ET À L'AIL

FRESH MUSHROOM SALAD WITH PARMESAN SHAVINGS
SALADE DE CHAMPIGNONS AU PARMESAN

SAUTÉED RED PEPPERS WITH GARLIC AND THYME
SALADE DE POIVRONS ROUGES AU THYM

GUINEA HEN ROASTED ON A BED OF POTATOES
PINTADE RÔTIE AUX POMMES DE TERRE CONFITES

GOLDEN SUNBURST APPLE TART
TARTE FINE AUX POMMES

SALADS

·················

Salades

FIELD SALAD WITH FRESH HERBS

Salade aux Herbes Fraîches

. . . .

Joël Robuchon likes to say, "I made my reputation on salad and mashed potatoes." But what salad, and what mashed potatoes! It's indicative of his personality—he can be only "the best"—to try to woo diners with a perfect salad. One morning I watched as the chefs at Jamin prepared the daily green salad: They snipped off only the very tips of the freshest, most tender salad greens, a mix of red- and green-tipped oak-leaf lettuce, white- and green-tipped curly endive, radicchio, watercress, lamb's lettuce (or mâche), dandelion greens, arugula. (The "insides" of the leaves, the less tender portions, were set aside for the staff lunch.) To that the chefs added a medley of the freshest of herbs, including chervil, sage, tarragon, dill, basil, marjoram, flat-leaf parsley, and mint. The choice, of course, is unlimited (purslane, sorrel, and nasturtium blossoms are also welcome additions). The point is to come up with a salad of varied colors, textures, and pungencies.

1 cup mixed fresh herb leaves—washed, dried, and loosely packed (preferably a mix of chervil, sage, tarragon, dill, basil, marjoram, flat-leaf parsley, and mint)

1 quart bite-size pieces of mixed salad greens—washed, dried, and loosely packed (preferably a mix of curly endive, radicchio, watercress, lamb's lettuce, dandelion greens, and arugula)
1 tablespoon minced black truffles (optional)
About ⅓ cup vinaigrette (page 328)

1. In a large shallow salad bowl, combine the herbs and salad greens, and toss with your hands. Add the minced truffle and toss again.

2. Pour the vinaigrette over the salad and toss, gently and thoroughly, until all the herbs and greens are lightly but evenly coated. They should not "swim" in dressing. Serve immediately.

Yield: 4 TO 6 SERVINGS

THE RED AND THE BLACK: RADICCHIO AND BLACK TRUFFLES

Salade Maraîchère aux Truffes

The ultimate of luxurious salads, this mixture of colors, textures, and flavors serves as a perfect foil for the avalanche of fresh black truffles arranged over the greens. It would be a marvelous beginning to a romantic dinner for two. Note that here, as elsewhere, the salad is served on a dinner plate: There's just never enough room for salad on small plates.

2 heads radicchio	Sea salt to taste
About 5 ounces curly endive, inner white portion only	½ cup peanut oil
	⅓ ounce black truffles, chopped
About 3 ounces lamb's lettuce	2½ ounces black truffles, thinly sliced
1½ ounces dandelion greens	(see box, pages 52–53)
1½ ounces mesclum	Freshly ground white pepper to taste
2 tablespoons freshly squeezed lemon juice	

1. Trim and wash the greens; drain and dry well. Place the radicchio in a bowl. Place the other greens in another bowl and toss to blend.

2. Prepare the vinaigrette: In a small bowl, mix together the lemon juice and salt. Whisk in the peanut oil, and taste for seasoning.

3. Neatly trim the outer edge of each radicchio leaf so that when arranged on the plate, they will form an even circle. Add just enough vinaigrette to the leaves to moisten them, and toss to thoroughly coat. Flattening the leaves as much as possible, carefully arrange the radicchio in a circle on 4 dinner plates.

4. Toss the remaining greens with the chopped truffles in the remaining vinaigrette. Mound the greens in the center of the radicchio circles, and cover the mounds completely with the sliced truffles, overlapping the slices to form a little mountain. You

should be able to see only the outer border of radicchio leaves. Season the truffles with freshly ground white pepper, and serve immediately.

Yield: 4 SERVINGS

Wine Suggestion: A HEADY GOLDEN RHÔNE VALLEY WHITE, SUCH AS A HERMITAGE

THIS THING CALLED

MESCLUM

Mesclum, also known as mesclun, is a Provençal blend of up to ten different salad greens and herbs, each varying in flavor, texture, and color. A mix might include red- and green-tipped oak-leaf lettuce, rocket or arugula, romaine, chervil, colorful red radicchio or trevise, curly white as well as green endive, escarole, and bitter dandelion greens. Add fresh herbs to this mixture (I'm partial to sage, dill, and tarragon) and you've a whole meal. If a wide variety of mixed greens and herbs is not available locally, order the "wild and exotic" salad mixture from Northwest Select, which offers a mesclum-style mixture that could include wild sorrel, land cress, mâche, violet leaves, and wild mustard. Northwest Select, 14724 184th Street NE, Arlington, WA 98223; tel. 203-435-8577.

BLACK TRUFFLES

Delicate, highly perfumed, and increasingly rare, black truffles remain one of the world's great luxuries. Fresh black truffles—unearthed in Provence from late November through late February—are firm, round black nuggets that range in size from a tiny pea to an oversized orange. Gently brushed of dirt, lightly peeled, and trimmed, truffles are served raw as well as cooked, and can be served whole, sliced into thin disks, finely minced, or cut into julienne strips to add an earthy, exotic fragrance, firm texture, and flavor to any dish. At Jamin, Chef Robuchon uses a generous quantity of fresh black truffles in season. At home, they're an obvious luxury, although top-quality preserved truffles can be substituted. When selecting preserved truffles, always purchase those in a glass jar, so you can see what you are purchasing. Buy only *truffes brossées au naturel*, truffles that have been sterilized in water and salt, with no alcohol or spices used to mask or heighten their flavors. (Do not use truffle peelings, truffle pieces, or preserved truffle juice: They are generally a disappointment and a bad buy.)

Joël Robuchon and truffle cultivator Yvon Bontoux, with his truffle dog Pamela, unearthing black truffles on a winter's day in Richerenches, in northern Provence

A sack full of freshly unearthed truffles, with a special metal pick for lifting them carefully from the ground

A LIVING HERB GARDEN

. . . .

If I had to list the ten most valuable lessons learned from this book, the virtues of fresh herbs would be near the top of the list. I cannot emphasize enough their value in adding bright, fresh flavors, honest colors, simple goodness. Both in my Paris apartment and my home in Provence, herbs hold a place of honor. At any one time, at least nine months of the year, my balconies and garden hold several kinds of sage, tarragon, fresh chervil, parsley, bay leaves, summer savory, rosemary, and chives. I promise you, once you make fresh herbs a habit, you'll never revert to using the dried variety, generally sorry substitutes. Fresh, potted herbs can be found at garden centers in season. If a wide variety of herbs is not available locally, a selection of twelve live herb plants can be ordered from The Herb-farm, 32804 Issaquah-Fall City Road, Fall City, WA 98024; tel. 206-784-2222 or 1-800-866-HERB.

RED CABBAGE SALAD WITH ANCHOVY DRESSING

Salade de Chou Rouge et de Poivron à l'Anchoïade

. . . .

With its strong, vibrant flavors, this is a colorful salad for those who like a generous hit of anchovies and garlic. The salad may be served as a part of a buffet, as a first-course salad, or even on its own as a simple luncheon dish, accompanied by crusty homemade bread. Any leftover salad makes a great filling for ham, turkey, or chicken sandwiches. It also suggests infinite variations: In place of the red cabbage and green pepper, try green cabbage and red pepper. (In this case, marinate the cabbage in lemon juice or white wine vinegar, not red wine vinegar, which would color the green cabbage.) Another variation may be prepared with finely chopped fennel (also marinated in lemon juice or white wine vinegar), adding red pepper or green pepper or both, for a colorful mixture.

Add garlic according to personal taste, and remember that although the salad may be served right away, it takes well to a bit of "aging." Just be aware that it will become more potent with age. Although many cooks use a food processor for shredding and grating, I find the results disappointing. This simple dish deserves a little extra effort, so grate the cabbage with the medium disk of a vegetable grater.

½ **head red cabbage (about 1½ pounds), grated**

3 **tablespoons best-quality red wine vinegar**

ANCHOVY DRESSING
1 **can (1.7 ounces) flat anchovy fillets in olive oil, drained, oil reserved**

3 **to 5 plump fresh garlic cloves (or to taste), degermed and coarsely chopped (see box, page 120)**

2 **tablespoons fresh flat-leaf parsley leaves, snipped with a scissors**

1 **green bell pepper, cored, seeded, and finely diced**

1. Several hours before serving: Place the cabbage in a large bowl. In a small saucepan, bring the vinegar to a boil over moderately high heat. Pour it immediately over

the cabbage and toss thoroughly. Cover, and set aside at room temperature for several hours. (The recipe may be prepared to this point 1 day in advance. Cover securely and refrigerate. Return to room temperature before serving.)

2. Prepare the dressing: Finely chop the anchovies with the reserved oil. Add the garlic and parsley, and chop together. The mixture should be rather coarse.

3. In a large serving bowl, combine the cabbage, anchovy dressing, and green pepper. Toss thoroughly. Serve at room temperature.

Yield: 4 TO 6 SERVINGS

BEETS WITH CREAMY HORSERADISH DRESSING

Betteraves, Sauce Crème au Raifort

. . . .

Horseradish is a highly underutilized condiment. When it is combined with the sweetness of beets, you have a powerful, intense collaboration. This is a delightful dish to pep up a gray winter day. Toss the salad while the beets are still warm, so that they thoroughly absorb the dressing.

EQUIPMENT: A steamer

3 to 4 medium beets (about 1 pound),
  well scrubbed

DRESSING
1 teaspoon best-quality red wine
  vinegar
1 teaspoon best-quality sherry wine
  vinegar

Sea salt to taste
2 tablespoons extra-virgin olive oil
1 tablespoon vegetable oil
Freshly ground white pepper to taste
2 tablespoons heavy cream
1 tablespoon prepared horseradish (or
  to taste)

1. Cook the beets: Place the beets in the top of a steamer. Cover, and steam over moderate heat until tender, about 45 minutes. (Alternatively, place the beets in a microwave-safe dish, add ¼ cup water, cover, and microwave at full power until tender, 10 to 15 minutes.) When cool, remove the skin and cut into ¾-inch dice. Place in a medium-size bowl and set aside.

2. Prepare the dressing: In a small bowl, whisk together the vinegars and salt. Gradually whisk in the oils until well blended. Season with pepper. Add the cream and horseradish, and stir to blend. Taste for seasoning.

3. To serve, pour the dressing over the beets and toss to coat evenly. (The recipe may be prepared 3 to 4 hours in advance. Cover securely and refrigerate. Return to room temperature before serving.)

Yield: 4 TO 6 SERVINGS

LAMB'S LETTUCE, POTATO, AND BLACK TRUFFLE SALAD

Salade de Mâche, Pommes de Terre, et Truffes

. . . .

A friend once described truffles as nature's way of saying "The earth is wonderful. To get a sense of the earth, eat truffles." Why not combine two wonders that grow beneath the soil—truffles and potatoes! This is a sublime salad, a layered crown of black truffles and steamed potatoes that have been steeped in a flavorful truffle vinaigrette. Truffles are an incredible luxury, and fresh truffles are a triple luxury. This recipe really should be prepared with fresh truffles, but top-quality truffles preserved in a jar are a worthy substitute.

Serve this with plenty of crusty grilled country-style bread.

EQUIPMENT: A steamer

1 to 2 whole black truffles (2 ounces)
²/₃ cup vinaigrette (page 328)
10 small potatoes (about 3 ounces each), scrubbed but not peeled

A handful of lamb's lettuce, rinsed and patted dry, for garnish
Coarse sea salt, for garnish
Small bunch of fresh chives, very finely minced, for garnish

1. At least 5 hours before you plan to serve the salad, begin the preparation: With a sharp knife or a vegetable peeler, carefully trim the truffles to form an even ball. Place the whole truffles in an airtight container and refrigerate. Save the truffle peelings for the vinaigrette.

2. Prepare the vinaigrette in a large bowl, and stir in the truffle peelings. Set aside.

3. Place the potatoes in a steamer, and steam until a skewer or fork inserted into a potato comes away easily, 15 to 20 minutes.

4. While the potatoes are still hot, peel them and slice into thin, even rounds ¼-inch

thick (the thickness of three quarters stacked together). Place them in the bowl with the truffle vinaigrette, and toss thoroughly. Cover, and set aside at room temperature for at least 4 hours, to allow the potatoes to absorb the vinaigrette.

5. When you are ready to serve the salad, drain the potatoes, reserving the vinaigrette. Set both aside.

6. Remove the truffles from the refrigerator. With a sharp knife, slice them as evenly and thinly as possible. Dip the slices into the reserved vinaigrette (don't douse or soak the truffle slices; you simply want to add a hint of the vinaigrette flavor).

7. On each salad plate, arrange the lamb's-lettuce leaves petal fashion, just inside the edge of the plate. Now arrange the outer ring of alternating potato and truffle slices, working clockwise and slightly overlapping the lamb's lettuce. Arrange the second ring working counterclockwise, again alternating the slices of truffle and potato, and slightly overlapping the outer ring. For the third ring, slightly overlap the second ring. Place a single slice of truffle in the center of the "crown." Carefully sprinkle each truffle with salt, and each potato with chives. Serve immediately.

Yield: 4 SERVINGS

Wine Suggestion: A PERFUMED SPICY RHÔNE VALLEY WHITE, SUCH AS A CHÂTEAUNEUF-DU-PAPE

Jean-Pierre Clot, with the tiny "ratté" variety of potatoes grown specially for Joël Robuchon's famed potato purée

POTATO POINTERS

To ensure even cooking, choose potatoes that are relatively the same size. When steaming or boiling, small potatoes are best, for they will cook more evenly. For the best flavor, steam rather than boil whole potatoes: Cook them in their skins, either in a colander set above boiling water or in a special vegetable or couscous steamer. There is no need to salt the water, for it will not be absorbed by the potatoes.

CELERY AND ROQUEFORT SALAD

Salade de Céleri-Branche au Roquefort

. . . .

Celery and Roquefort is a classic combination, and no wonder. Everyone loves the crunch of celery, and the intensity of the Roquefort helps perk up the delicately flavored vegetable.

8 to 10 tender celery ribs, preferably from the interior (about 1 pound), root end and leaves trimmed

DRESSING
1 teaspoon best-quality red wine vinegar

2 teaspoons best-quality sherry wine vinegar
Sea salt to taste
3 tablespoons extra-virgin olive oil
¼ cup crumbled Roquefort cheese
Freshly ground white pepper to taste

1. Slice each celery rib crosswise into thin half-moon shapes. Place in a large bowl and set aside.

2. Prepare the dressing: In a small bowl, whisk together the vinegars and salt. Gradually whisk in the oil until well blended. Add the Roquefort and crush with a fork to blend.

3. To serve, pour the dressing over the celery and toss to coat evenly. Season with pepper to taste.

Yield: 4 TO 6 SERVINGS

ASSORTED RAW VEGETABLE SALADS

Crudités

. . . .

Crudités, or assorted raw vegetables, have become such mundane fare in France that one is apt to forget how beautiful and enjoyable they can be when treated with some attention and care. Here is an assortment of small vegetable salads, to be made one by one or several at a time, for a simple family lunch or a grand buffet. The recipes are simply blueprints to suggest which dressings and seasonings have an affinity for which fresh vegetables.

GRATED CARROT SALAD WITH LEMON

Carottes Râpées au Citron et à l'Ail

. . . .

I love the tang of lemon juice alongside the sweet flavor of fresh carrots. The addition of a touch of garlic transforms this from an ordinary salad into one with great personality.

DRESSING
2 tablespoons freshly squeezed lemon
    juice
Sea salt to taste
1½ tablespoons extra-virgin olive oil
1½ tablespoons peanut oil

1 pound carrots, peeled
2 plump fresh garlic cloves (or to taste),
    degermed and minced (see box,
    page 120)
3 tablespoons fresh flat-leaf parsley
    leaves, snipped with a scissors

1. Prepare the dressing: In a small bowl, whisk together the lemon juice and salt. Gradually whisk in the oils until well blended. Taste for seasoning and set aside.

2. With the fine disk of a vegetable grater or a food processor, finely grate the carrots. In a medium-size bowl, combine the carrots and garlic. Pour the dressing over the carrots, and toss to coat evenly. (The salad may be prepared to this point up to 1 day in advance. Cover securely and refrigerate. Return to room temperature before serving.)

3. Sprinkle with parsley and serve.

Yield: 6 TO 8 SERVINGS

A WORD ABOUT SALT

Salt is essential to good cooking and should not be considered an optional seasoning. Salt actually helps bring to life the natural flavors of an ingredient, adding body to stocks and sauces, enlivening the flavors of pastries and cakes, giving balance to the final dish. I use only French unrefined sea salt from Brittany, which serves as a subtle, delicate, in fact refined, flavor booster. (Sea salt is extracted from sea water by evaporation, while the more common rock salt is found in its crystalline state in the ground.) I prefer coarse sea salt for general seasoning, selecting fine sea salt when the coarse version might be too emphatic or would not have time to dissolve, as in preparing breads and pastries. Both in the kitchen and at the table, I grind coarse sea salt from a salt grinder, instead of a standard salt shaker. Kosher salt is not a satisfactory substitute for sea salt: It has the same chemical properties as common table salt, and the flavors of both are too aggressive and too chemical. They are poor imitations of the real thing. Sea salt—both refined and unrefined—can be found in most supermarkets and specialty stores. It's more expensive, but a little goes a long way. Once convinced, you'll be a convert for life. English sea salt and a Lucite salt mill can be ordered from Select Origins, Box N, Southampton, NY 11968.

FRESH MUSHROOM SALAD WITH PARMESAN SHAVINGS

Salade de Champignons au Parmesan

. . . .

This is a particular favorite among the assorted fresh vegetable salads: I would have never thought of combining fresh mushrooms with thin shavings of Parmesan cheese, and when you add a touch of lemon juice, you have a real eye-opener. Do make the effort to prepare this with fresh herbs. If all the suggested assortment is not available, try to use at least two: tarragon, thyme, and mushrooms are terrific together. (For even shavings of Parmesan cheese, shave with a cheese plane or a vegetable peeler.)

DRESSING
3 tablespoons extra-virgin olive oil
1 plump fresh garlic clove, degermed and finely minced (see box, page 120)
2 tablespoons fresh flat-leaf parsley leaves
2 tablespoons fresh basil leaves
2 tablespoons fresh tarragon leaves
1 teaspoon fresh thyme leaves

Freshly ground white pepper to taste

¼ cup freshly squeezed lemon juice
Sea salt to taste
8 ounces mushrooms, trimmed and cleaned
2 ounces Parmesan cheese, thinly shaved

1. Prepare the dressing: In a small bowl, combine the oil and garlic. With a scissors, snip the parsley, basil, tarragon, and thyme leaves. Add to the dressing, and stir to blend. Season with pepper to taste. Set aside.

2. In a medium-size bowl, combine the lemon juice and salt, and stir to dissolve. Thinly slice the mushrooms, and toss them with the lemon juice. Pour the dressing over the mushrooms, and toss to coat evenly (The salad may be prepared 2 to 3 hours in advance. Cover securely and refrigerate. Return to room temperature before serving.)

3. Sprinkle the salad with the Parmesan shavings, and serve.

Yield: 6 TO 8 SERVINGS

CREAMY CUCUMBER SALAD WITH CURRY

Salade de Concombre à la Crème au Curry

. . . .

DRESSING

2 tablespoons *crème fraîche* (page 339)
 or heavy cream
3 tablespoons plain whole-milk yogurt
Curry powder to taste

Sea salt to taste

1 European or hothouse cucumber,
 peeled and thinly sliced

1. Prepare the dressing: In a small bowl, combine the *crème fraîche,* yogurt, curry powder, and salt. Stir to blend, and taste for seasoning.

2. To serve, place the cucumbers in a shallow bowl. Pour the dressing over the cucumbers and toss to coat evenly. (This salad should be tossed just before serving, for cucumbers will give off a good deal of liquid, even if they have been salted and drained beforehand.)

Yield: 4 TO 6 SERVINGS

CUCUMBER TRUCS

. . . .

For a pleasing presentation, try scoring the peeled cucumbers along their length with a fork. Also, so the water in the cucumbers does not drown the dressing, peel and slice them, place them in a bowl, and sprinkle lightly with salt. Cover with several ice cubes and place in the refrigerator for 1 hour. This will allow the cucumbers to crisp up while they give off liquid. Drain and pat dry, discarding the liquid and the ice cubes, and toss with a favorite dressing. Serve immediately.

GREEN BEAN SALAD WITH TOMATOES, GARLIC, AND SHALLOTS

Haricots Verts aux Tomates,
à l'Ail et aux Échalotes

....

B right and full-flavored, this is an ideal summertime salad. The dressing and beans may be prepared several hours in advance, but don't combine them until the very last minute so the salad will be crisp and fresh-tasting. Since some palates find the combination of raw garlic and shallots a bit pungent, the garlic and shallots are marinated in oil beforehand to soften the flavors. For best results, use vine-ripened tomatoes.

DRESSING
1 tablespoon best-quality sherry wine
    vinegar
Sea salt to taste
3 tablespoons extra-virgin olive oil
2 plump fresh garlic cloves, degermed
    and minced (see box, page 120)

2 shallots, minced

2 firm, medium, vine-ripened tomatoes
2 tablespoons coarse sea salt
1 pound young, tender green beans
3 tablespoons fresh flat-leaf parsley
    leaves, snipped with a scissors

1. About 1 hour before serving the salad, prepare the dressing: In a small bowl, whisk together the vinegar and salt. Set aside. In another bowl, combine the oil, garlic, and shallots. Set aside to mellow for about 1 hour.

2. Core, peel, seed, and chop the tomatoes. Place in a fine-mesh sieve and sprinkle lightly with some of the coarse salt. Set aside to drain.

3. Rinse the beans thoroughly, and trim the ends. Cut into 1-inch lengths.

4. Prepare a large bowl of ice water.

5. Fill a large pot with water and bring to a boil over high heat. Add the remaining salt and the beans, and cook until crisp-tender, about 4 minutes. Immediately drain the

beans and plunge them into the ice water so they cool down as quickly as possible. Drain the beans and wrap in a thick towel to dry.

6. To finish: Combine the vinegar and oil mixtures, and stir to blend; taste for seasoning. Transfer the beans to a bowl, pour the dressing over the beans, and toss to coat evenly. Add the tomatoes and parsley, and toss to blend. Taste for seasoning. Serve immediately.

Yield: 4 SERVINGS

KEEPING IT GREEN

....

For crisp green vegetables—such as the green beans here—blanch the vegetables in boiling salted water, drain, and plunge directly into ice water for 1 or 2 minutes. The colder the bath the better, for the cold will instantly stop cooking, allowing the vegetables to retain their bright color. Once cooled, drain thoroughly. If they stay too long in water they will become waterlogged and quickly lose flavor.

SAUTÉED RED PEPPERS WITH GARLIC AND THYME

Salade de Poivrons Rouges au Thym

. . . .

This is a vibrant summer salad, the kind of dish to make in quantity for a large buffet. I love the way the flavorful pepper oils mingle with the olive oil and vinegar, all made even more pungent by a good dose of herbs and garlic.

3 tablespoons extra-virgin olive oil

4 red bell peppers, cored, seeded, and sliced lengthwise into eighths

5 plump fresh garlic cloves, minced

2 teaspoons fresh thyme leaves

1 tablespoon best-quality sherry wine vinegar

1. In a large skillet, heat the oil over high heat. When it is hot, add the peppers and reduce the heat to moderate. Cook, stirring occasionally, until the peppers are softened, 10 to 15 minutes. Add the garlic and thyme, and continue cooking for 1 to 2 minutes. Do not let the garlic burn.

2. Add the vinegar and toss to coat evenly. Transfer to a serving bowl. Serve warm or at room temperature.

Yield: 4 SERVINGS

Beets and Walnuts with Walnut Oil Dressing

Betteraves et Noix à l'Huile de Noix

. . . .

Beets and walnuts have a lovely affinity for each other, and the addition of the lemon and walnut oil vinaigrette makes for a salad that's both homey and elegant.

EQUIPMENT: A steamer

3 to 4 medium beets (about 1 pound), well scrubbed

DRESSING
1 tablespoon freshly squeezed lemon juice

Sea salt to taste
3 tablespoons best-quality walnut oil

3 tablespoons freshly cracked walnut halves
Freshly ground black pepper to taste

1. Cook the beets: Place the beets in the top of a steamer. Cover and steam over moderate heat until tender, about 45 minutes. (Alternatively, place the beets in a microwave-safe dish, add ¼ cup water, cover, and microwave at full power until tender, about 10 minutes.) When cool, remove the skin and cut into ¾-inch dice. Place in a medium-size bowl and set aside.

2. Prepare the dressing: In a small bowl, whisk together the lemon juice and salt. Gradually whisk in the oil until well blended. Taste for seasoning.

3. To serve, pour the dressing over the beets and toss to coat evenly. (The recipe may be prepared to this point 3 to 4 hours in advance. Cover securely and refrigerate. Return to room temperature before serving.)

4. Just before serving, add the walnuts and toss. Season generously with pepper, and serve.

Yield: 4 TO 6 SERVINGS

CELERY ROOT AND APPLES IN CREAMY MUSTARD DRESSING

Salade "Bonne Femme"

. . . .

A lovely, almost mysterious variation on the classic *céleri rémoulade*, this salad might be considered the king of crudités. I love Chef Robuchon's addition of the apple, for although you don't see it mixed in with the bone-white celery root (also called celeriac), your palate detects the pleasant tartness. Note that sizes of celery root vary tremendously. The amount of dressing here is enough to nicely coat 1 pound of grated celery root, so adjust according to weight. Any leftover dressing can be used as a dip with other raw vegetables, such as carrots, celery, or cucumbers.

DRESSING
2 tablespoons freshly squeezed lemon
    juice
Sea salt to taste
2 tablespoons imported Dijon mustard
    (or to taste)
1 cup *crème fraîche* (page 339) or
    heavy cream

1 small to medium celery root (about 1
    pound)
1 tart green apple, such as Granny
    Smith, peeled and cored

1. Prepare the dressing: In a large bowl, whisk together the lemon juice and salt. Add the mustard and *crème fraîche,* and stir to blend. Taste for seasoning and set aside.

2. Cut the celery root into quarters, and peel it. With a hand grater or food processor, coarsely grate the celery root. Add to the dressing and toss to coat evenly.

3. With a hand grater or food processor, coarsely grate the apple. Add to the celery root and toss to coat evenly. Taste for seasoning. (The salad may be prepared several hours in advance. Cover securely and refrigerate.) Serve chilled or at room temperature.

Yield: 4 TO 6 SERVINGS

WARM FIRST COURSES

....

Entrées Chaudes

SAVORY TOMATO AND BASIL TARTS

Tarte Friande

aux Tomates, Poivrons, et Basilic

. . . .

This is one of Chef Robuchon's most spectacular creations, a truly savory, highly seasoned vegetable tart set atop layers of golden phyllo pastry. In the dining room at Jamin, the waiters like to joke that this is the best pizza in town! Indeed it is. Take one look at the photograph and you're daunted, but in truth this is not a terribly complicated dish to make. If you want a picture-perfect tart, it's rather labor-intensive, but your work will be aesthetically as well as gastronomically rewarded. Many obvious variations come to mind: The tart may be prepared as one large circle or rectangle, covered with the thick tomato sauce, then topped with the tomatoes and peppers. Or substitute ratatouille for the tomato sauce, then top with thin rounds of zucchini. Like a traditional tart shell, the phyllo may be baked several hours in advance, then held at room temperature. Prepare this in season, when tomatoes are most flavorful.

EQUIPMENT: One 1-inch round metal pastry cutter; one 5-inch round metal pastry cutter (or substitute a homemade cardboard stencil); baking parchment

About 16 large plum tomatoes
5 to 6 large green bell peppers

TOMATO SAUCE
1 large onion, finely chopped
1 tablespoon extra-virgin olive oil
Sea salt to taste
4 plump fresh garlic cloves
Bouquet garni: several parsley stems, celery leaves, and sprigs of thyme, wrapped in the green part of a leek and securely fastened with cotton twine

2 tablespoons tomato paste
1 tablespoon sugar

3 tablespoons unsalted butter, melted
4 sheets phyllo dough
2 tablespoons chopped fresh basil leaves
About 1 tablespoon extra-virgin olive oil
Coarse sea salt and coarsely ground white pepper to taste
1 teaspoon fresh thyme leaves

1. Prepare the tomato disks: Core the tomatoes, and peel them with a vegetable peeler. Halve each tomato lengthwise, and squeeze slightly to remove the seeds. Discard the seeds. With a small spoon, remove the tomato pulp. Finely chop the pulp, place in a medium-size bowl, and reserve for the tomato sauce. Carefully flatten each tomato half. With the 1-inch cutter, cut the tomatoes into even disks. Arrange the disks side by side on a baking sheet or platter. You will need 24 tomato disks for each tart. Chop any leftover pieces of tomato and add to the tomato pulp. Set aside. (These may be prepared several hours in advance. Cover and refrigerate.)

2. Prepare the pepper disks: With a vegetable peeler, peel the peppers. Cut the peppers in thirds lengthwise. Remove and discard the seeds and core. Carefully flatten the pieces, halve the peppers horizontally, and with the 1-inch cutter, cut the peppers into even disks. You will need 16 pepper disks for each tart. Prepare a large bowl of ice water. Bring a large pot of water to a boil. Salt the water, add the pepper disks, and blanch for 10 seconds. Remove with a slotted spoon and transfer to the ice water. When cool, drain thoroughly and place side by side on a baking sheet or platter. Set aside. (These may be prepared several hours in advance. Cover and refrigerate.)

3. Prepare the tomato sauce: In a large skillet, combine the onion, oil, and salt over moderate heat. Cook until soft and translucent, 3 to 4 minutes. Add the garlic, bouquet garni, reserved chopped tomatoes, tomato paste, and sugar. Taste for seasoning. Cook, uncovered, over moderate heat until the sauce thickens, about 10 minutes. Remove and discard the garlic and bouquet garni. Transfer the sauce to a food processor or food mill, and purée. Set aside.

4. Place a layer of baking parchment on a baking sheet and butter the parchment. With the 5-inch cutter, prepare 20 disks of phyllo dough. Place 1 disk of dough on the baking sheet, and lightly brush the top with melted butter. Cover with another disk of dough, butter the top, and repeat with 3 more disks of dough, to make a stack five layers high. Do not butter the top layer. Repeat for three more tarts. Cover the tarts with another piece of baking parchment (do not butter this parchment). Weight by placing another baking sheet of about the same size on top. Refrigerate until the butter has hardened, about 30 minutes.

5. Preheat the oven to 400°F.

6. Place the phyllo dough, still sandwiched between the baking sheets, in the center of the oven. Bake until the dough turns an even golden brown, about 15 minutes. Watch carefully, for ovens vary. Remove from the oven, remove the top baking sheet and the

top sheet of parchment, and set aside to cool. (The dough may be prepared to this point several hours in advance. Reserve at room temperature.)

7. In a small saucepan, reheat the tomato sauce over low heat. Taste for seasoning. Stir in the basil. Carefully spoon 1/4 cup tomato sauce on top of the baked phyllo disks, dividing the sauce evenly among the 4 tartlets. Do not spread the sauce all the way out to the edge, or it may drip down the sides. Smooth with the back of a spoon.

8. Prepare the outermost ring of tomato and pepper disks: Select 14 tomato and 7 pepper disks. Working clockwise, arrange petal-fashion, 2 tomato disks for each green pepper disk on top of the sauce, overlapping slightly. Prepare the second ring: Select 6 tomatoes and 6 peppers. Working counterclockwise, alternate single disks of tomato and pepper, overlapping slightly. Prepare the third ring: Select 3 tomatoes and 3 peppers. Working clockwise, alternate single disks of tomato and pepper, overlapping slightly. In the center, place a single tomato disk. (Do not season the vegetables at this point or they will give up too much liquid when they cook.) Repeat for the remaining 3 tartlets. (Depending upon the size of your disks, and the tightness of your rings, you may not use all the vegetable disks.)

9. Place the tartlets in the center of the oven and bake until warmed through, 2 to 3 minutes. Remove from the oven, and with a pastry brush, coat lightly with oil. Season with salt, white pepper, and thyme. Return to the oven, 2 to 3 minutes.

10. To serve: Place each tart in the center of a warmed dinner plate and serve immediately.

Yield: 4 SERVINGS

FRESH BOUQUET GARNI

Most good cooking is simply a search for a distilled essence of flavors. A bouquet garni—no more than a mixture of fresh herbs wrapped securely with cotton twine—is one of these culinary extras that subtly improves the flavor of a dish by adding fresh, herbal essences. Try preparing the same dish twice, with and without the addition of a fresh bouquet garni, and you'll see what I mean. There is no "standard" recipe for a bouquet garni, but it might include sprigs of fresh thyme, parsley, tarragon, bay leaf, celery leaves, a rib of celery, or rosemary. One convenient way to hold it all together is to wrap the fresh herbs in the green part of a leek, then fasten it securely with cotton twine.

Wine Suggestion: A FLINTY, FRUITY WHITE, SUCH AS A LOIRE VALLEY POUILLY-FUMÉ

TRUFFLE, ONION, AND BACON TARTLETS

Tarte Friande de Truffes aux Oignons et Lard Fumé

. . . .

This is a wildly extravagant dish, but there are occasions that demand a certain lavishness: a layer of thinly sliced truffles, a layer of peppery onion, bacon and cream. Add a few sips of chilled Burgundy, pass the grilled garlic bread, and you're in heaven! (Note: It is important that the bacon be minced rather fine. If you chill the bacon in the freezer for 30 minutes or so, it will be easier to cut.)

This recipe is also extraordinary when cooked in little ramekins, without the luxury of truffles. You'll finish by saying, "Is my mouth happy!"

4 black truffles (about 1½ ounces each)	Sea salt and freshly ground black pepper to taste
1 plump fresh garlic clove, halved	
2 tablespoons unsalted butter, melted	4 very thin slices bacon (about 4 ounces), chilled
8 medium onions (about 2 pounds)	
2 tablespoons goose fat (see box, pages 84–85)	⅓ cup heavy cream
	Fine sea salt, for garnish

1. Prepare nine 5-inch rounds of waxed paper.

2. With a sharp knife or vegetable peeler, carefully trim the truffle to form an even ball. Slice the truffles into thin, even rounds. Mince the truffle peelings and set aside.

3. Rub one side of the waxed paper rounds with the garlic halves. With a brush, generously coat the same side with butter. Beginning in the center, arrange truffle slices in a spiral pattern on one of the buttered papers, first brushing the underside of each slice with butter so that the slices stay together. The truffle slices should overlap slightly. When the truffle slices are arranged, brush the entire surface with a generous layer of butter and top with another paper round, butter side down. Press down firmly. Repeat to make 3 more tart bases. Refrigerate the tart bases for at least 1 hour to harden the butter. (These truffle rounds may be prepared 6 to 8 hours in advance. Cover securely and refrigerate.)

4. Preheat the oven to 475°F.

5. Cut the onions in half, place them cut side down on a work surface, and cut into thin, almost transparent, slices.

6. In a large skillet, combine the onions and goose fat over high heat. Season, and cook 10 minutes, stirring constantly. The onions should not brown. Set aside.

7. Trim the fat from the bacon and cut the meat into very tiny cubes. Bring a small saucepan of water to a boil. Place the bacon in a fine-mesh sieve and submerge in the boiling water for 10 seconds. Set aside to drain.

8. Add the truffle peelings to the skillet containing the onions, and warm over low heat, about 30 seconds. Add the bacon, pepper generously, and stir constantly for 1 minute. Add the cream and cook 1 minute more, stirring constantly. Taste for seasoning. The mixture should be quite peppery.

9. Divide the onion mixture among 4 dinner plates, and flatten to form circles the size of the truffle rounds. Use the extra paper round as a guide (but do not place under the onions).

10. To assemble the tarts: Remove the truffle rounds from the refrigerator, take off the top piece of paper, and invert onto the onion rounds, leaving the top paper round intact. Place the plates in the oven for 1 minute, or just long enough to melt the butter that is holding the truffles together. Remove from the oven as soon as the butter melts, and carefully pull away the top layer of paper. Sprinkle with the fine sea salt and pepper. Serve with grilled country bread rubbed with garlic.

Yield: 4 SERVINGS

Wine Suggestion: A GREAT WHITE BURGUNDY, SUCH AS A CORTON-CHARLEMAGNE

NOTE: To prepare individual onion-bacon ramekins: Spoon the onion and bacon mixture into four ½-cup ramekins, and even out with the back of a spoon. Cover with plastic wrap and reheat either in a microwave for 1 minute on high or in a steamer. To serve, unmold onto warmed salad plates. Serve immediately, with grilled country bread rubbed with garlic.

SMALL IS BEAUTIFUL

. . . .

The way in which ingredients are chopped or cut can dramatically alter flavor. In the truffle, onion, and bacon tart, for example, it's amazing how tiny cubes of bacon can release such a wealth of flavor.

WARM OYSTERS WITH FENNEL AND CURRY

Huîtres Chaudes au Fenouil et au Curry

. . . .

Rich and ethereal, with that wonderfully salty, briny sea essence, these warm oysters bathed in a rich sauce make for a very elegant first or main course. For best results, prepare this dish just before serving. Your actual cooking time will be greatly reduced if you have all the equipment at hand and do all the chopping and measuring in advance. Do not open the oysters until the last minute, however.

3 shallots, minced

1²/₃ cups dry white wine, preferably a Chardonnay

8 tablespoons unsalted butter, chilled

Unsalted butter, softened, for the baking dish

24 freshly shucked oysters, liquor strained and reserved

1 medium onion, minced

1 small fennel bulb, minced

1 cup heavy cream

Large pinch of curry powder

Freshly ground white pepper to taste

¼ cup salmon roe (optional; see Note)

¼ cup snipped fresh chives

1. In a small saucepan, combine the shallots, wine, and 1 tablespoon of the butter over moderately high heat. Bring to a boil and reduce by half, about 10 minutes.

2. Generously butter a shallow flameproof baking dish. Arrange the oysters in a single layer in the dish. Set aside.

3. Add the reserved oyster liquor to the reduced wine mixture. Return to a boil, and then strain the hot mixture through a fine-mesh sieve directly over the oysters. Place the dish over moderate heat, turning the oysters after 30 seconds. As soon as the liquid begins to tremble, 1 to 2 minutes, remove from the heat.

4. Transfer the oysters to a plate to cool. With a scissors, trim the small dark beards, or mantles, from the oysters, for a more aesthetic presentation. Reserve the oyster liquid that remains in the dish.

5. In a medium-size saucepan, combine 5 tablespoons of the butter with the onion and fennel, and cook until softened, 3 to 4 minutes. Whisk in the oyster liquid, cream, and curry, and reduce over moderate heat for 5 to 6 minutes. Taste for seasoning.

6. Line a fine-mesh sieve with moistened cheesecloth, and strain the sauce into another saucepan. Whisk in the remaining 2 tablespoons butter. Add the oysters to the sauce and heat just until warmed through, about 1 minute.

7. Transfer the oysters to warmed shallow soup bowls. Stir the salmon roe into the sauce, and spoon over the oysters. Garnish with the chives and serve immediately.

Yield: 4 SERVINGS

Wine Suggestion: A NONSPARKLING CHAMPAGNE, SUCH AS A COTEAUX CHAMPENOIS

NOTE: If caviar, salmon roe, or preserved truffles are not available locally, they can be ordered from Petrossian, a reliable source for many quality food products. Orders can be placed by fax (212-245-2812) or phone (1-800-828-9241) from Petrossian, Inc, 182 West 58th Street, New York, NY 10102-0852.

MAKE REDUCING A

ROUTINE

As home cooks, there are many routine professional procedures that we shun altogether, and one of them is the practice of reducing a liquid to obtain richer, more intense flavors, and often a thicker sauce. I'm not sure why we resist, but I have a feeling that we fear we're wasting good liquid as we reduce. Nothing could be further from the truth. This recipe, for instance, benefits from a classic reduction of wine and shallots, a step that requires no effort on your part, other than the 10 minutes it takes for the shallots, wine, and butter to be transformed from three unrelated ingredients into a unified, rich sauce. Taste the sauce before and after reducing it, and you'll quickly see what I mean. At last, a culinary "truc" that requires no special equipment, no particular culinary efficiency, just a few minutes of time that will pay you back in spades!

. . . .

Fresh chives are one of the prettiest and most flavorful of herb garnishes. For fresh chivelike greens year-round—garden or no garden—plant 5 or 6 shallot bulbs, root end down, side by side in a flower pot. Do not plant them too deeply; cover with just a thin layer of soil. Place the pot near a window or on a well-lit kitchen counter. Within a few days little "chives" will begin sprouting. They will easily grow to 6 to 8 inches within about 10 days. To harvest, snip with scissors. Indoors, the shallots may give out after 3 or 4 weeks but will grow for months on a balcony. I keep several pots going at all times, planting a new batch every few weeks.

FOIE GRAS WITH SMOOTH LENTIL CREAM SAUCE

Foie Gras à la Crème de Lentilles

. . . .

I love seemingly contradictory combinations like this one: regal foie gras with commonplace lentils. Of course there's nothing commonplace about this dish, a sure-fire winner for foie gras lovers. The French call lentils "poor man's caviar," and that they are, especially if you can secure the prized dark slate-green *lentilles de Puy*, which have a very crisp, earthy, wholesome flavor that marries well with the rich, smooth, elegant foie gras. If the imported variety is not available, substitute the same quantity of large green lentils. The cooking method for the foie gras—a simple steaming—makes for a very quick and special dish. While this souplike dish serves 4 very generously as a main course, it can easily serve 8 as a rich first course.

EQUIPMENT: An immersion mixer (optional); a steamer

1 fresh duck foie gras (1 to 1½ pounds) (see Note)

1 tablespoon sea salt

1⅔ cups French *lentilles de Puy* (see Note)

2 cups chicken stock (page 334)

2 cups water

2½ ounces slab bacon, rind removed

1 plump fresh garlic clove, halved

1 onion stuck with 1 clove

1 carrot

Bouquet garni: several parsley stems, celery leaves, and sprigs of thyme, wrapped in the green part of a leek and securely fastened with cotton twine

Sea salt and freshly ground white pepper to taste

6 tablespoons unsalted butter, chilled, cut into small pieces

GARNISH

Coarse sea salt

1 tablespoon coarsely ground white peppercorns

¼ cup fresh chervil leaves or flat-leaf parsley leaves

1 small bunch of chives, snipped with a scissors

1. At least 6 hours before preparing the dish, prepare the foie gras: Note that a duck liver consists of two lobes, one small, one large. With the tip of a small sharp knife, carefully remove any traces of green from the surface of the foie gras. With your hands, separate the larger lobe from the smaller one by gently pulling them apart. Cut each lobe crosswise into 5 to 6 pieces, each about 1 inch thick. Again with the tip of a small sharp knife, remove the thin transparent skin surrounding each piece of duck liver. With the tip of the knife remove and discard the thin red blood vessel that runs lengthwise through the inside of each lobe. (You may, indeed, need to poke around with your fingers to find the vessels, but it is worth it. Leaving the vessels in will make for unsightly foie gras.) Prepare a large bowl of ice water, add 1 tablespoon salt for each 1½ quarts water, and place the foie gras pieces in the water. Cover and refrigerate for 6 hours. The salt will help to draw out the blood, making for a clean, even-colored foie gras.

A WORD ON FOIE GRAS

. . . .

Foie gras—which literally means "fat liver" in English—is the oversized liver of fattened, specially bred geese and ducks. The liver of a fattened goose can weigh up to two pounds, while a fatted duck liver generally weighs about one pound. A good liver is pale, ivory pink in color, and is rich, succulent, unctuous, and luxurious. The most popular method of preparing foie gras is in a terrine: The seasoned foie gras is cooked, matured, then served in slices with toasted bread. Foie gras can also be seared in slices, roasted whole, or added as a flavoring to sauces. When a recipe calls for foie gras, do not substitute the liver of a standard duck; the results just won't be the same.

2. Prepare the lentils: Place the lentils in a colander and rinse under cold running water. Transfer them to a large saucepan and add cold water to cover. Bring to a boil over high heat. When the water boils, remove from the heat, drain, and rinse the lentils under cold running water. Return the lentils to the saucepan, add the chicken stock and the 2 cups water, and bring to a boil over high heat. With a slotted spoon, skim any impurities that rise to the surface. Add the bacon, garlic, onion, carrot, and bouquet garni. Season with salt and pepper. Reduce the heat to very low, cover securely, and cook until the lentils are tender, 40 to 45 minutes for French lentils, about 35 minutes for domestic lentils. Stir from time to time to prevent the lentils from sticking. Skim as necessary.

3. Remove the pan from the heat and discard the carrot, onion, and bouquet garni. Remove the bacon and cut it into fine dice. In a small saucepan, combine the bacon with 2 tablespoons of the lentils. Set aside.

4. With a slotted spoon, remove the remaining lentils from the cooking liquid. Do not discard the cooking liquid. Place the lentils in a food mill or food processor, and blend to a purée. Return the lentils to a medium-size saucepan over moderate heat. Whisk in enough cooking liquid to obtain a thin sauce. Force the lentils through a food mill once again (or purée in a food processor) and return to the saucepan. Reduce the heat to low, and whisk in 3 tablespoons of the butter. Do not boil. Remove from the heat, and whisk in the remaining 3 tablespoons butter, until thoroughly incorporated. The sauce should be thin, almost like a rich cream soup. (If you have an immersion mixer, use it here to lighten and fluff up the sauce.) Taste for seasoning. Set aside and keep warm. (The sauce may be prepared up to 30 minutes in advance. Reheat in the top of a double boiler over low heat.)

5. Prepare twelve 7½-inch squares of baking parchment. Soak the parchment in water to make it pliable, then drain and pat dry to remove excess liquid. Remove the foie gras from the water and pat thoroughly dry. Wrap each piece of foie gras in moistened parchment, then tightly twist each end to secure. Set aside.

6. In a steamer, bring 2 cups water to a boil over high heat. Place the wrapped foie gras in the steamer, reduce the heat

POIVRE MIGNONNETTE

. . . .

Historically, a *mignonnette* was a small muslin sachet fillet with peppercorns and cloves, used to flavor soups and stews much in the way we use a bouquet garni today. A *mignonnette* containing ginger, cloves, coriander, nutmeg, and hot pepper was also often dipped into a dish at the last minute, to add a touch of spice. Today the term *poivre mignonnette* more commonly refers to coarsely ground white peppercorns. For maximum flavor, grind whole peppercorns—either in a small spice grinder or with a mortar and pestle—just before using them.

LENTILS

. . . .

Although some cooks suggest soaking lentils before cooking them (theoretically to puff them up a bit and make them more digestible), Chef Robuchon advises against it. Soaking lentils actually causes them to begin the sprouting process, and in fact they begin to ferment, making for disagreeable, indigestible lentils. Rather, blanch them first, to remove any traces of bitterness.

to moderate, cover, and cook just until the foie gras begins to melt and is warmed through, 4 to 6 minutes.

7. Meanwhile, reheat the bacon-lentil mixture over moderately high heat. Add it to the creamy lentil sauce, and stir to blend. If the lentil sauce is too thick, add a little more cooking liquid. Set aside and keep warm.

8. Remove the foie gras from the steamer, and with a pair of scissors, cut away one end of the parchment. Drain off and discard all the liquid that has melted from the foie gras. Cut off the other side and carefully unwrap the foie gras: It will be quite fragile. Drain, and pat dry if necessary. Arrange 2 pieces of foie gras in each warmed shallow soup bowl. Nap with the creamy lentil sauce. Sprinkle with the coarse sea salt and coarsely ground white pepper. Decorate with chervil leaves and minced chives, and serve immediately.

Yield: 8 FIRST-COURSE SERVINGS, 4 MAIN-COURSE SERVINGS

N O T E : Fresh foie gras can be ordered from D'Artagnan, Inc., 399–419 Saint Paul Avenue, Jersey City, NJ 07306; tel. 800-DAR-TAGN or 201-792-0748; fax 201-792-0113. Ask for Moulard Duck foie gras A Prime. The foie gras arrives vacuum-packed in heavy plastic, and before opening has about a 10-day shelf life. *Lentilles de Puy* can be ordered from Dean & DeLuca, 110 Greene Street, New York, NY 10012.

T H E   G O O D   O F   G O O S E   F A T

. . . .

Goose fat is the smooth ivory-colored fat of a fattened goose. The fattening process produces both high-quality fat and a smooth and unctuous liver, known as foie gras d'oie ("fat goose liver"). Traditionally goose fat has been used to preserve poultry, meats, and terrines, but in cooking it can be used interchangeably with any solid animal fat, such as butter, chicken or duck fat, or suet. Try sautéeing potatoes in goose fat and you'll become an instant convert: Your potatoes will be golden, moist, more richly flavored.

Goose fat burns less than butter, "fixes" the flavors of ingredients, and it can be heated to a higher temperature than other fats, such as butter. This means, spoonful for spoonful, you'll need less goose fat than other fats to achieve the same moist, well-flavored results when sautéeing. Goose fat can be purchased in jars and cans, and sometimes at German and Hungarian butchers. I always use goose fat when sautéeing potatoes and find it is an excellent vehicle for bringing out the flavors of shellfish, such as shrimp or lobster. For a depth of flavors, use a combination of goose fat and olive oil or goose fat and butter when sautéeing. Goose fat, which melts to a golden liquid when heated, returns to a solid state at room temperature. It can be stored indefinitely, refrigerated in a well-sealed container.

Nutritionally, goose fat has half the saturated fat of butter, and almost four times the (healthy) polyunsaturated fat and twice the monounsaturated fat (thought to be harmless).

French goose fat can be purchased in a 12-ounce can from Maison Glass Delicacies, 111 East 58th Street, New York, NY 10022; tel. 212-755-3316 or 800-U-CALL-MG.

MAKE-AHEAD DINNER

·················

As much as I love cooking with friends at my side, there are days when you want most of the dinner to be prepared in advance so you can join the party. In this menu, the foie gras is prepared three to four days ahead and the ratatouille the day before, as are the raspberry gratins. The chicken is grilled at the last minute. Begin the meal with a chilled Alsatian Gewürztraminer, then enjoy a Beaujolais with the chicken. If you're in a celebratory mood, finish off with a bubbling pink Champagne.

·················

TERRINE OF FRESH DUCK LIVERS
TERRINE DE FOIE GRAS DE CANARD

CHARCOAL-BROILED HALVED CHICKEN WITH HOT MUSTARD
POULET GRILLÉ EN CRAPAUDINE

PROVENÇAL VEGETABLES
RATATOUILLE

FIELD SALAD WITH FRESH HERBS
SALADE AUX HERBES FRAÎCHES

INDIVIDUAL RASPBERRY GRATINS
GRATINS DE FRAMBOISES

COLD FIRST COURSES

. . . .

Entrées Froides

BAY SCALLOPS WITH THYME AND LEMON BUTTER

Marinière de Pétoncles

. . . .

Easy, elegant, and impressive. What more can one ask of a dish? This is an ultimate appetizer, rather fun and uncomplicated to make, and pretty to serve. Use your imagination when choosing the shells you use, as well as the base for the shells on the serving platter (we used coarse sea salt). Most of the elements can be prepared just before your guests arrive, with the final arranging done at the last moment.

3 baby leeks, green portion only (or substitute the greens of 3 fresh scallions)

Coarse sea salt

8 bay scallop shells (or substitute clam shells, large scallop shells, any cleaned shells gathered from the beach)

2 teaspoons unsalted butter, softened

24 fresh bay scallops, rinsed and patted dry

Freshly ground coarse white pepper to taste

2 teaspoons fresh thyme leaves

5 tablespoons unsalted butter

3 shallots, finely minced

6 tablespoons dry white wine, preferably a Chardonnay

1 tablespoon heavy cream

1 tablespoon freshly squeezed lemon juice

1. Rinse the leek or scallion greens and cut them into thin diagonal slices (you will need 24 slices for the garnish). Prepare a large pot of boiling water. Salt the water, add the greens, and blanch for 2 minutes. Rinse under cold running water, drain, and set aside.

2. Scatter an even layer of coarse sea salt on a large round serving platter. Arrange the scallop shells on top of the salt. Set aside.

3. Lightly brush an ovenproof platter with some of the softened butter, and arrange the scallops on the platter in a single layer. Brush the scallops lightly with softened

butter, and season them generously with freshly ground coarse white pepper, a touch of finely ground sea salt, and half the thyme leaves. Set aside.

4. Preheat the broiler.

5. In a medium-size saucepan over moderate heat, combine 3 tablespoons of the butter, the shallots, and a pinch of salt. Cook until the shallots begin to soften, 2 to 3 minutes. Do not let them brown. Add the wine, and reduce for 2 to 3 minutes. Whisk in the cream and lemon juice, and taste for seasoning. Off the heat, whisk in the remaining 2 tablespoons butter until well incorporated into the sauce. (The sauce may be prepared up to 30 minutes in advance. Keep it warm, uncovered, in the top of a double boiler over low heat.)

6. Place the platter of scallops beneath the broiler, about 3 inches from the heat. Broil for 1 minute. The scallops should be heated but not cooked. Remove from the heat.

7. With a small spoon, spoon the shallot and butter sauce into the scallop shells. Arrange 3 scallops on top of the sauce in each shell. Arrange 3 slices of leek or scallion green like a three-leaf clover on top of the scallops. Sprinkle with the remaining thyme leaves, and serve 2 shells per serving.

Yield: 4 SERVINGS

Wine Suggestion: A PERFUMED, FLORAL WHITE, SUCH AS A CHABLIS GRAND CRU

THE FINE AND THE COARSE

. . . .

As a seasoning, whole white or black peppercorns, ground at the last moment from a pepper mill, add unparalleled flavor. But there are times when a bit more assertive flavor is welcome, and that's when it's time to consider the virtues of freshly ground coarse pepper. At home I grind whole peppercorns in a small electric spice or coffee mill (being sure to thoroughly clean the mill after use, so no odors remain). Alternatively, the peppercorns can be crushed by hand, using two different methods. On a work surface, crush the peppercorns with a heavy mallet or with the bottom of a heavy skillet. Or crush the peppercorns in a mortar with a pestle.

TOMATO-MINT SORBET

Sorbet Tomate à la Menthe

. . . .

Simple and satisfying, this is a marvelous first course for a luncheon on a steamy summer day. Make this with "meaty" plum tomatoes, and serve it in clear glass bowls with a sprig of mint for garnish. Note that the method of making the tomato purée—baking the tomatoes, then peeling them—is also a good quick way to make a basic tomato sauce.

EQUIPMENT: One 1-quart capacity ice cream maker

3 pounds plum tomatoes
1¼ cups confectioners' sugar
1 tablespoon freshly squeezed lemon
   juice

Pinch of salt
1 tablespoon chopped fresh mint leaves
Several whole fresh mint leaves, for
   garnish

1. Preheat the oven to 400°F.

2. Halve the tomatoes horizontally, and squeeze gently to remove the juice and seeds. Arrange the tomatoes, cut side down, on a baking sheet. Place it in the center of the oven and bake until the skin pulls away from the flesh, about 10 minutes.

3. Remove the baking sheet from the oven and place it on a rack. Set aside to cool.

4. When the tomatoes are cool enough to handle, peel them and remove the cores. Place the tomatoes in a food processor, and process until smooth. Strain through a fine-mesh sieve into a large bowl. Add the sugar, lemon juice, salt, and chopped mint to the tomato purée, and stir until well blended.

5. Refrigerate until thoroughly chilled (the sorbet mixture should feel cold to the touch). Then transfer the mixture to an ice cream maker and freeze according to the manufacturer's instructions. Serve immediately.

Yield: 3 CUPS SORBET

MARINATED MUSHROOM SALAD

Champignons, Légumes, et Raisins Marinés à la Coriandre

. . . .

Highly seasoned and exotically heightened with the flavors of coriander and the sweetness of raisins, this salad is served as a refreshing first course at Jamin. I've also prepared simplified versions, deleting the raisins and using only the ground coriander, not the whole grains, which some palates can't tolerate. In warm weather it is delicious as a side dish to grilled meats or roast chicken.

The salad (without the garnishes) may be prepared one day in advance, to give the flavors some time to mellow. Just be sure to remove it from the refrigerator at least 30 minutes before serving so that it can reach room temperature.

2½ pounds firm, fresh mushroom caps (about 3 pounds whole mushrooms)

⅔ cup extra-virgin olive oil

1 medium onion, minced

3 tablespoons whole coriander seeds

Sea salt and freshly ground white pepper to taste

1 bottle dry white wine, preferably a Chardonnay

2 tablespoons freshly ground coriander

Bouquet garni: several parsley stems, celery leaves, and sprigs of thyme, wrapped in the green part of a leek and securely fastened with cotton twine

6 tablespoons freshly squeezed lemon juice

1 can (14½ ounces) imported plum tomatoes, drained and puréed in a food processor or blender

½ cup tomato paste

¾ cup golden raisins

¾ cup black currants

VEGETABLE GARNISH

About 16 small green asparagus stalks, tender tips only

8 small leeks, white and green tender parts, well rinsed

16 fresh baby onions (or substitute pearl onions)

1 cup cauliflower flowerets

1 cup fresh peas

Several tablespoons vinaigrette (page 328)

HERB GARNISH

1 small bunch of chives, snipped with a scissors

¼ cup fresh mint leaves, snipped with a scissors

1. One day before serving: Rinse the mushrooms under cold running water, and drain. Twist off the stem ends, to leave perfect caps. (The stems will not be used in this recipe, but may be reserved for preparing stocks or a mushroom soup.) If the mushroom caps are large, quarter them. Set aside.

2. In a large deep skillet, combine the oil, onion, whole coriander seeds, salt, and pepper over moderately high heat. Cook until the onions are softened, 2 to 3 minutes. Add the wine, ground coriander, and bouquet garni. Increase the heat to high and bring to a boil. Boil to help burn off the alcohol in the wine, about 5 minutes, then reduce the heat to low. Add the mushrooms and the lemon juice. Cover, increase the heat to high, and cook for 5 minutes. The mushrooms will give off a good deal of liquid.

3. With a slotted spoon, transfer the mushrooms to a sieve set over a large bowl. Set aside to drain. Add the tomato purée and tomato paste to the liquid in the skillet. Cover, and cook over high heat until reduced to about 1 quart, about 10 minutes.

4. Meanwhile, prepare the raisins and currants: Rinse well and combine in a small saucepan. Cover with cold water. Bring to a boil over high heat, and cook for 2 minutes. Drain thoroughly and set aside.

5. To complete the basic salad, remove and discard the bouquet garni from the sauce. Add the raisins, currants, and mushrooms, and cook for 1 minute. Taste for seasoning. Transfer to a bowl, cover, and refrigerate for 24 hours, to allow the flavors to blend and mellow.

6. Several hours before serving, prepare the garnish vegetables: Prepare a large bowl of ice water. Bring a large pot of water to a boil. Salt the water and add the asparagus. Cook until tender, 2 to 3 minutes. With a slotted spoon, transfer the asparagus to the ice water and leave until thoroughly chilled. Drain, and set aside. Repeat for the leeks, onions, cauliflower, and peas, but change the cooking water for each vegetable.

7. To serve: With a slotted spoon, transfer the mushroom mixture (draining off any excess sauce) to individual salad plates. Toss the garnish vegetables in the vinaigrette and arrange on top of the salad. Sprinkle with the chives and mint, and serve.

Yield: 8 TO 12 SERVINGS

Wine Suggestion: A FLINTY WHITE SANCERRE

QUATRE ÉPICES

Quatre Épices

....

*Q*uatre épices, literally "four spices," is a classic French mixture designed to season terrines of pork or duck liver. Use the best-quality spices you can find, and grind them yourself in a spice or coffee mill. I generally prepare only the amount I will need for each terrine

¼ **teaspoon freshly ground cinnamon**
¼ **teaspoon freshly ground allspice**
¼ **teaspoon freshly ground cloves**
¼ **teaspoon freshly ground nutmeg**

Combine all the ingredients in a small bowl and stir thoroughly. Use immediately.

Yield: 1 TEASPOON *QUATRE ÉPICES*

FESTIVE SHRIMP SALAD

Salade de Crevettes en Boléro

. . . .

This is a bright and lively seafood salad that can be prepared with shrimp or lobster. I like to serve it as a luncheon dish, with plenty of crusty toasted homemade bread.

2 cups aromatic shrimp bouillon
   (page 333)
72 medium-size raw shrimp in the shell
   (about 2¼ pounds)
2 large tomatoes, cored, peeled, and
   seeded
6 tablespoons freshly squeezed lemon
   juice

2 Granny Smith apples
2 medium avocados
1 tablespoon peanut oil
1 cup seafood vinaigrette (page 325)
2 tablespoons minced fresh chives
¼ cup minced black truffles (optional)
Fresh chervil or flat-leaf parsley leaves,
   for garnish

1. In a small saucepan, bring the shrimp bouillon to a boil over high heat. Add the shrimp and cook just until they change color, 4 to 5 minutes. Remove the shrimp with a slotted spoon and set aside to cool. Then peel and devein them, discarding the shells.

2. With a ¼-inch diameter melon baller, cut balls out of the tomato flesh. (Alternatively, chop the flesh into even ¼-inch dice.) Set aside.

3. Divide the lemon juice between 2 small bowls. With a ¼-inch melon baller, cut balls out of the apples (or chop into even ¼-inch dice). Place the apple balls in one of the bowls with the lemon juice, and toss to prevent the fruit from discoloring. Drain and set aside. Repeat with the avocados.

4. Place 1 tablespoon each of tomato, apple, and avocado in each of 4 small bowls. Drizzle with the oil and toss to coat evenly. (Reserve the remaining apple, avocado, and tomato balls.) Set aside.

5. To assemble: Coat the bottoms of 4 salad plates with seafood vinaigrette. Add the shrimp to the remaining vinaigrette, and toss to coat evenly. Transfer the shrimp to a strainer to drain excess dressing.

6. Arrange a ring of 18 shrimp on each plate, placing them tightly side by side. In

the center of each shrimp ring, place the contents of the bowls containing the apple, avocado, and tomato mixture. Place the remaining fruit balls outside the shrimp ring, alternating apple, avocado, and tomato. Sprinkle the chives, and truffles if using, over the mixture in the center. Place 1 chervil or parsley leaf on every other shrimp. Serve immediately.

Yield: 4 SERVINGS

Wine Suggestion: A FRESH, AROMATIC CHARDONNAY, SUCH AS A RULLY PREMIER CRU, FROM BURGUNDY

TERRINE OF FRESH DUCK LIVERS

Terrine de Foie Gras de Canard

. . . .

Rich, luscious, mellow, this is a sure-win recipe for the true gourmand. I've tasted a lot of foie gras in my life—the great, the good, the indifferent, the horrible. I've never tasted better than this: Smooth and silky, it melts in your mouth with an explosive, velvety richness. Chef Robuchon's method of soaking the liver in salt water first makes for a pure, evenly colored foie gras. The only trick here (besides securing top-quality fresh duck livers) is the task of carefully removing the blood vessels that run through the livers. Be sure to order your fresh duck liver one week advance, allowing time for preparation and ripening.

Serve foie gras as an elegant first course, accompanied by freshly toasted homemade bread and a glass of either chilled Sauternes or a perfumed late-harvest Gewürztraminer, *vendange tardive*.

EQUIPMENT: One 1½-quart oval or rectangular porcelain or enameled cast-iron terrine, with a cover; cooking thermometer; baking parchment

2 fresh duck foie gras (2 to 3 pounds total; see Note)
About 1 tablespoon fine sea salt

SEASONING, FOR EACH 2 POUNDS OF FRESH DUCK LIVER
1 tablespoon fine sea salt

½ teaspoon freshly ground white pepper
1 teaspoon superfine sugar
1 teaspoon *quatre épices* (page 95)
¼ teaspoon freshly grated nutmeg

1. The day before you plan to cook it, prepare the foie gras: Note that a duck liver consists of two lobes, one small, one large. With your hands, separate the larger lobe of each liver from the smaller one by gently pulling them apart. With a small sharp knife, gently scrape away any traces of green bile. With a small sharp knife trim away a strip (about ¾ inch wide) on the thinnest edge of each of the large lobes. (This will allow the salt to penetrate the livers and draw out the blood, making for a clean, even-colored foie gras.) Prepare a large bowl of ice water, add 1 tablespoon salt for each

1½ quarts water, and place the foie gras pieces in the water. Cover with plastic wrap and refrigerate for 6 hours.

2. Remove the pieces of duck liver from the salt water, gently pat dry, and place them on a large clean towel. (The livers can be slippery; the towel will keep them from sliding around as you work with them.) With a small sharp knife, scrape off and lift away the clear membrane that covers the outside of each lobe of duck liver. Then, beginning with the small lobe, use the point of a knife to guide your fingers into the interior of the lobe, in search of the large blood vessel that runs down the inside. Wherever sinews or vessels are visible, pull gently but firmly to remove them, using your fingers and the point of a knife to go deeply into the foie gras. You may have to poke around a bit to find the vessel, but work slowly and methodically, handling the liver as little as possible. Set aside. Repeat with the large lobe, again working from the inside of the lobe, noting that it has a network of vessels. As necessary, split the lobe open with the knife to probe and get at the vessels. Trim off and discard any visible blood spots or any greenish parts, which would turn the terrine bitter.

3. In a shallow bowl, combine the salt, pepper, sugar, *quatre épices,* and nutmeg; blend thoroughly. Reshape the lobes as best you can. Gently rub the seasonings as evenly as possible over each piece of duck liver. Do not overhandle the fragile livers. Return them to a clean bowl, cover with plastic wrap, and refrigerate for 8 to 12 hours.

4. The next day, preheat the oven to 250°F.

5. Select a deep pan slightly larger than the terrine to serve as a water bath. Cut a piece of baking parchment to fit the bottom of this pan, and make several parallel incisions in the center of the paper. Place this in the bottom of the pan and set aside. (The paper will prevent the water from boiling and splashing up into the foie gras.) Cut another piece of parchment to fit the top of the terrine; set aside.

6. Beginning with one of the large lobes, place the duck liver, smooth side down, in the terrine, pressing down gently to eliminate any air pockets. Place the smaller lobes and any pieces of liver in the middle. Top with the remaining large lobe, smooth side up. Cover with the prepared piece of parchment, pressing down gently to even out the livers. (Even pressure will result in a finer, more compact terrine.) Discard any liquid that remains in the bowl. Refrigerate the terrine for 30 minutes.

7. Meanwhile, heat a large pot of water to 176°F, or just below the simmering point. Remove the terrine from the refrigerator, and place it in the prepared water-bath pan. Add the warm water, leaving a generous ¾-inch gap between the water level and the top of the terrine. The water temperature will naturally drop to around 158°F, and this

is where it should stay for the duration of the cooking time. Place the terrine in its water bath in the center of the oven, and cook for 50 to 75 minutes (25 minutes per pound).

8. Remove the pan from the oven, and remove the terrine from the water bath. Carefully pour off all the liquid in the terrine into a large glass cup with a spout. Allow the liquid to settle for several minutes. All the cooking juices will sink to the bottom, leaving a clear layer of golden melted duck fat on top. Don't be surprised at the quantity; the livers will give off 1 to 2 cups of fat. Gently ladle the fat over the terrine, fully covering the duck livers. Discard the cooking juices in the bottom of the cup. Allow the terrine to rest, uncovered, until cool, about 3 hours. During this time do not weight down the terrine.

9. When the terrine is thoroughly cooled, place the cover on it. Refrigerate until the fat has hardened and the liver is firm, about 12 hours. Then remove the cover and securely cover the terrine with plastic wrap. (Do not cover it with foil, for foil will discolor foie gras.) Refrigerate for 3 to 4 days, to allow the foie gras to ripen. Once the terrine has been sliced, it should be consumed within 2 to 3 days.

10. To serve: Remove the foie gras from the refrigerator 15 to 30 minutes before serving (the time will depend upon the temperature of your refrigerator), for it should be served cool but not chilled. Cut it carefully into thin, even slices. The terrine should be slightly marbled, a pleasing rosy pink, and smooth and buttery. Place each slice on a small plate, and pass thin slices of toasted country bread.

Yield: 10 TO 12 SERVINGS

Wine Suggestion: A GRAND SAUTERNES OR A GEWÜRZTRAMINER, *VENDANGE TARDIVE*

NOTE: Fresh foie gras can be ordered from D'Artagnan, Inc., 399–419 Saint Paul Avenue, Jersey City, NJ 07306; tel. 800-DAR-TAGN or 201-792-0748; fax 201-792-0113. Ask for Moulard Duck foie gras A Prime. The foie gras arrives vacuum-packed in heavy plastic, and before opening has about a 10-day shelf life.

SOME FOIE GRAS

POINTERS

. . . .

1. Careful and thorough cleaning of duck livers is essential for a smooth and even-textured foie gras.

2. The more carefully you handle duck livers, the less they will "melt" during cooking. Work slowly and patiently.

3. Do not add truffles, Sauternes, Cognac, or Armagnac to a fresh duck liver terrine. It will only mask the pure, rich flavor of the duck liver.

4. Sugar is added to the seasoning mixture to keep the liver from discoloring during cooking.

5. Temperature is important: A duck liver is fragile and must be cooked at a very low temperature to avoid its turning tough and hard.

6. Undercooked duck liver will be grainy and unappetizing. Overcooked liver runs the risk of melting.

7. Do not weight down a warm terrine. Allow it to cool thoroughly—uncovered and unweighted—before refrigerating.

SALAD OF SEA SCALLOPS, WILD MUSHROOMS, AND CAVIAR

Salade de Noix de Saint-Jacques aux Girolles et au Caviar

· · · · · · · · · · · · · · · · · ·

Fresh and vibrant, this is a salad full of explosive flavor combinations and varied textures, perfumes, colors. It's really four recipes in one; the cider vinegar vinaigrette can be used in many other dishes. Do not attempt to prepare this luxurious and expensive salad unless you have top-rate caviar and the freshest of fresh scallops, which in this preparation are served raw.

8 large sea scallops (1½ to 2 inches)
2 tablespoons extra-virgin olive oil
Small pinch of saffron threads
Sea salt and freshly ground white
    pepper to taste

**BELGIAN ENDIVE IN CIDER VINEGAR
    VINAIGRETTE**
2 tablespoons best-quality cider vinegar
Sea salt to taste
½ cup peanut oil
Freshly ground white pepper to taste
2 Belgian endives, leaves separated,
    rinsed, and dried
1 small head radicchio, leaves
    separated, rinsed, and dried

FENNEL AND MUSHROOM GARNISH
4 ounces wild chanterelle mushrooms
    (or substitute domestic mushrooms),
    trimmed and brushed clean
3 tablespoons extra-virgin olive oil
1 small onion, minced
1 small fennel bulb, minced
Sea salt and freshly ground white
    pepper to taste

2 tablespoons sevruga caviar
Fresh chervil or flat-leaf parsley leaves,
    for garnish

1. Prepare the scallops: Rinse the scallops and pat dry. Remove and discard the little muscle on the side of the scallops. Slice each scallop horizontally into four equal slices. (To slice evenly, use a thin sharp knife. Press down on the scallop, slicing from the bottom up, as if you were slicing a genoise or pound cake to make layers.) Place the

scallop slices side by side in a single layer on a large platter. In a shallow dish, combine the oil, saffron, salt, and pepper. With a brush, coat both sides of the scallop slices with the saffron oil. Cover with plastic wrap and refrigerate.

2. Prepare the vinaigrette: In a medium-size bowl, combine the vinegar and salt. Whisk in the oil, and season to taste with pepper. Set aside.

3. Layer the leaves of Belgian endives, one on top of the other, and slice crosswise into matchstick-size strips. In a small bowl, toss the endives with half of the vinaigrette. Set aside.

4. In another small bowl, toss the remaining vinaigrette with the radicchio leaves. Set aside.

5. Prepare the fennel and mushroom garnish: If you are using wild mushrooms, leave them whole if small or quarter if large. If you are using domestic mushrooms, coarsely chop them. In a medium-size skillet, combine the oil, onions, and fennel over moderate heat. Cook until the vegetables are soft and the onions are translucent, 2 to 3 minutes. Stir in the mushrooms and cook until softened, 3 to 4 minutes. Taste for seasoning, and set aside.

6. Prepare the plates: On 4 chilled dinner plates, arrange the dressed radicchio in a large circle. Spoon the dressed endives around the inside edge of the ring, half filling in the center of the plate.

7. Remove the scallops from the refrigerator. Carefully cover the endive salad with the scallop slices, overlapping them slightly. Dot the scallops with caviar. Place a chervil or parsley leaf on top of each dot of caviar. Spoon the fennel and mushroom mixture into the center of the plates. Serve immediately.

Yield: 4 SERVINGS

Wine Suggestion: A WHITE BORDEAUX, SUCH AS A GRAVES

In the Mood for Fish

....

It doesn't take much to put me in the mood to create menus made up of fish and shellfish. Obviously the day's menu depends on what's fresh and available, but when I spy fresh oysters and whole daurade, or red snapper, in the market, these are the recipes I reach for. If time permits and you're in a very ambitious mood, serve a platter of glazed spring vegetables alongside. With the meal, plan on a good white Burgundy. As an uncomplicated dessert, serve fragrant vanilla custards, or pots de crème, with a good vintage Port.

....

WARM OYSTERS WITH FENNEL AND CURRY
HUÎTRES CHAUDES AU FENOUIL ET AU CURRY

FISH BAKED IN COARSE SALT
DAURADE EN CROÛTE DE SEL

GLAZED SPRING VEGETABLES
PRINTANIÈRE DE LÉGUMES

INDIVIDUAL VANILLA CUSTARDS
PETITS POTS DE CRÈME À LA VANILLE

SMOKED SALMON ROLLS WITH FRESH SALMON "CAVIAR"

Frivolités de Saumon Fuméaux Oeufs de Saumon

. . . .

I adore this dish. It's beautiful, flavorful, and remarkably easy to prepare. The colorful little smoked salmon rolls are perfect for an elegant dinner party, for they're prepared ahead of time. The only trick here is to obtain top-quality hand-cut salmon, sliced paper thin. It's possible that you will have some leftover salmon mousse, since proportions will vary according to the quantity of salmon trimmings. Spread the mousse on small squares of toast, or pipe them into tiny rounds and arrange alongside the salmon rolls.

6 large paper-thin slices smoked salmon
(about 13 ounces)

SALMON MOUSSE
1 teaspoon unsalted butter, softened
1/4 cup aromatic shrimp bouillon
(page 333)
1 1/2 teaspoons powdered gelatin

2 drops Tabasco sauce
1 drop Worcestershire sauce
1/2 cup heavy cream, chilled

GARNISH
3 ounces salmon roe (see Note, page 79)
6 thin lemon slices

1. Place a small mixing bowl in the refrigerator to chill.

2. Prepare the salmon: Trim each slice to a 3 × 6 1/2-inch rectangle. Reserve the trimmings for the mousse. Set aside.

3. Prepare the mousse: In a food processor, combine the salmon trimmings and butter, and process just until blended. Do not overmix or the machine may heat up the salmon. Set aside.

4. In a small saucepan, warm the bouillon over low heat. Add the gelatin and stir to dissolve. Add the bouillon to the butter mixture in the food processor, along with the Tabasco and Worcestershire sauces. Turn the machine on and off, 2 to 3 times, to just blend. Transfer to a large bowl.

5. In the chilled bowl, whip the cream until it holds stiff peaks. Add one third of the cream to the salmon mixture. With a spatula, fold the two mixtures gently but thoroughly. Gently fold in the remaining cream.

6. To assemble: Place a piece of plastic wrap slightly larger than a salmon slice on a flat work surface. Place a slice of salmon on the plastic wrap. Spoon about 3 tablespoons of the salmon mousse in a thin line, lengthwise, in the center of the salmon. Using the plastic wrap to help you push, roll the salmon up lengthwise, cigar-style, to enclose the mousse. The two long edges of the salmon rectangle should just meet. Gently twist the ends of the plastic to secure. Repeat for the remaining salmon rectangles, arranging them in a single layer on a dish. Refrigerate the salmon rolls for at least 2 hours, but not more than 24 hours.

7. To serve: Remove the plastic wrap. With a sharp knife, cut the salmon rolls in half at an angle. Place two rolls, seam side up, on each of 6 chilled plates, arranging them in a "V" formation. Place a thin line of salmon roe along the top of each roll, covering the seam. Place 1 lemon slice on each plate, and serve immediately.

Yield: 6 SERVINGS

Wine Suggestion: A WHITE FULL OF VITALITY, SUCH AS A LOIRE VALLEY SAVENNIÈRES

FISH AND SHELLFISH

....

Poissons, Coquillages, et Crustacés

IVORY TURBANS OF SHRIMP AND PASTA

Turbans de Langoustines en Spaghetti

. . . .

I'll admit that after having sampled this dish many times at Jamin, and having witnessed the preparation, I was daunted. Twirl spaghetti around the insides of a savarin mold? My husband and I attacked it one Saturday afternoon, and found that once you get the hang of the spaghetti lining, it's child's play. And our home version had every bit of the flavor, elegance, finesse of the restaurant version—so rich and pure, I shiver with pleasure just thinking of it! While Chef Robuchon uses fresh *langoustines* from Brittany, the little "turbans" are also delicious when prepared with fresh shrimp.

EQUIPMENT: Six 3½-inch savarin or ring molds, preferably nonstick; a steamer

Unsalted butter, softened, for the
    molds

Coarse sea salt

1 tablespoon olive oil

2 ounces spaghetti

1½ pounds medium-size raw shrimp in
    the shells, peeled and deveined,
    shells reserved

About 3 tablespoons unsalted butter,
    softened

Sea salt and freshly ground white
    pepper to taste

¼ cup heavy cream

SAUCE

6 tablespoons extra-virgin olive oil

1 small fennel bulb, minced (about 3
    ounces)

1 shallot, minced

1 small celery rib, minced (about 2
    ounces)

1 small onion, minced

Bouquet garni: several parsley stems,
    celery leaves, and sprigs of thyme,
    wrapped in the green part of a leek
    and securely fastened with cotton
    twine

Sea salt to taste

3 cups heavy cream

Freshly ground white pepper to taste

1 tablespoon unsalted butter, chilled

About 1 teaspoon freshly squeezed
    lemon juice

About 1 teaspoon Cognac

1 tablespoon fresh white truffle
    shavings, or 1 small bunch fresh
    chervil or flat-leaf parsley leaves, for
    garnish

1. With a pastry brush, very generously butter the insides of the molds, using about 2 tablespoons of the butter. Chill the molds in the refrigerator until the butter is firm, about 15 minutes.

2. Meanwhile, bring a large pot of water to a boil. Add 1 tablespoon salt per quart of water. Add the oil and the spaghetti, and cook for 6 minutes. Remove from the heat and let the spaghetti sit in the water for 1 minute. Drain, refresh under cold running water, drain again, and set aside. Cover the spaghetti with plastic wrap so it does not dry out.

3. Line the molds: Separate out a single strand of spaghetti. Beginning at the bottom of the mold, gently and tightly wind the spaghetti around the center tube, working your way to the top. Begin again at the bottom, this time working in the opposite direction, winding the spaghetti strands toward the top of the outer edge. Repeat until each mold is lined with a single concentric layer of spaghetti. Chill in the refrigerator until the butter is firm again, about 15 minutes.

4. Place the shrimp on a clean plate; pat dry with paper towels. With a pastry brush, paint the shrimp with the remaining softened butter. Season with salt and pepper.

5. In a food processor or blender, combine 4 ounces of the shrimp (about four) with the cream and blend until fluffy and mousselike. Set aside.

6. Prepare six 4-inch squares of aluminum foil. Brush one side of each with butter, and set aside.

7. With a pastry brush, liberally paint the chilled, lined molds with the mousse, using it all up. Arrange about 3 whole shrimp side by side on top of the mousse. (You may need to halve some of the shrimp to fit the molds evenly.) Cover each mold with a piece of foil, butter side down. Transfer the molds to the refrigerator.

8. Prepare the sauce: In a small skillet, combine 3 tablespoons of the oil with the fennel, shallots, celery, onions, and bouquet garni over moderately high heat. Season with salt, and cook until softened, 3 to 4 minutes. Set aside.

9. In a large skillet, heat the remaining 3 tablespoons oil over moderately high heat. When the oil is very hot, almost smoking, add the shrimp shells. Shake the pan over high heat to sear the shells, cooking for 3 to 4 minutes. Do not be concerned if some of the shells stick to the pan. Add the softened vegetables, the cream, and a touch of salt and pepper, and bring to a boil. Reduce the heat to low and simmer gently for 15 minutes. Remove from the heat and let rest for 10 minutes.

10. Line a fine-mesh sieve with moistened cheesecloth, and set the sieve over a large skillet. Strain the contents of the first skillet through the sieve, pressing down to extract as much liquid as possible. Discard the solids. Return the strained sauce to a small saucepan and bring to a boil, 3 to 4 minutes, reducing to about 1 cup. Remove from the heat, whisk in the butter, and season to taste with lemon juice and Cognac. Keep warm, loosely covered, in the top of a double boiler over low heat.

11. Prepare a large vegetable or couscous steamer: Fill the bottom portion with enough water to steam for several minutes. Remove the molds from the refrigerator, and with the foil still in place, carefully arrange them in a single layer in the top of the steamer. Cover and steam until warmed through, about 3 minutes. (If necessary, steam in batches.)

12. To serve, remove the foil from the molds and carefully unmold each onto a warmed salad plate. Spoon a bit of the sauce in the center of the mold, and spoon the remaining sauce around the edge. Shower with freshly shaved white truffles or snipped fresh herbs, and serve immediately.

Yield: 6 SERVINGS

Wine Suggestion: A LIGHT PROVENÇAL WHITE, SUCH AS BELLET, FROM NORTH OF NICE

The makings of one of many versions of a bouquet garni, a mixture of herbs and spices used to impart aromatic flavors to stocks and sauces: Here, a sprig of fresh bay leaves, bundles of fresh thyme, rosemary, and parsley, a few grains of white and black peppercorns, with cheesecloth and string for wrapping in a bundle.

Spring Lobster with Fresh Baby Vegetables

Homard Printanière

. . . .

No dish says "springtime" like this brilliantly colored mixture of lobster and baby vegetables garnished with fresh herbs. This extravagant, elegant preparation is one of my favorites of Chef Robuchon's dishes, for it sings of freshness, delicacy, richness, and vivacity. If you are able to obtain female lobsters, be sure to reserve the precious dark green coral. The coral can be mixed with butter and cream and quickly cooked at the last minute to create a bright red lobster sauce, one of Chef Robuchon's signatures. If baby vegetables are not available, trim standard-size fresh vegetables down to size. You don't need to slavishly follow the suggested number and variety of vegetables, but for a colorful presentation choose a combination of at least four. In this recipe, much of the preparation can be done in advance, with a few moments of last-minute cooking at serving time.

EQUIPMENT: Four bamboo skewers

1 recipe ginger shellfish court bouillon (page 329)

4 live Maine lobsters (1 pound each), preferably female

1 to 4 tablespoons unsalted butter, softened (for the coral)

VEGETABLES

16 baby carrots, peeled, greens trimmed to 1 inch from base

3 tablespoons sugar

7 tablespoons unsalted butter

Sea salt and freshly ground white pepper to taste

16 baby purple-top white turnips, scrubbed, greens trimmed to 1 inch from base

16 fresh baby onions (or substitute pearl onions)

7 ounces snow peas, ends trimmed, strings removed

1 pound baby green asparagus, tough ends trimmed, tied in a bundle with cotton twine

8 ounces fresh chanterelle mushrooms, trimmed and brushed clean (or substitute domestic mushrooms caps, trimmed, cleaned, and quartered)

1 tablespoon freshly squeezed lemon juice (for domestic mushrooms)

SAUCE
7 tablespoons unsalted butter, chilled
Sea salt and freshly ground white
    pepper to taste
1 tablespoon freshly squeezed lemon
    juice (optional)

1 tablespoon heavy cream
3 tablespoons minced fresh ginger
Small bunch fresh chervil or flat-leaf
    parsley leaves, for garnish

1. Blanch the lobsters: In a large pot, bring the court bouillon to a rolling boil. Thoroughly rinse the lobsters under cold running water. With a scissors, remove the rubber bands restraining the claws, and plunge the lobsters, head first, into the court bouillon. Counting from the time the lobster hits the water, cook for 2 minutes. With tongs, remove the lobsters from the court bouillon, and drain. (Note that the lobster meat will not be fully cooked at this point.) Reserve 1⅓ cups of the court bouillon for the sauce.

2. Remove the lobster meat: Twist each large claw off the body of the lobster. Gently crack the claw shells with a nutcracker or hammer, trying not to damage the meat. Extract the meat with a seafood fork; it should come out in a single piece. Set aside. To remove the meat from the tail, use a scissors to cut lengthwise through the back of the lobster, and extract the tail meat in a single piece. With a small knife, remove the long, thin intestinal tract running the length of the tail meat.

Remove and discard the lumpy head sac, located near the eyes. Remove and reserve the soft green strip of tomalley

STORING

LIVE LOBSTER

. . . .

Live lobsters should be cooked as soon as they come from the market. If they will not be cooked immediately, rinse the lobsters under cold water and drain. Transfer to a large pan, cover with a moistened towel, and refrigerate until cooking time. Rinse again just before cooking.

LOBSTER BUTTER

. . . .

Lobster tomalley and coral can both be used to prepare a quick lobster butter. Combine one or both in a blender or small food processor with several tablespoons of softened butter, and process until smooth. Spread on grilled homemade bread, to eat as a snack or to serve alongside a salad.

(liver) from the upper portion of the body cavity (see page 124). Remove and carefully reserve the dark green coral that runs parallel to the liver, if present. Pass the coral of each lobster through a fine-mesh sieve, and mix with 1 tablespoon butter for each coral. The lobster butter will be used later to prepare the sauce. Cover securely and refrigerate.

Gently roll the tail meat into a neat spiral, securing it with a bamboo skewer. Trim the skewers if necessary. Place all the lobster meat on a clean plate, cover securely, and refrigerate until just before serving time. The lobster can be prepared to this point up to 4 hours in advance.

If desired, carefully rinse the head and feathery antennae, and, with a scissors, cut the shell in half lengthwise to use as garnish. Cover securely and refrigerate.

3. Prepare the root vegetables: In a small saucepan with a tight-fitting lid, combine the carrots, 1 tablespoon of the sugar, and 1 tablespoon of the butter over moderate heat. Season, cover, and cook until tender, shaking the pan from time to time, 10 to 15 minutes. (Cooking time will vary according to the size and freshness of the vegetables.) Drain and set aside. Repeat with the turnips and onions, cooking each with 1 tablespoon sugar and 1 tablespoon butter.

MALE VS. FEMALE

When compared side by side, it is relatively easy to distinguish a male from a female lobster: The female will be broader through the "hip" than the male. With the lobster on its back, examine the first of the two tiny claws: The female's will be feathery, the male's bony. Female lobsters are desirable, for the flesh is more tender and more flavorful, and the female is generally heavier than a male of the same size. The female also offers delicious roe, used to flavor sauces as well as lobster butter.

4. Prepare the snow peas: Prepare a large bowl of ice water. Bring a large pot of water to a boil. Add 1 tablespoon salt per quart of water, and add the snow peas. Cook until tender, about 4 minutes. Remove with a slotted spoon and transfer to the ice water. Once cooled, drain and set aside.

5. Prepare the asparagus: Bring a small deep saucepan of water to a boil. Add the asparagus, standing up, and cook just until the lower portions are crisp-tender, about 4 minutes. Add boiling water to cover the tips, and continue cooking for 2 to 3 minutes. Remove with tongs and place in the ice water. Drain, and set aside, removing the twine.

6. Prepare the mushrooms: In a medium skillet, combine the mushrooms and

the remaining 1 tablespoon butter over moderate heat. (If you are using domestic mushrooms, add the lemon juice along with the butter.) Season, cover, and cook until tender, about 5 minutes. Drain and set aside.

7. Finish cooking the lobster: In a large nonstick skillet, heat 4 tablespoons of the butter over moderately high heat. Generously season the lobster pieces with salt and pepper. Sauté the lobster gently for 3 to 4 minutes on each side, removing the faster-cooking claw meat as soon as the meat firms up and turns a bright sunset red. As the lobster cooks, spoon the butter over the meat to keep it moist. Remove the lobster from the pan, transfer to a large serving platter, and keep warm. In the same skillet, add the reserved 1⅓ cups court bouillon to the butter over high heat; reduce for 2 to 3 minutes. Add the lemon juice, and whisk to blend. Add the cream to the coral-butter mixture, and stir to blend. Add this to the sauce, whisking constantly. Do not let the sauce boil. The coral should turn the sauce a bright red. Add the minced ginger. Off the heat, swirl in 3 tablespoons chilled butter. Taste for seasoning.

8. In a large skillet, combine all the reserved vegetables with the remaining 3 tablespoons butter over moderate heat. Heat just to warm through, stirring gently, about 1 to 2 minutes. Taste for seasoning.

9. To serve: Remove the skewers from the lobster. Spoon the sauce over the lobster, and arrange the vegetables on top. If desired, place the reserved lobster shells decoratively around the edges of the platter. Sprinkle with the chervil or parsley leaves, and serve immediately.

Yield: 4 SERVINGS

Wine Suggestion: AN INTENSE WHITE, SUCH AS A BÂTARD-MONTRACHET, FROM BURGUNDY

Joël Robuchon with two lobster fishermen on the Brittany coast

GARLIC-STUDDED MONKFISH IN FENNEL CREAM SAUCE

Blanc de Lotte Piqué à l'Ail à la Crème de Fenouil

. . . .

A lively, simple preparation, this recipe uses a technique that works for all sorts of fish: The monkfish is pan-fried quickly, then transferred to a hot oven to complete the cooking process. I love the symphony of flavors in the sauce—a blend of saffron, fennel, and a touch of cream.

EQUIPMENT: One oval baking dish just slightly larger than the fish (about 10 × 16 inches)

PASTA SAUCE
¼ cup extra-virgin olive oil
Generous pinch of saffron threads, crumbled

2½ pounds fresh monkfish, membrane removed, bone in
3 plump fresh garlic cloves, cut in thin slivers

SAUCE
1 tablespoon unsalted butter
1 large fennel bulb (about 13 ounces), minced

1 large onion (about 15 ounces), minced
Sea salt to taste
1 cup dry white wine, preferably a Chardonnay
⅔ cup heavy cream

3 tablespoons unsalted butter, chilled
1 tablespoon extra-virgin olive oil
Sea salt and freshly ground white pepper to taste

2 tablespoons coarse sea salt
3 tablespoons olive oil
6 ounces fresh tagliatelle or fettuccine

1. One day before serving, prepare the pasta sauce: In a small bowl, combine the oil and saffron. Stir to blend. Cover securely and leave overnight at room temperature to infuse.

2. The day of serving, preheat the oven to 450°F.

3. Rinse the monkfish and pat dry. With a sharp knife, cut along the backbone to separate the fillets. Reserve the bone. Cut each fillet crosswise into three equal portions. (Or ask your fishmonger to do this for you.) Set aside.

4. Prepare a small saucepan of boiling water. Place the garlic in a fine-mesh sieve and submerge it in the boiling water for 10 seconds to blanch. Set aside to drain.

5. With a small knife, make incisions at regular intervals in the fish, and fill them with the garlic slivers. Set aside.

TO DEGERM OR

NOT TO DEGERM

. . . .

Almost every cook, at one time or another, has asked the question: "Should I remove the tiny green sprout that runs through the center of a clove of garlic?" In cases where the garlic will be cooked and the dish will be eaten immediately, there's really no need. But when raw garlic is added to a dish, it's always best to remove this "germ," for it will begin to ferment, making, for some, an indigestible dish. Garlic is more than a pungent flavoring agent in cooking: When the germ is removed, it also helps to preserve foods that you might want to keep for several days, such as a tomato sauce or ratatouille.

6. Prepare the sauce: Cut the monkfish bone into several pieces. In a medium saucepan, melt the 1 tablespoon of butter over moderately high heat. When hot, add the monkfish bones, fennel, and onion, and stir to blend. Season, and cook until the vegetables are soft, about 5 minutes. Slowly add the wine and continue cooking for 3 minutes more. Add the cream and cook 3 minutes more. Remove the monkfish bones. Transfer the sauce to a food processor and blend until smooth. Strain it through a fine-mesh sieve into a clean saucepan, and set aside.

7. In a large skillet, melt 1 tablespoon of the butter and the 1 tablespoon oil over moderately high heat. When hot, add the fish and cook until lightly browned, 1 minute per side. Season each side with salt and pepper to taste after cooking. Transfer to a baking dish. Cover with aluminum foil and place in the center of the oven. Roast until opaque through, about 10 minutes more. (Roasting time will vary according to the thickness of the fish.)

8. Meanwhile, prepare the pasta: Strain the saffron oil to remove the saffron threads, which taste bitter on their own. (If using ground saffron, there is no need to strain.)

In a large pot, bring 2 quarts water to a boil over high heat. Add the salt and oil. Add the pasta, and cook just until tender. Remove the pasta with a slotted spoon and place in a colander to drain. Toss well to eliminate as much water as possible. Transfer the pasta to a large bowl, pour the saffron oil over it, and toss to coat. Set aside and keep warm.

9. Return the sauce to the heat and warm over low heat. Add the remaining 2 tablespoons butter, a few pieces at a time, whisking constantly after each addition, until all the butter is incorporated and the sauce is smooth and creamy. Taste for seasoning and transfer to a sauceboat.

10. Place a portion of fish on each of 6 warmed dinner plates. Spoon the sauce over the fish. Garnish with the pasta and serve immediately.

Yield: 6 SERVINGS

Wine Suggestion: A DRY, WELL-BALANCED WHITE, SUCH AS A RIESLING

THAT   GOLDEN   SAFFRON

Saffron—from the dried stigmas of the saffron crocus bulb—is one of the world's most prized and expensive condiments. Fortunately, a little goes a long way.

True saffron has a pungent aroma and a slightly bitter taste that is not at all disagreeable. The fine threads of the best saffron are deep, almost blood red, with just a tinge of yellow. I prefer saffron threads to powdered saffron because one has a clearer idea of what one is purchasing. Powdered saffron could easily be a blend, or a way of concealing lower quality. (Safflower threads, which are similar in color and form but have little flavor, are often passed off as the real thing. Likewise, powdered turmeric, from a rhizome that's popular in Asia, is often sold as powdered saffron.)

When saffron threads are marinated to add color and flavor, strain out the threads, for the saffron could turn bitter during the marinating period. When added to a sauce near the end of the cooking time, the threads need not be strained. Top-quality Spanish saffron can be ordered from The Mail Order Spice House Ltd., P.O. Box 1633, Milwaukee, WI 53201; tel. 414-768-8799.

LOBSTER WITH GINGER AND SPRING VEGETABLES

Nage de Langoustes aux Aromates

. . . .

I adore preparing and serving this elegant shellfish dish, with the house fragrant with the scents of ginger and orange. It's not quite a soup, but almost, for the aromatic ginger broth is enriched with cream and another dose of ginger, then poured over the shellfish and served with a medley of tiny vegetables and fresh herbs. In it you'll find numerous Robuchon signatures: an explosion of ginger, the lemon zest, the tiny balls of vegetables, and a flourish of fresh herbs. This is a fine recipe for entertaining, for most of the preparation can be done in advance. While at Jamin the dish is served with *langouste,* the delicious French spiny lobster, it is equally spectacular when prepared with fresh lobster.

4 live Maine lobsters (1 pound each)
1 recipe ginger shellfish court bouillon
   (page 329)

VEGETABLES
1 small carrot, peeled
½ small cucumber, peeled
6 mushroom caps, trimmed and cleaned
1 shallot, cut into thin rings
½ cup fresh peas
2 tablespoons grated lemon zest (yellow
   rind)
1 tablespoon unsalted butter, softened

BROTH
6 tablespoons heavy cream
3 tablespoons trimmed, peeled, and
   minced fresh ginger
2 teaspoons freshly squeezed lemon
   juice
2 tablespoons unsalted butter
Sea salt and freshly ground white
   pepper to taste

GARNISH
Small bunch of fresh tarragon, snipped
   with a scissors
Small bunch of fresh chives, snipped
   with a scissors

1. Cook the lobsters: Thoroughly rinse the lobsters under cold running water. In a large pot, bring the court bouillon to a rolling boil. With a scissors, remove the rubber bands restraining the claws, and plunge the lobsters, head first, into the court bouillon.

Counting from the time the lobster hits the water, cook for 5 minutes. (The lobsters may be cooked one at a time.) Remove the pot from the heat, and leave the lobsters in the court bouillon for at least 30 minutes or up to 1 hour. The shellfish will continue to cook as they rest, and the meat will remain moist.

2. Prepare the vegetables: With a ¼-inch diameter melon baller, cut balls out of the flesh of the carrot, cucumber, and mushrooms. (Alternatively, chop the flesh into neat ¼-inch dice.) Toss the carrots, cucumbers, mushrooms, shallots, peas, and lemon zest with the softened butter. Set aside.

3. At serving time, preheat the oven to 200°F.

4. Carefully remove the lobsters from the court bouillon. Drain thoroughly, reserving the court bouillon. Remove the meat from the lobster: Twist each large claw off the body of the lobster. Gently crack the claw shells with a nutcracker or hammer, trying not to damage the meat. Extract the meat with a seafood fork; it should come out in a single piece. Set aside. Gently detach the tail from the rest of the body. With a scissors, carefully cut lengthwise through the back of the lobster, and extract the tail meat in a single piece. With a small knife, remove the long, thin intestinal tract running the length of the tail meat.

Remove and discard the lumpy head sac, located near the eyes. Remove and reserve the pale green tomalley (liver) from the upper portion of the body cavity. Remove and carefully reserve the dark green coral, if present. (The tomalley and coral will not be used in this recipe. For preparation, see box, page 116.)

If desired, carefully rinse the head and feathery antennae, and, with a scissors, cut the shell in half lengthwise to use as a garnish. Place all the lobster meat on a warmed platter, cover, and transfer to the oven to keep warm while finishing the broth.

5. Finish the broth: Remove and strain 2 cups of the court bouillon, and transfer to a medium-size saucepan. Warm over low heat, and then whisk in the cream. Add the fresh ginger, lemon juice, and butter, and taste for seasoning. Add the buttered vegetables, and heat just until warmed through.

6. To serve: Arrange the pieces of meat from one lobster in each of 4 warmed shallow soup bowls. Spoon the broth over the lobster meat, and garnish with the herbs. If desired, place the reserved lobster shells decoratively around the edges of the bowls, and serve. (Alternatively, prepare all in an elegant soup tureen and serve at the table.)

Yield: 4 SERVINGS

Wine Suggestion: A TOP-QUALITY WHITE BURGUNDY, SUCH AS A BÂTARD-MONTRACHET

Whole Grilled Salmon Fillet with Red Shallot Sauce

Saumon Grillé au Beurre Rouge

. . . .

Chef Robuchon's method for cooking a whole side of salmon—broil it, then bake it—is truly spectacular. The result is a salmon that's moist, not dry, and perfectly cooked. It's delicious warm with a rich red shallot sauce, but can also be served with just a touch of freshly squeezed lemon juice and a garnish of fresh dill. At room temperature, the salmon is excellent as a summer luncheon dish, served with a sauce of extra-virgin olive oil in which you have marinated fresh basil and chopped fresh tomatoes. The first time I prepared this salmon I served tender steamed spring potatoes tossed in a mixture of garlic, oil, and parsley. We were in heaven. I don't know how to be more convincing! This recipe is simplified if you have two ovens. If not, simply broil the fish first, then adjust the oven heat and finish baking in the same oven.

1 whole salmon fillet, skin attached (about 2 pounds)	2 shallots, minced
2 teaspoons peanut oil	2 cups red wine, preferably a Syrah
Sea salt and freshly ground black pepper to taste	16 tablespoons (1 cup) unsalted butter, chilled and cut into pieces

1. Preheat the broiler. If you have a second oven, preheat it to 425°F. Cover a broiling pan with a large piece of aluminum foil, leaving a slight overhang to facilitate turning the fish.

2. Brush both sides of the salmon with the oil, then season with salt and pepper. Place the salmon in the broiling pan, skin side up. Set the pan 5 to 6 inches from the heat, so that the fish broils gently without burning, and broil 5 minutes. Remove the pan from the oven, and pulling the foil up slightly from one side, gently turn the salmon

skin side down. Return it to the oven and broil for 5 minutes more. Remove the pan from the oven and carefully transfer the salmon, leaving it skin side down, to a shallow baking dish.

3. If you are using one oven, adjust the heat to 425°F.

4. Place the baking dish in the center of the oven, and bake—turning once—until the salmon is opaque in the center and slightly firm, about 18 minutes total.

5. Meanwhile, prepare the red shallot sauce: In a medium-size saucepan, combine the shallots and red wine and season very lightly with salt and pepper. Bring to a boil over moderately high heat, and reduce to about 3 tablespoons, 20 to 25 minutes. Remove the pan from the heat, and whisk in 2 tablespoons of the cold butter. Return the pan to low heat, whisking until the butter has melted. Then remove it from the heat and whisk in 2 more tablespoons butter. Repeat until three fourths (12 tablespoons) of the butter has been used. Taste for seasoning. Add the rest of the butter, whisking until well blended. Never allow the sauce to boil. (If a smooth sauce is desired, strain through a fine-mesh sieve to remove the shallots.) Keep warm, uncovered, in the top of a double boiler over low heat.

6. Remove the salmon from the oven, and carefully peel off the skin (see Note). Carefully transfer the salmon to a serving platter, turning it one more time; the prettier, more golden side will be the inner portion of the fillet. At the table, cut the salmon into thick serving pieces. Serve the red shallot sauce separately in a warmed sauceboat.

Yield: 8 SERVINGS

Wine Suggestion: A FRAGRANT, SILKY RED—SUCH AS A VOLNAY, FROM BURGUNDY—SERVED JUST SLIGHTLY CHILLED, AT 58°F TO 61°F

N O T E: As a special treat, the grilled salmon skin can be chopped and lightly sautéed in a small skillet until crisp. Add it, still warm, to a tossed salad, or serve it alongside the grilled salmon, seasoned with a touch of lemon juice.

SALMON ON A BED OF CREAMY CABBAGE

Saumon Poêlé au Chou

. . . .

This is a quick, simple, elegant recipe, and one that demands no particular technical skills. Just make sure you have the freshest of salmon. Cabbage is a highly under-utilized and underestimated vegetable, and I love the combination of colorful green cabbage, smothered in a creamy butter sauce, with the brilliant, crispy salmon. This could serve 8 as a first course or 4 as a main course.

½ large head green cabbage (about 1½ pounds)
8 tablespoons unsalted butter
Sea salt and freshly ground white pepper to taste
6 tablespoons heavy cream
1 shallot, minced
¼ cup dry white wine, such as a Chardonnay

¼ cup best-quality sherry wine vinegar
1½ pounds fresh salmon fillet, skin attached but scaled, cut into 4 or 8 equal portions
1 tablespoon extra-virgin olive oil
Fresh chives, snipped with a scissors, for garnish
Handful of whole chervil or flat-leaf parsley leaves, for garnish

1. Trim the cabbage, discarding any tough outer leaves and the tough inner core. Slice by hand into thin slivers. Bring a large pot of water to a boil. Salt the water, add the cabbage, and cook for 1 minute to blanch. Remove the cabbage and drain well.

2. In a large skillet, combine the cabbage with 2 tablespoons of the butter and cook over low heat for 2 to 3 minutes. Season, cover, and cook until slightly wilted but still crunchy, about 5 minutes. Stir in 5 tablespoons of the cream and continue cooking until warmed through, 1 to 2 minutes. Set aside and keep warm.

3. Prepare the sauce: In a small saucepan, combine the shallot with 1 tablespoon butter and a pinch of salt. Cook over low heat until soft and translucent, 3 to 4 minutes. Add the wine and vinegar, and bring to a boil. Cook until reduced by two thirds, 2 to 3 minutes. Remove from the heat. Gradually whisk in the remaining 1 tablespoon cream and 5 tablespoons butter. Whisk until all the butter is incorporated and the sauce is

smooth and creamy. Taste for seasoning. Transfer to the top of a double boiler set over gently simmering water. Cover loosely and keep warm over low heat.

4. Prepare the salmon: With a sharp knife, score the salmon in a crisscross pattern, cutting through the skin and just slightly cutting into the flesh. Generously season both sides of the salmon.

5. In a large nonstick skillet, heat the oil over moderately high heat. When hot, place the salmon fillets, skin side down, in the skillet. Cook without turning until the skin is very crisp, 2 to 3 minutes (cooking time will depend upon the thickness of the salmon). With a wide spatula, turn the salmon over and cook it barely 30 seconds. Leave the salmon in the pan and remove it from the heat. The salmon will continue to cook as you dress the plates.

6. Spoon the cabbage into the center of 4 to 8 warmed dinner plates. Top with a slice of salmon, skin side up, and spoon the warm sauce around the cabbage. Garnish with herbs and serve immediately.

Yield: 8 FIRST-COURSE SERVINGS OR 4 MAIN-COURSE SERVINGS

Wine Suggestion: A RICH DRY WHITE, SUCH AS A CHASSAGNE-MONTRACHET, FROM BURGUNDY

ZUCCHINI-WRAPPED SHRIMP WITH WILD MUSHROOMS

Fricassée de Langoustines aux Courgettes et Champignons

. . . .

This is a delightful dish for entertaining: It's light, complex, full-flavored, and probably different from anything else you're likely to sample. Fresh *langoustines* or large shrimp are wrapped in thin strips of zucchini, then browned in a touch of goose fat. Alongside, you'll serve a blend of two different wild mushrooms, flavored with a bit of garlic and thyme. If wild mushrooms are not available, substitute a mix of domestic mushrooms such as shiitake and common white mushrooms (do not use dried mushrooms).

2 small, very firm, fresh zucchini (about 6 ounces), carefully scrubbed but not peeled

16 large raw shrimp, peeled

2 tablespoons peanut oil

8 ounces fresh chanterelle mushrooms, trimmed and brushed clean

Sea salt and freshly ground white pepper to taste

2 shallots, minced

2 tablespoons unsalted butter

8 ounces fresh oyster mushrooms, trimmed and brushed clean

2 plump fresh garlic cloves, minced

2 tablespoons fresh flat-leaf parsley leaves, snipped with a scissors

2 tablespoons goose fat

Pinch of fresh thyme leaves

Fresh chervil or flat-leaf parsley leaves, for garnish

1. With a vegetable peeler, peel the zucchini lengthwise into 16 thin, even slices. Rinse the shrimp and pat dry. Wrap a zucchini strip, spiral fashion, around each shrimp, securing it with a toothpick. Set aside.

2. In a large nonstick skillet, heat the oil over high heat. When hot, add the chanterelle mushrooms. Season with salt and pepper, and add the shallots. Cook until softened, about 5 minutes. Transfer to a bowl, set aside, and keep warm.

3. In the same skillet, melt the butter over high heat. When hot, add the oyster

mushrooms. Season with salt and pepper and cook until softened, 2 to 3 minutes. Return the chanterelle mushrooms to the skillet, add the garlic, and toss to blend. Sprinkle with the parsley. Transfer to a bowl, set aside, and keep warm.

4. In the same skillet, melt the goose fat over high heat. When hot, add the wrapped shrimp and cook until slightly firm, 2 to 3 minutes on each side. Season with salt, pepper, and thyme.

5. To serve, remove the toothpicks and arrange 4 wrapped zucchini bundles in the center of each of 4 warmed dinner plates. Spoon the mushroom mixture on either side. Garnish with the herbs and serve immediately.

Yield: 4 SERVINGS

Wine Suggestion: A RICH AND GLORIOUS DRY WHITE, SUCH AS A PULIGNY-MONTRA-CHET, FROM BURGUNDY

ON CLEANING

MUSHROOMS

· · · · · · · · · · · · · · · · ·

In an ideal world, mushrooms would arrive devoid of grit, sand, and dirt—but of course they usually don't. Because wild mushrooms are very perishable, clean them with a soft pastry brush, not an abrasive brush sold for cleaning mushrooms. Do not immerse them in water, but rather rinse them quickly and individually under cold running water. Pat dry with a soft towel.

FAT FIXES FLAVOR

· · · · · · · · · · · · · · · · ·

When I was spending days in the kitchen at Jamin, I was always amazed to witness the studied use of different kinds of fat. Here is an example, where butter, peanut oil, and goose fat are used, each to its best advantage, to make for a dish with a depth of flavors.

ROASTED MONKFISH WITH TOMATOES, ZUCCHINI, LEMON, AND THYME

Lotte au Plat aux Tomates, Courgettes, Citron, et Thym

. . . .

This is an uncomplicated summery fish dish that is spectacular in its simplicity. As ever, search for the freshest and most flavorful ingredients and you're more than halfway to success. Instead of monkfish, you may use any white fish fillets, such as red snapper, West Coast halibut, or tilapia.

EQUIPMENT: One baking dish just slightly larger than the monkfish (about 9 × 13 inches)

3 medium onions, sliced into thin
  rounds
12 shallots, halved
3 tablespoons extra-virgin olive oil
2 imported bay leaves
Large bunch of fresh thyme sprigs
Sea salt to taste
2 pounds fresh monkfish, membrane
  removed, rinsed and patted dry, cut
  into 4 equal pieces

4 medium tomatoes, cored and thinly
  sliced
4 small zucchini, trimmed and thinly
  sliced
1 lemon, scrubbed and thinly sliced
2 cups dry white wine, preferably a
  Chardonnay

1. Preheat the oven to 350°F.

2. Layer the onions and shallots on the bottom of the baking dish. Drizzle with 1 tablespoon of the oil. Add the bay leaves, half of the thyme, and salt. Place the fish on top. Arrange the tomatoes, zucchini, and lemon on top of and around the fish. Add the wine to cover halfway. Add the remaining 2 tablespoons oil and thyme.

3. Place in the oven and bake, uncovered, until the fish is opaque throughout but

still resilient, 30 to 40 minutes, depending upon the thickness of the fish. Remove and discard the thyme and bay leaves. Serve immediately.

Yield: 4 TO 6 SERVINGS

Wine Suggestion: A FRAGRANT INTENSE WHITE, SUCH AS THE RHÔNE VALLEY'S CHÂTEAU GRILLET

ON KITCHEN ODORS

. . . .

As cooks, we often forget that kitchen equipment can transfer unwelcome flavors. At Jamin, every time a cook picks up a piece of equipment—a strainer, a pastry brush, a pan—he takes a sniff before proceeding. Strainers and brushes are major culprits, and off odors caused by less than perfect cleaning can easily pass through to delicate sauces. So make a habit of sniffing your own equipment, and wash it again if necessary.

FISH BAKED IN COARSE SALT

Daurade en Croûte de Sel

. . . .

A classic fish preparation, this dish is found along the Atlantic coast near Arcachon, as well as in the Basque region along the Spanish/French border. It's one of the finest, most flavorful, and simplest ways to prepare fish, for the salt crust acts as a moist "oven," enveloping the entire fish, baking it gently and evenly. These are the rules: Begin with the freshest of fish and pay careful attention to the weight of the fish, to the oven temperature, and to the size of dish in which the fish is baked. Respect those elements, and a 2-pound fish should bake perfectly in 30 minutes, a 3-pound fish in 40 minutes. The fish should be gutted but not scaled, for the scales themselves impart flavor. Traditionally, the dish is prepared with no other seasoning, not even pepper, allowing the pure flavor of the fish to dominate. And despite what one might think, the fish does not end up tasting particularly salty, for the salt serves not so much as a seasoning as a vehicle for sealing in juices and flavor. Try this with whole red snapper, rockfish, striped bass, or even a small salmon. As accompaniments, serve ratatouille (page 229), freshly grilled bread, and a rich white wine.

EQUIPMENT: One oval baking dish large enough to hold the fish (about 8½ × 14 inches)

One 3-pound whole fish, gutted but not scaled, head left on, tail and fins trimmed

7 to 8 cups (about 4 pounds) coarse sea salt or kosher salt (see Note)
Extra-virgin olive oil and fresh lemon sections, for garnish

1. Preheat the oven to 450°F.

2. Rinse the fish thoroughly inside and out until there is no trace of blood. If the gills have not been removed, do so to avoid bitterness. Pat dry.

3. Evenly spread 1 cup of the salt on the bottom of the baking dish. Place the fish on top of the salt, and pour the remaining 6 to 7 cups salt over the fish to completely cover it from head to tail. It should look as though you have a baking dish mounded

with nothing but salt. (If the fish is large, there's a chance the tail fin will extend outside the baking dish. That won't alter the baking of the fish.)

4. Place the dish in the center of the oven, and bake for 40 minutes for a 3-pound fish or until an instant-reading thermometer inserted in the thickest part reads 130°F. Adjust baking times by about 5 minutes either way for each ½ pound of fish.

5. Remove the dish from the oven. Brush away as much salt as possible from the fish, so it won't get on the flesh when you remove the skin. (This is a rather awkward procedure, and it helps to have two pairs of hands, one to hold the baking dish, another to carefully scrape off the salt.) Using the blade of a sharp knife, gently scrape the skin from the top fillet of the fish and discard. Using two large spoons, gently remove the top fillet in neat pieces and transfer to 2 warmed dinner plates. With the spoons, carefully remove the center bones and discard. Remove the bottom fillet in pieces and transfer to 2 additional warmed dinner plates.

6. Serve immediately, passing a cruet of olive oil and bowl of lemon wedges for seasoning.

Yield: 4 SERVINGS

Wine Suggestion: A RICH DRY WHITE, SUCH AS A CHASSAGNE-MONTRACHET, FROM BURGUNDY

NOTE: In general, I advise using unrefined sea salt for cooking, preferably *sel de Guérande* from Brittany. But when the salt is used solely as a cooking vessel and won't be consumed, refined sea salt or kosher salt, both of which are far less expensive, is a perfectly adequate substitute.

SEA SCALLOPS WITH FRESH GINGER SAUCE

Noix de Saint-Jacques au Gingembre Frais

. . . .

Luxurious, exotic, romantic, this is a heavenly dish, and one that is exceptionally simple to make. Serve it as the first course of a formal dinner party, with an equally elegant Rhône Valley white. The dish is subtly laced with a fresh hint of ginger, and the normally mundane leek—often relegated to the stockpot—takes on a new uptown personality. At Jamin, the scallops are seared very quickly—for about 30 seconds—just until browned around the edges. For scallops cooked all the way through, sear for 1 minute on each side.

8 large fresh sea scallops (1½ to 2 inches)

ACCOMPANIMENT
2 tablespoons unsalted butter
2 leeks, white part only, trimmed, well rinsed, and cut into 2-inch matchsticks
Sea salt and freshly ground white pepper to taste

SAUCE
5 shallots, minced
2 tablespoons unsalted butter

2 leeks, green part only, coarsely chopped
6 tablespoons dry vermouth
3 tablespoons finely julienned fresh ginger (matchstick size)
Bouquet garni: several parsley stems, celery leaves, and sprigs of thyme, wrapped in the green part of a leek and securely fastened with cotton twine
2 cups heavy cream
1 teaspoon blanched, minced fresh ginger

1. Prepare the scallops: Rinse the scallops and pat dry. Remove and discard the little muscle on the side of the scallops. Cut each scallop in half horizontally, and set aside.

2. Prepare the accompaniment: In a small skillet, melt the butter over moderate heat. When hot, add the matchstick leeks and cook just until soft, 2 to 3 minutes. Season to taste. Set aside and keep warm.

3. Prepare the sauce: In a medium saucepan, combine the shallots and 1 tablespoon

of the butter over moderate heat. Cook until the shallots brown, 1 to 2 minutes. Add the chopped leeks and cook 1 to 2 minutes more. Add the vermouth, matchstick ginger, and bouquet garni, and cook until most of the liquid is absorbed, 2 to 3 minutes. Add the cream and cook until reduced by half, 8 to 10 minutes more. Strain through a fine-mesh sieve into a clean saucepan. Whisk in the remaining 1 tablespoon butter, and add the minced ginger. Taste for seasoning. (The sauce may be prepared up to 30 minutes in advance. Keep it warm, loosely covered, in the top of a double boiler over low heat.)

4. Prepare the plates: Spoon 4 small mounds of matchstick leeks in the center of each of 4 warmed dinner plates. Spoon the sauce evenly over the plates, covering the leeks. Set aside.

5. Adding no fat, heat a large nonstick skillet over high heat. Add the scallops and cook just until they brown around the edges, 30 seconds to 1 minute on each side. Season each side after it has cooked. (Cooking time will vary according to the size of the scallops. For scallops that are cooked all the way through, sear for 1 minute or more on each side.)

6. Carefully transfer the scallops to the prepared plates. Place a scallop on top of each mound of leeks, with the side that was cooked last facing up (this side will be more moist and have more eye appeal). Serve immediately.

Yield: 4 SERVINGS

Wine Suggestion: A RICH RHÔNE VALLEY WHITE, SUCH AS A HERMITAGE

CREAMY SCALLOP AND CAVIAR PILLOWS

Étuvée de Noix de Saint-Jacques au Caviar

. . . .

Seemingly simple and thoroughly elegant, this is a rich dish best served in small batches. Imagine caviar sandwiches—dollops of black caviar between slices of sweet scallops—all bathed in a sauce of multiple flavors. I love the way the coarse white pepper interacts with the delicate flavor of the scallops, making for a dish with layers of personality. It goes without saying that you should search out the freshest of scallops and the best-quality caviar.

8 large sea scallops (1½ to 2 inches)
2 tablespoons unsalted butter, melted
2 tablespoons sevruga caviar
Coarsely cracked white pepper to taste

SAUCE
Zest (yellow peel) of 1 lemon, cut into
   matchsticks
2 shallots, very finely minced
3 tablespoons unsalted butter
¼ cup white wine, such as a
   Chardonnay

¼ cup mussel cooking liquid
   (page 148)
1½ cups heavy cream
1 teaspoon freshly squeezed lemon
   juice
Sea salt and freshly ground white
   pepper to taste
1 tablespoon sevruga caviar

2 tablespoons fresh chives, snipped with
   a scissors, for garnish
Sea salt, for garnish

1. Prepare the scallops: Rinse the scallops and pat dry. Remove the little muscle on the side of the scallops and discard. Slice each scallop horizontally into 4 equal slices. (To slice evenly, use a thin sharp knife. Press down on the scallop, slicing from the bottom up, as if you were slicing a genoise or pound cake to make layers.) With a brush, very lightly butter one side of each scallop slice. On a small chilled ovenproof salad plate, arrange 4 scallop slices, buttered side down, in a circle; the slices should not overlap. Place a small spoonful of caviar on top of each scallop slice. Place a scallop slice, buttered side up, on top of the caviar, to form little scallop sandwiches. Repeat this on 3 other salad plates. Sprinkle with several grains of coarsely cracked (not ground) white pepper. Cover with plastic wrap and refrigerate while preparing the sauce.

2. Preheat the oven to 350°F.

3. Prepare the sauce: Bring a small saucepan of water to a boil. Place the lemon zest in a fine-mesh sieve and submerge it in the boiling water for 10 seconds. Drain. Mince the zest and set aside.

4. In a small saucepan, combine the shallots and 2 tablespoons of the butter over moderate heat. Cook until soft and translucent, 2 to 3 minutes. Add the wine, bring to a boil, and boil for 2 to 3 minutes to burn off the alcohol. Strain through a fine-mesh sieve into a large saucepan. Add the mussel cooking liquid, cream, lemon zest, and lemon juice. Cook over high heat until reduced by half, about 5 minutes. Remove from the heat and whisk in the remaining 1 tablespoon butter, whisking constantly until all the butter is incorporated and the sauce is smooth and creamy. Taste for seasoning. (The sauce may be prepared up to 30 minutes in advance. Keep it warm, uncovered, in the top of a double boiler over low heat.)

A WORD ON

SEA SCALLOPS

. . . .

Scallops, or *coquilles Saint-Jacques,* are hermaphrodites, and the coral often attached to the scallops will tell you the sex of the mollusk: pale white for male scallops, reddish orange for female. While some people love the soft, rich flavor of the coral, true connoisseurs insist that the most flavorful scallops are those without coral.

5. Remove the prepared scallops from the refrigerator, and place the plates in the preheated oven for just 1 minute. The scallops should just begin to warm, no more. Add the caviar to the sauce and stir to blend. Remove the scallops from the oven, and divide the sauce among the 4 plates, evenly covering the scallops. Sprinkle each plate with chives and salt, and serve immediately.

Yield: 4 SERVINGS

Wine Suggestion: A WINE OF GREAT CLASS, SUCH AS THE WHITE BURGUNDY CHEVALIER MONTRACHET

TINY FISH FILLETS WITH VEGETABLE CONFETTI

Rouget à l'Émulsion d'Huile d'Olive

. . . .

If there is a dish that's quintessential Robuchon, this is it. A trinity of very, very finely diced vegetables unite to form a colorful saffron-flecked confetti, spooned atop freshly sautéed fish fillets. Visually exciting, the dish is equally rewarding to the palate. The sauce is a stunning blend of highly reduced fish stock that's laced with flavors of fresh fennel, shallots, and basil, and extra-virgin olive oil that is whisked in at the end to form a rich emulsion. The result is an intense condensation of flavors, of essences. Zucchini, red peppers, and mushrooms never tasted better. At Jamin, Robuchon uses tiny *rouget,* or red mullet, fillets with their skin still attached. Other fish that might be served in this manner are red snapper and porgy. If time is limited, prepare only the fish and the sauce, deleting the vegetable coating.

FISH STOCK

3 tablespoons extra-virgin olive oil

3 shallots, finely minced

2 small fennel bulbs, finely minced

Bouquet garni: several parsley stems, celery leaves, and sprigs of thyme, wrapped in the green part of a leek and securely fastened with cotton twine

1 pound fish bones, heads, and trimmings (gills removed), well rinsed and cut up

Sea salt to taste

VEGETABLE CONFETTI

1 red bell pepper, cored and seeded

1 small, very firm fresh zucchini (about 3 ounces), scrubbed

1 pound mushrooms, cleaned and patted dry

Pinch of saffron threads

1 teaspoon fresh thyme leaves

1 tablespoon extra-virgin olive oil

Sea salt to taste

SAUCE

3 tablespoons extra-virgin olive oil, at room temperature

¼ cup fresh basil leaves

1 small tomato, cored, peeled, seeded, and very finely chopped

Sea salt to taste

2 tablespoons extra-virgin olive oil

4 to 8 fish fillets (4 to 8 ounces each) such as red mullet, red snapper, or porgy

Sea salt to taste

1. Prepare the fish stock: In a medium-size saucepan, combine the olive oil, shallots, and fennel over moderately high heat. Cook until the shallots and fennel are softened, 4 to 5 minutes. Add the bouquet garni and fish bones, and cook for 2 minutes more. Add a pinch of salt and water to barely cover. Simmer gently for 20 minutes.

2. Remove the pan from the heat and let the stock rest for 10 minutes. Line a sieve with moistened cheesecloth and place it over a medium-size saucepan. Ladle the stock through the sieve. You should have about 2 cups stock. Place the saucepan over high heat and reduce the stock to ½ cup, about 10 minutes. Set aside.

3. Prepare the vegetable confetti: Mince the pepper into very tiny cubes. With a vegetable peeler, slice the zucchini (with peel) into thin strips, and with a very sharp knife cut into very tiny cubes.

4. Prepare a medium-size saucepan of boiling water. Place the zucchini in a fine-mesh sieve and submerge in the boiling water for 10 seconds to blanch. Drain, and set aside. Repeat for the red pepper. Combine the drained zucchini and red pepper in a clean cloth and wring, pressing to squeeze out all the liquid. Place the vegetable mixture in a small bowl and set aside.

5. Cut the mushrooms into the same tiny cubes. Add to the zucchini and red peppers, and toss to combine. The mixture should resemble a bright confetti. With a thin, sharp knife, chop the saffron and add to the vegetable mixture. Add the thyme and toss thoroughly.

6. In a large skillet, combine the vegetables and oil over high heat. Toss to coat with the oil and cook until warmed through, about 3 minutes. Do not overcook; the vegetables should remain crisp. Season to taste. Set aside and keep warm.

7. Prepare the sauce: If the fish stock is not hot, reheat until boiling. With a wisk or an immersion mixer, blend in the olive oil, bsail, and tomato. Mix until well blended and frothy. Taste for seasoning. Keep warm, uncovered, in the top of a double boiler over low heat.

8. Prepare the fish: In a large nonstick skillet, heat the oil over moderately high heat. When hot, add the fish and cook until opaque through but not firm or dry, 2 to 3 minutes on each side, seasoning each side after cooking.

9. To serve, spoon the sauce in the center of 4 warmed dinner plates. Place the fish, skin side up, in the center. Spoon the vegetables on top of the fish, and serve.

Yield: 4 SERVINGS

Wine Suggestion: A YOUNG, DRY, LOW-ACID WHITE, SUCH AS A MEDITERRANEAN CASSIS

BAY SCALLOP BUNDLES WITH OYSTERS AND CAVIAR

Huîtres et Noix de Pétoncles au Caviar

. . . .

I sampled this dish on one of my first visits to Jamin, in 1982. It has remained a personal favorite ever since—there's a lovely briny, salty tang in the combination of oysters, scallops, and caviar. And the bright, springy look of the small spinach-wrapped scallop bundles just makes me smile. Much of the work for this dish can be done in advance, which means it's a good, impressive dish for entertaining. (And easy as well!) If oysters in the shell are not available, use top-quality preshucked oysters.

EQUIPMENT: Six ½-cup ramekins

20 to 24 tender fresh spinach leaves, deveined

10 ounces bay or sea scallops

Sea salt and freshly ground white pepper to taste

6 tablespoons unsalted butter, melted

18 freshly shucked oysters, liquor strained and reserved

1 small fennel bulb, minced

1 small onion, minced

½ cup dry white wine, preferably a Chardonnay

1 cup *crème fraîche* (page 339) or heavy cream

Generous pinch of saffron threads

6 teaspoons sevruga caviar (optional)

1. Prepare a large bowl of ice water. Bring a large pot of water to a boil. Salt the water, add the spinach, and cook just to wilt, about 30 seconds. Immediately drain the spinach and plunge the leaves into the ice water to cool. Once cooled, drain thoroughly and arrange the leaves on paper towels, so they will be easier to work with later. Set aside.

2. Finely chop the scallops. Place in a medium-size bowl and season. Toss with 1 tablespoon of the butter. Set aside.

3. Prepare the ramekins: Line the molds with spinach leaves, placing the outside of the leaves (generally the darker side) against the sides of the mold, allowing some overhang. Fill each mold with the scallop mixture. Cover the top of each mold with the overhanging spinach leaves. Set aside. (The recipe may be prepared to this point 3 to 4 hours in advance. Cover each mold securely and refrigerate. Remove from the refrigerator 30 minutes before baking.)

4. Prepare the oysters: In a medium saucepan, combine the oysters, their liquor, and 1 tablespoon of the butter over high heat. Bring to a boil, remove immediately from the heat, and strain, reserving the liquor. Place the oysters in a covered ovenproof dish and set aside.

5. Prepare the sauce: In a small saucepan, combine the remaining 4 tablespoons butter, the fennel, and the onion over low heat. Cook until softened, about 10 minutes. Add the wine, reserved oyster liquor, and *crème fraîche*, and continue cooking for 2 to 3 minutes more. Line a sieve with moistened cheesecloth, set the sieve over a large bowl, and strain the sauce into the bowl. Return the sauce to the pan and add the saffron. Cook over moderate heat, stirring occasionally, until smooth and glossy and reduced by half, about 10 minutes. Taste for seasoning. (The sauce may be prepared up to 30 minutes in advance. Keep it warm, uncovered, in the top of a double boiler over low heat.)

6. Preheat the oven to 350°F.

7. Place the molds in the center of the oven and bake until firm to the touch, about 15 minutes. Place the oysters, covered, in the oven and bake just until warmed through, about 5 minutes.

8. Unmold each spinach and scallop bundle onto the center of a warmed dinner plate. Surround each bundle with 3 oysters, and spoon the sauce over the oysters. If you are serving caviar, place 1 teaspoon on top of each mold. Serve immediately.

Yield: 6 SERVINGS

Wine Suggestion: A NONSPARKLING CHAMPAGNE, SUCH AS A COTEAUX CHAMPENOIS

MUSSELS WITH CREAM, MUSHROOMS, LEEKS, AND FENNEL

Mouclade Façon Joël Robuchon

. . . .

Marvelously elegant, this dish is half soup, half sauced mussels, and is a specialty of Joël Robuchon's native Poitou. I like his addition of mushrooms, leeks, and fennel, which lend a festive note. The mussels are served in the shell, and may be placed either on a large serving platter or in individual shallow soup bowls. Be sure to pass the pepper mill, for mussels and freshly ground pepper are truly complementary flavors. Mouclade may be seasoned with either saffron or curry, to suit individual tastes.

1 small leek, white and tender green parts

3 tablespoons unsalted butter

½ small fennel bulb, cut in julienne strips

4 mushrooms, brushed clean, cut in julienne strips

3 pounds fresh mussels in their shells

2 shallots, minced

2 cups dry white wine, preferably a Chardonnay

Handful of fresh flat-leaf parsley stems, tied in a bundle with cotton twine

Freshly ground white pepper to taste

2 teaspoons fresh thyme

½ cup heavy cream

Pinch of curry powder or saffron threads, or to taste

Handful of fresh flat-leaf parsley leaves, snipped with a scissors

1. Prepare the leek: Trim the leek at the root. Split it lengthwise for easier cleaning. Rinse well under cold running water, and transfer to a bowl of cold water to soak. When all the grit has settled to the bottom of the bowl, remove the leek and dry thoroughly. Cut into julienne strips. Set aside.

2. In a small skillet, combine 1 tablespoon of the butter, the leeks, and the fennel over moderate heat. Cook until softened, about 3 minutes. Add the mushrooms and continue cooking until all the vegetables are tender, about 3 minutes more. Set aside.

3. Thoroughly scrub the mussels, and rinse with several changes of water. If an open mussel closes when you press on it, it is good; if it stays open, the mussel should be discarded. Beard the mussels. (Do not beard the mussels in advance or they will die and spoil; see Note.)

4. In a very large skillet, combine the shallots, wine, parsley stems, and the remaining 2 tablespoons butter over high heat. Boil for 5 minutes. Add the mussels, sprinkle generously with pepper, and stir. Cover, and cook until the mussels just open, about 5 minutes. Remove the mussels as they open. Do not overcook. Discard any mussels that do not open.

5. Transfer the mussels to a large warmed serving platter, removing the top of each mussel shell. Cover loosely with foil. Set aside and keep warm. (Alternatively, arrange the mussels in individual shallow soup bowls.)

6. To finish: Strain the cooking liquid through a fine-mesh sieve lined with moistened cheesecloth into a medium-size saucepan. Add the thyme, and cook over moderately high heat until reduced by half, 2 to 3 minutes. Stir in the cream and the curry powder or saffron threads. Continue cooking until the mixture just boils. Add the mushroom mixture and stir to blend.

7. Spoon the sauce over the mussels and sprinkle with the parsley. Serve immediately, with finger bowls.

Yield: 4 TO 6 SERVINGS

Wine Suggestion: A DRY WHITE SAUVIGNON, SUCH AS THE LOIRE VALLEY'S SOFT AND SMOKY POUILLY-FUMÉ

N O T E : In some markets mussels are pre-prepared, in that the small black beard that hangs from the mussel has been clipped off but not entirely removed. These mussels need only be rinsed before cooking.

A BISTRO-STYLE FEAST

. . . .

I don't know anyone who doesn't fall on his knees at the thought of a luscious golden roast chicken paired with a crusty potato gratin and a sip of a fragrant red Volnay, from Burgundy. Start off the meal with tiny brochettes of baby scallops, served with a blanc de blancs *Champagne. For dessert, serve thick slices of lemon cake with tangerine marmalade, along with a young Sauternes.*

. . . .

BROCHETTES OF BAY SCALLOPS
BÂTONNETS AUX PÉTONCLES

GRANDMOTHER'S ROAST CHICKEN
POULET RÔTI "GRAND-MAMAN"

THE "UPPER CRUST" POTATO GRATIN
LE GRATIN DES GRATINS

LEMON CAKE WITH DOUBLE CHOCOLATE ICING
MARBRÉ AU CITRON, CONFITURE D'ORANGES
SANGUINES

STEAMED MUSSELS WITH PEPPER AND PARSLEY

Moules à la Marinière

. . . .

*M*oules à la marinière always reminds me of Saturday lunch in the country, when there's often a hungry crowd. I cook up a healthy batch of mussels and serve them with fresh crusty homemade bread and plenty of chilled white Muscadet. Let's hear it for simplicity! When Chef Robuchon's staff prepares mussels in the restaurant kitchen, they're always careful to season them with plenty of freshly ground black pepper just before cooking—a trick worth following for all shellfish, for it adds that extra bit of zest. This recipe may also be used for preparing small, sweet steamed clams. Serve this with a simple green salad and plenty of crusty country bread.

4 pounds fresh mussels in their shells

4 shallots, minced

2 cups dry white wine, such as a
    Chardonnay

Handful of fresh flat-leaf parsley stems,
    tied in a bundle with cotton twine

2 tablespoons unsalted butter

Freshly ground black pepper to taste

Handful of fresh flat-leaf parsley
    leaves, snipped with a scissors

1. Thoroughly scrub the mussels, and rinse them in several changes of water. If an open mussel closes when you press on it, it is good; if it stays open, the mussel should be discarded. Beard the mussels. (Do not beard the mussels in advance or they will die and spoil. See Note, page 144.)

2. In a very large skillet, combine the shallots, wine, parsley stems, and butter over high heat. Boil for 5 minutes. Add the mussels, sprinkle generously with pepper, and stir. Cook, covered, until the mussels just open, about 5 minutes. Remove the mussels as they open. Do not overcook. Discard any mussels that do not open.

3. Transfer the mussels in their shells to a warmed serving platter. Line a fine-mesh sieve with moistened cheesecloth, and strain the cooking liquid through it. Pour the strained liquid over the mussels, sprinkle with the parsley, and serve immediately, with finger bowls.

Yield: 4 TO 6 SERVINGS

Wine Suggestion: A YOUNG WHITE CHARDONNAY, SUCH AS BURGUNDY'S SAINT-ROMAIN

NOTE: This recipe also serves as an all-purpose method of cooking mussels. If you need cooked mussels but not the cooking liquid, strain the juice and reserve it to use as you would any good fish stock. This recipe should yield about 1 cup of mussel cooking liquid. Cover securely and refrigerate for 2 to 3 days, or freeze for up to 1 month.

PARSLEY TRUC

Parsley, like salt and pepper, has become such a commonplace ingredient that we forget that it is capable of transforming an ordinary dish into a spectacular one. Try carefully snipping the leaves of flat-leaf parsley with a sharp scissors rather than chopping them with a knife. Sprinkle them as a garnish at the last minute, and you'll quickly see the difference.

POULTRY
AND MEATS

....

Volailles et Viandes

PHEASANT ROASTED ON A BED OF BRAISED ENDIVE

Poule Faisane aux Endives en Cocotte Lutée

Chef Robuchon's method for roasting poultry is ingenious. The bird is seared first on the stove, then in the oven, then roasted in a hermetically sealed container—a technique that eliminates fat and gives the juices a richer, almost caramelized taste. (The same procedure can be followed for duck; see page 154.) Although the idea of pheasant stuffed with foie gras sounds almost decadent, it's really very clever: The foie gras instantly flavors the frame and the richness spreads out into the meat. (Because a small amount of foie gras is used, it will actually melt into the juices and all but disappear.)

This recipe also makes use of an extremely simple, impressive, and practical technique, that of wrapping the casserole with luting pastry, or *repère,* a flour and egg white pastry. The pastry—which takes seconds to prepare—hardens as it dries in the oven and seals the casserole. No juices are allowed to evaporate and all the flavors are retained, making for a moist and flavorful bird. When preparing this dish at Jamin, the chefs use puff pastry to seal the roasting pan, but this simple pastry is easier to handle and just as effective.

EQUIPMENT: One 1½-quart oval earthenware or enameled cast-iron casserole, with a lid

LUTING PASTRY
1 cup all-purpose flour
3 to 4 large egg whites

1 female pheasant (about 1 pound),
    wing tips, gizzard, and heart reserved
Sea salt and freshly ground white
    pepper to taste
3 ounces fresh foie gras (or substitute
    best-quality foie gras terrine)

3 tablespoons unsalted butter
1 carrot, coarsely chopped
1 onion, coarsely chopped
3 plump fresh garlic cloves, unpeeled
1½ cups water
1 recipe braised endives (page 227)
2 large egg yolks
1 tablespoon water

1. Prepare the luting pastry: In the bowl of a heavy-duty electric mixer fitted with a flat paddle, combine the flour and 3 egg whites and mix until the dough is soft and pliable. If necessary, add the additional egg white. If the dough is still too firm, add several teaspoons of water to soften. Set aside. (The pastry may be prepared to this point several hours in advance. Wrap securely and store at room temperature.)

2. Chill the lid of the casserole in the refrigerator for at least 20 minutes, so the luting pastry will adhere more easily when applied.

3. Preheat the oven to 475°F.

4. Generously season the interior of the pheasant with salt and pepper. Place the foie gras in the cavity of the bird, and truss. Generously season the outside. Set aside.

ROASTING TIPS

. . . .

When roasting poultry, always place the breast end—the largest part of the bird—toward the back of the oven. Since ovens are generally hotter in the back, the bird will cook more evenly. Likewise, always select a skillet or roasting pan just large enough to hold the poultry, so that the maximum amount of cooking juices is retained.

5. In an ovenproof skillet just large enough to hold the pheasant, melt the butter over moderately high heat. Place the bird on its side in the pan and brown for 3 minutes. Turn and brown the other side for 3 minutes more. Turn the bird on its back and brown for 4 minutes more, for a total of 10 minutes browning time.

6. Surround the bird with the carrots, onion, garlic, and reserved wing tips, gizzard, and heart. Turn the bird on its side. Place the skillet in the oven, with the thicker part of the bird (the breast end) toward the back of the oven. Roast, uncovered, for 3 minutes. Turn the bird over and roast the other side for 3 minutes more. Turn the bird on its back and roast for 4 minutes more, for a total of 10 minutes roasting time.

7. Remove the skillet from the oven, and transfer the bird to a plate. Season generously with salt and pepper. Return the skillet with the cooking juices, vegetables, and giblets to the heat and continue browning over high heat, 2 to 3 minutes. Spoon off and discard any fat on the top. Add the 1½ cups water to deglaze, scraping up any bits

that cling to the bottom. Continue cooking to reduce, 5 to 6 minutes. Strain through a fine-mesh sieve, pressing down firmly on the giblets and aromatics to extract as much juice as possible. Measure the liquid: You should have at least 1 cup.

8. Reduce the oven temperature to 425°F.

9. Crisscross the endives on the bottom of the casserole. Place the pheasant on top, breast side up. Pour the cooking juices over the bird.

10. Prepare the glaze: In a small bowl, whisk the egg yolks with 1 tablespoon water. Set aside.

11. Cut the luting pastry in half, and roll each half into a strip 4 inches wide and long enough to wrap halfway around the casserole. Place the lid on the casserole and wrap the pastry strips around its edge, pressing to make a tight seal. With a brush, coat the surface of the pastry with the glaze.

12. Place the casserole in the center of the oven, and roast for 15 minutes per pound of pheasant. Remove from the oven but do not break the pastry seal. Let rest at room temperature for at least 10 minutes but not more than 30 minutes.

13. To serve, break the seal and discard the pastry. Transfer the pheasant to a carving board. Arrange the endives around the edges of a large warmed serving platter. Carve the pheasant and arrange the slices in the center of the platter. Spoon cooking juices over all. Transfer any remaining cooking juices to a bowl to pass.

Yield: 2 LARGE OR 4 SMALL SERVINGS

Wine Suggestion: A MEATY RED BURGUNDY, SUCH AS A CHAMBERTIN

PROPER TRUSSING

FOR A

COMPACT SHAPE AND

EVEN COOKING

. . . .

Securing the wings and legs of a bird tight to the body—a technique known as trussing—not only helps make for a much more attractive presentation but also forms a compact shape that will cook more evenly. The technique is suitable for all poultry to be roasted, poached, or braised. To truss: Thread a trussing needle with cotton twine. Push the needle through the upper part of the wings to fix them to the body. Pass the needle in the opposite direction through the thighs. Tie the ends of the twine together and trim the excess.

ROASTED DUCK WITH SAUTÉED APPLES, HONEY, AND CIDER VINEGAR

Canette Rôtie aux Pommes Poêleés, Sauce au Miel, et au Vinaigre

. . . .

Duck is delicious, but too often it's rejected as too fatty or too complicated to cook. Try this method and you'll soon see that it's as easy as roasting a chicken. Here the duck is actually seared on all sides in a very hot oven, then continues to cook while it rests. All the fat is discarded, but not the flavorful cooking juices produced by the duck trimmings and aromatic vegetables and herbs. The sauce is an exuberant blend of lime, orange, and grapefruit zest, bolstered by honey and cider vinegar. The duck is garnished with wedges of golden caramelized apples. The first time I prepared this, I served the dish with a salad of nasturtium leaves and blossoms, and tossed a spoonful of the sauce into the vinaigrette, amplifying the flavors and offering a rewarding complement to the poultry.

EQUIPMENT: One ovenproof skillet just large enough to hold the duck

- 1 duck (2½ to 4 pounds), liver reserved, trimmings (neck, heart, wing tips) chopped (see Note)
- Sea salt and freshly ground white pepper to taste
- 3 plump fresh garlic cloves
- 1 small carrot, cut into thick diagonal slices
- 1 small onion, cut into thick slices
- 1 sprig fresh thyme
- Grated zest (orange peel) of 1 small orange
- Grated zest (yellow peel) of 1 small grapefruit
- Grated zest (green peel) of 1 lime
- 4 tablespoons clarified butter (page 326)
- 4 cooking apples, cored, peeled, and cut into 6 even slices each
- 1 tablespoon honey
- 3 to 4 tablespoons best-quality apple cider vinegar
- About ½ cup water
- 3 tablespoons unsalted butter, chilled

1. Preheat the oven to 425°F.

2. Season the duck, inside and out, with salt and pepper. Place the duck liver in the cavity, and truss (see box, page 153). Place the duck on its side in the skillet, and set it in the oven with the fullest part of the duck (the breast portion) toward the back. Roast, uncovered, for 10 minutes. Turn the duck on the other side and roast for 10 minutes more. Turn the duck on its back and roast for 10 minutes more.

3. Remove the skillet from the oven and surround the duck with the chopped trimmings and the garlic, carrot, onion, and thyme. Remove the trussing string from the bird, and season the legs with salt. (At this point the bird will hold its shape on its own. Without the string, the legs will cook more evenly.) Return the skillet to the oven and roast the duck for a total of 13 to 15 minutes per pound (the time will vary according to the size of the duck and your flavor preference). Select the longer roasting time for a smaller duck, the shorter time for a large duck. (Thus, total roasting time for a 2½-pound duck would be about 37 minutes, for a 5-pound duck, 1 hour and 5 minutes.) Spoon the cooking juices over the duck 3 or 4 times to keep it moist as it roasts.

4. Remove the duck from the oven, and once again season generously. Transfer the duck to a platter, reserving the skillet and its contents, and place the duck at an angle against the edge of a baking dish, with its head down and tail in the air. (This heightens the flavor by allowing the juices to flow down through to the breast meat.) Cover the duck loosely with aluminum foil. Turn off the oven and place the duck in the oven, with the door ajar. Let it rest for at least 20 minutes and up to 1 hour. The duck will continue to cook as it rests.

5. Prepare the zests: Bring a medium-size saucepan of water to a boil. Place the

REMOVING THE GLANDS

The duck's fat glands, two small nodules found on the upper side of the bird's tail, help keep its feathers nice and shiny. Unfortunately, when a duck is cooked, the fat can impart a bitter flavor. Usually, the butcher will have removed the glands, but if they are still intact, you'll have to remove them yourself: Place the bird breast side up, and use the tip of a sharp knife to cut out the portion of tail flesh that contains the glands.

orange, grapefruit, and lime zest in a fine-mesh sieve, and submerge it in the boiling water for 2 minutes to blanch. Rinse under cold running water, drain, and set aside.

6. Prepare the apples: In a large nonstick skillet, heat the clarified butter over moderately high heat. When hot, add the apples in a single layer, and cook until golden brown on one side before turning. Cook until soft, 5 to 10 minutes. Drain, arrange around the edge of an ovenproof platter, cover with foil, and keep warm.

7. Prepare the sauce: Place the skillet with the trimmings over high heat. Cook until nicely browned, 1 to 2 minutes. Drain and discard the liquid in the pan (it will be mostly fat). Add the honey, stir, and cook 1 to 2 minutes more. Deglaze with several tablespoons of vinegar, and cook for 1 minute. Add about ½ cup water, and simmer for 5 minutes more.

8. Strain the sauce through a fine-mesh sieve placed over a clean skillet, pressing down on the trimmings. To this, add any cooking juices that have drained from the duck as it rested. Bring the sauce to a boil over high heat. Taste, and if necessary, add another teaspoon or two of vinegar. Remove the pan from the heat and add the chilled butter, a few pieces at a time, working on and off the heat so that the butter melts gently to thicken the sauce. Stir in the reserved zest.

9. To serve: Carve the duck and arrange the meat in the center of the platter, surrounded by apple slices. Spoon about half the sauce over the duck. Pour the reserved sauce into a warmed sauceboat. Serve immediately.

Yield: 4 SERVINGS

Wine Suggestion: A TOP-QUALITY RHÔNE VALLEY RED, SUCH AS A CÔTE-RÔTIE

NOTE: Top-quality fresh duck can be ordered from D'Artagnan, Inc., 399–419 Saint Paul Avenue, Jersey City, NJ 07306; tel. 800-DAR-TAGN or 201-792-0748; fax 201-792-0113. Ask for a female Muscovy duck (for 2) or male Muscovy (for 4).

A FLAVOR BONUS

....

To extract the maximum flavor from all poultry trimmings—such as the neck, heart, and wing tips—chop them as fine as possible with a cleaver. For a quick and delicious sauce, sauté them quickly in fat, add aromatics such as carrots, onions, garlic, and thyme, then deglaze with a bit of water or wine. Over low heat, reduce for 4 to 5 minutes, then strain.

WHOLE ROASTED FOIE GRAS WITH CARAMELIZED TURNIPS

Foie Gras Rôti Entier aux Navets

. . . .

What a great marriage: rich and silken foie gras with tender caramelized turnips. Most of the work can be done in advance, leaving the turnips in the skillet to rewarm at the last minute, and the foie gras cooks in no time—so this is an ideal dish for entertaining. (It is also a versatile recipe for turnips; try preparing them this way with a simple roast duck or game. And it's a marvelous way to prepare fresh foie gras, for you don't need to denerve the livers in this recipe.)

Serve the dish in the early spring, when first-of-the-season turnips are available. If you are preparing it in the winter, blanch the turnip rounds first in plenty of salted boiling water, to soften the flavor a bit. Once again, it's that final seasoning and deglazing that make all the difference. If you happen to have cooked poultry that day or the day before, be sure to save some of the cooking juices, and add them to the pan with the vinegar when deglazing. Try to specify a smaller, 1-pound liver when ordering for this recipe; it's plenty for 4 generous servings.

1 fresh duck foie gras (1 to 1½ pounds; see Note, page 84)

1 tablespoon fine sea salt

1½ pounds round white purple-top turnips, about 2 inches in diameter, cut into rounds about 1 inch thick

5 tablespoons unsalted butter

Sea salt and freshly ground white pepper to taste

2 tablespoons sugar

1 cup chicken stock (page 334)

2 teaspoons extra-virgin olive oil

1 tablespoon balsamic vinegar

Chicken cooking juices (optional)

GARNISH

Coarse sea salt

1 tablespoon coarsely ground white peppercorns

1 tablespoon finely minced fresh chives

1. About 8 hours before serving time, prepare the foie gras: Note that a duck liver consists of two lobes, one small, one large. With your hands, separate the larger lobe from the smaller one by gently pulling them apart. With a small sharp knife, gently scrape away any traces of green bile. With the knife, trim away a strip (about ¾ inch wide) on the thinnest edge of the large lobe. (This will allow the salt to penetrate the liver and draw out the blood, making for a clean, even-colored foie gras.) Prepare a large bowl of ice water, add the 1 tablespoon sea salt for each 1½ quarts water, and place the foie gras pieces in the water. Cover with plastic wrap and refrigerate for 6 hours.

2. Meanwhile, prepare the turnips: In a 12-inch skillet, preferably with a tight-fitting lid, combine the turnips and butter over moderate heat. Season with salt and pepper, then sprinkle with the sugar. Cook slowly, turning the turnips from time to time, until lightly browned, about 10 minutes. Add ¼ cup of the stock, cover, and continue cooking over moderate heat until much of the liquid has been reduced, 5 to 6 minutes. Continue, adding stock and reducing it, until all the stock has been used and the turnips are evenly golden brown and meltingly tender. The entire cooking process should take about 30 minutes. Set the turnips aside in the skillet.

3. Preheat the oven to 475°F.

4. Prepare the foie gras: Remove the pieces of foie gras from the salt water, and gently pat dry. Season the liver generously with salt and pepper. Add the oil to a medium-size nonstick ovenproof skillet, and place the two lobes of foie gras in the skillet. Place the skillet in the center of the oven, and roast the foie gras for 4 to 5 minutes on one side. Then turn the foie gras and roast for 6 to 7 minutes more. The foie gras should be golden, almost caramelized, on the outside. (To test for doneness, place a metal skewer in the thickest part of the larger lobe, and leave it there for 30 seconds. Remove the skewer and touch it to your bottom lip. If the skewer is cold, the foie gras is underdone; return it to the oven for 1 to 2 minutes more. If the skewer is warm, the foie gras is perfectly cooked.)

5. While the foie gras is cooking, return the turnips to the heat and allow them to reheat gently.

6. Remove the skillet from the oven, and leaving the foie gras in it, carefully drain off the fat. Place the skillet over moderately high heat, and deglaze with the vinegar and, if you are using them, the chicken cooking juices. Scrape up any bits that cling to the bottom of the pan. Continue cooking for 1 to 2 minutes, scraping and stirring,

constantly spooning the juices up and over the foie gras to moisten and season it, until the liquid is thick and almost caramelized. The foie gras will continue to cook, and melt, as you cook the sauce.

7. Transfer the liver and the sauce to the center of a warmed platter. Arrange the turnip rounds around the foie gras, and sprinkle each piece of turnip with coarse salt and coarsely ground white pepper. Down the center of each lobe of foie gras, arrange a single row of coarsely ground white pepper, coarse salt, and finely minced chives. Serve immediately.

Yield: 4 SERVINGS

Wine Suggestion: A GRAND BORDEAUX, SUCH AS A POMEROL

RABBIT WITH MUSTARD, FAVA BEANS, AND BABY ONIONS

Lapin Sauté aux Fèves et aux Petits Oignons

....

Moist and tender, this is the most elegant rabbit with mustard you're ever likely to encounter. The key here is to cook the rabbit slowly over very low heat so it does not dry out. At Jamin, Chef Robuchon prepares this with rabbit shoulder, fresh rabbit liver, fava beans, and wild chanterelle mushrooms. For the home cook a whole rabbit is more practical. This is the sort of recipe that takes a fair amount of last-minute juggling—you need to keep dancing, and to keep your wits about you—but it's worth the effort. What you want to achieve here is a mingling of fresh, specific flavors and a certain succulence. As ever, it's the complex combination of flavors, the touch of fresh herbs, the little details, that work to make this dish a culinary triumph. When fresh fava beans aren't in the market, I prepare this with quickly blanched snow peas or baby asparagus for that essential touch of green.

1 large whole fresh rabbit (about 4 pounds), or 2 smaller rabbits, cut into serving pieces, liver reserved

3 tablespoons imported French mustard

1 tablespoon fresh thyme leaves

Sea salt and freshly ground white pepper to taste

2 tablespoons unsalted butter

2 tablespoons extra-virgin olive oil

1 cup chicken stock (page 334)

ONIONS

7 ounces fresh baby onions (or substitute pearl onions)

1 tablespoon sugar

1 tablespoon unsalted butter

Sea salt and freshly ground white pepper to taste

MUSHROOMS

8 ounces fresh chanterelle mushrooms, trimmed and brushed clean (or substitute domestic mushroom caps, trimmed, brushed clean, and quartered)

1 tablespoon extra-virgin olive oil

1 tablespoon freshly squeezed lemon juice (for domestic mushrooms)

FAVA BEANS

1 pound fresh unshelled fava beans, or about 1 cup shelled beans

BACON

1 tablespoon unsalted butter

4 ounces lightly smoked bacon, cut into very fine julienne

2 tablespoons unsalted butter

Sea salt and freshly ground white pepper to taste

1 tablespoon best-quality red wine vinegar

Several tablespoons fresh flat-leaf parsley leaves, snipped with a scissors

1 teaspoon fresh summer savory or fresh thyme leaves

1. Brush both sides of the rabbit pieces very generously with the mustard. Sprinkle generously with thyme, salt, and pepper. Crush the reserved bones and chop the reserved trimmings, and set aside.

2. Preheat the oven to 200°F.

3. Cook the rabbit: In a very large skillet, heat the butter and oil over moderately high heat. When hot but not smoking, add the reserved trimmings and the seasoned rabbit pieces. Immediately reduce the heat to low (to keep the rabbit meat from drying out). Cover and cook, shaking the pan from time to time, until the rabbit is tender but still moist, about 15 minutes per side. (Cooking time will vary according to the size of the pieces.) Leaving the trimmings in the skillet, transfer the rabbit meat to a large casserole. Season again with salt and pepper. Cover and place in the oven to keep warm until serving time.

4. Increase the heat to high and deglaze the skillet with the chicken stock, scraping up any bits that cling to the bottom. Reduce over high heat to 1 cup, 2 to 3 minutes, then strain the sauce through a fine-mesh sieve, discarding the solids. Cover and keep the sauce warm over very low heat, or place the saucepan, covered, in the warm oven.

CUTTING UP A

RABBIT

To cut up a whole rabbit for cooking, first remove the liver; cover and refrigerate it. Trim off the flaps of skin, tops of forelegs, and any excess bone; reserve. With a heavy knife or cleaver, divide the carcass crosswise into three sections—hind legs, saddle, and forelegs (including the rib cage). Cut between the hind legs to separate them into two pieces. Split the front carcass into two pieces to separate the forelegs. Split the saddle crosswise into three even pieces.

5. Prepare the onions: If you are using pearl onions, blanch them for 2 minutes in a large pot of boiling salted water, then drain.

In a small sauté pan with a tight-fitting lid, combine the onions, sugar, and butter over low heat. Season, cover, and cook until the onions are tender, 15 to 20 minutes. Shake the pan occasionally to prevent the onions from browning. Set aside, covered.

6. Prepare the mushrooms: In a medium-size saucepan, combine the mushrooms and olive oil over moderate heat. (If you are using domestic mushrooms, add the lemon juice along with the oil.) Season, cover, and cook until tender, about 5 minutes. Set aside, covered.

7. Prepare the fava beans: Shell the beans and discard the pods. Prepare a large bowl of ice water. Bring a large pot of water to a boil, adding 1 tablespoon of salt per quart of water. Add the beans and cook for 30 seconds, counting from the time the water returns to a boil. Remove the beans with a slotted spoon, and plunge them into the ice water to cool. As soon as the beans are cool, drain them. Peel off and discard the tough outer coating of the beans, as well as the germ, which can make the beans bitter (see box, page 164). Set aside.

8. Prepare the bacon: In a small skillet, combine the butter and bacon over moderate heat, and cook until soft, 2 to 3 minutes. The bacon should not brown or become crunchy. Set aside.

9. Finish the garnish: Drain the mushrooms and onions. In a large skillet, heat 1 tablespoon of the butter over moderate heat, and add the mushrooms and onions. Taste for seasoning, and sauté gently until heated through. Add the reserved bacon and fava beans, and heat just until warmed through. The mixture should be meltingly tender and moist. Cover and keep warm over very low heat.

10. Cook the rabbit liver: Liberally season the liver with salt and pepper. In a small skillet, melt the remaining 1 tablespoon butter over moderate heat, and add the liver. Cook for 1 to 1½ minutes on each side. If the liver seems to be cooking too quickly, remove the skillet from the heat and allow the liver to cook off the heat, shaking the pan from time to time. It should stay moist and tender. Transfer the liver to a plate. Deglaze the pan with the vinegar, then return the liver to the pan, rolling it in the deglazed juices.

11. To serve, divide the warm rabbit pieces among 4 warmed dinner plates. Spoon the onion, mushroom, bean, and bacon mixture over the rabbit. Cut the liver into 4 equal pieces and arrange alongside. Spoon the reserved sauce over the rabbit pieces

only, and sprinkle the rabbit pieces with the parsley. Sprinkle the pieces of liver with summer savory or thyme, and serve immediately.

Yield: 4 SERVINGS

Wine Suggestion: A STURDY RED, SUCH AS SANTENAY, FROM BURGUNDY

FAVA BEANS

Fava beans—also known as broad beans—are long and round, with almost velvety light green pods, not unlike lima beans. Known as *fèves* in French, fava beans are very tender when young, but as they mature, the skin covering the beans can become coarse and tough. Like fresh peas, the beans must be shelled before eating. Likewise, the tough outer skin of the bean must be removed, or slipped off by rolling with the tips of the fingers. Mature fava beans also contain a small germ, or tiny sprout, found at the tip of the bean. These, too, should be slipped off with the tips of the fingers and discarded, for they can impart a bitter flavor. Fava beans are relative newcomers to the American market, but they often can be found at farmers' markets or fine greengrocers. They can be eaten raw, and are delicious dipped in coarse sea salt, as an appetizer or snack.

ROAST LEG OF LAMB WITH PARSLEY CRUST

Gigot d'Agneau Rôti et Persillé

. . . .

To my taste, this is the ultimate leg of lamb recipe. I cook it often because it's ideal for entertaining: It's basically care-free and no-risk, and leftovers are delicious. Ask the butcher for a few bones and trimmings from the upper leg joint; this will add exceptional flavor.

EQUIPMENT: One oval baking dish just slightly larger than the lamb (about 9 × 13 inches)

Extra trimmings and bones from lamb upper leg
Bouquet garni: several parsley stems, celery leaves, and sprigs of thyme, wrapped in the green part of a leek and securely fastened with cotton twine
2 whole heads plump fresh garlic, unpeeled, cut in half horizontally

1 leg of lamb (about 5 pounds), bone in, carefully trimmed of fat and tied (ask your butcher to do this for you)
1 tablespoon unsalted butter, softened
Sea salt and freshly ground white pepper to taste

PARSLEY TOPPING
2 slices white bread, crusts removed
¼ cup fresh flat-leaf parsley leaves
Sea salt to taste

1¼ cups cold water

1. Preheat the oven to 425°F.

2. In the bottom of the baking dish, scatter the trimmings, bones, bouquet garni, and garlic, cut side down. Place the lamb on top and rub with the butter. Season generously. Place in the oven and roast about 50 minutes to 1¼ hours (10 to 12 minutes per pound for medium rare, 15 minutes for medium). Turn the lamb several times while it is cooking, and baste occasionally.

3. Meanwhile, prepare the topping: Place the bread in a food processor and process to fine crumbs. Add the parsley and process until well blended. For an even finer texture, force the crumbs through a fine-mesh sieve. Season, and set aside.

4. Remove the lamb from the oven, and again season generously. On a large platter, place a salad plate upside down on a dinner plate. Transfer the lamb to the platter and set it, exposed bone in the air, at an angle on the upside-down plate. Cover the lamb loosely with aluminum foil. Turn off the oven and place the lamb in the oven, with the door ajar. Let it rest for at least 25 minutes and up to 1 hour.

SEASONING MEAT

. . . .

Always salt and pepper meat immediately before placing it in a hot oven. If it is seasoned in advance, the meat will "sweat" and the salt will act like a magnet, drawing out all the flavorful juices. Always season again immediately after removing the meat from the oven, for this is what gives the meat a "seasoned" and finished flavor.

5. Prepare the sauce: Place the roasting pan with the trimmings and garlic over moderate heat. Cook to caramelize the drippings, 2 to 3 minutes. Be careful not to burn them. Spoon off any excess fat, and add the 1¼ cups cold water to deglaze the pan, scraping up any bits that cling to the bottom. Lower the heat and cook until reduced by half, 5 to 7 minutes. Strain through a fine-mesh sieve. Taste for seasoning and pour into a warmed sauceboat. Set aside and keep warm.

6. Preheat the broiler.

7. To finish the lamb: With your hands, spread a thin, even layer of the parsley-crumb topping all over the lamb. Place the meat about 3 inches from the broiler, and broil, turning, until the crust is golden brown, about 6 minutes total. Watch carefully and do not let it burn. Remove from the oven and carve. Serve with the sauce.

Yield: 8 SERVINGS

Wine Suggestion: A FINE WELL-BALANCED BORDEAUX, SUCH AS A SAINT-JULIEN

GARLIC BY THE HEAD

. . . .

If you love garlic, whenever you roast meat or poultry, take several unpeeled heads of garlic, slice them horizontally, and place the pieces on the bottom of the roasting pan. They will gently infuse the meat or poultry, and garlic lovers will have an extra treat to spread, soft clove by clove, on toast. Likewise, when roasting whole cloves of garlic, do not peel them: The garlic will be more difficult to eat, but the cloves will be far more flavorful and more moist than those that have been peeled.

A TASTY
VINAIGRETTE

. . . .

Should you have any pan juices left over from roasting a leg of lamb or even a chicken, use them to prepare a vinaigrette. I often substitute the juices for oil, or add a spoonful or two to oil and vinegar. You'll be surprised at the flavorful results.

At tableside in Patricia Wells's home in Provence: Potatoes "Chanteduc," Roast Leg of Lamb with Parsley Crust, Rustic Wheat and Rye Bread, and Pear, Vanilla, and Star Anise Clafoutis (on the hearth)

GUINEA HEN ROASTED ON A BED OF POTATOES

Pintade Rôtie aux Pommes de Terre Confites

. . . .

A simple, golden dish, this combination is ideal for those days when you want a good fresh meal but don't have lots of time to cook. I love roasting poultry on a bed of potatoes, for the delicious juices drip into the potatoes, giving them a wonderfully rich flavor. You could substitute a whole chicken, a pair of Cornish game hens, or several chicken breasts for the guinea hen; and fresh Belgian endives could be used instead of potatoes.

A salad of watercress or mixed greens is an excellent accompaniment.

EQUIPMENT: One ovenproof oval baking dish just slightly larger than the guinea hen
(about 9 × 13 inches)

1 fresh guinea hen (about 2 pounds),
   neck, wing tips, and liver reserved
1 sprig fresh rosemary
1 sprig fresh thyme
4 tablespoons unsalted butter

Sea salt and freshly ground white
   pepper to taste
2 pounds baking potatoes, such as
   Idaho Russets, peeled and cut into
   eighths

1. Preheat the oven to 425°F.

2. Place the neck, wing tips, liver, rosemary, and thyme inside the guinea hen and season the inside generously. Truss the hen (page 153). Rub the skin with 1 tablespoon of the butter, and season generously.

3. Rub the bottom of the baking dish with 1 tablespoon of the butter. Place the guinea hen on its side in the dish, and arrange the potatoes around it. Dot the potatoes with the remaining 2 tablespoons butter, and season them generously with salt and pepper.

4. Place the dish in the center of the oven and roast, uncovered, for 20 minutes, basting at the end of the roasting time. (When basting, also turn the potatoes so that they brown evenly.) Turn the hen on its other side and roast 20 minutes more. Baste,

and turn the guinea hen on its back. Roast for another 20 minutes. Baste, and roast for 15 minutes more. Test for doneness: Pierce the thigh with a skewer: the guinea hen is cooked when the juices run clear. This should take about 1¼ hours total.

5. Remove the dish from the oven and season generously with salt and pepper. Transfer the guinea hen to a platter, and place it at an angle against the edge of an overturned plate, with its head down and tail in the air. This heightens the flavor by allowing the juices to flow down through the breast meat. Cover loosely with foil. Turn off the oven and place the platter in the oven, with the door ajar. Let rest for at least 10 minutes or up to 30 minutes. The hen will continue to cook as it rests. At the same time, keep the potatoes covered in a warm oven.

6. Carve the guinea hen and place the pieces on a warmed platter. Arrange the potatoes around the platter, and serve.

Yield: 4 TO 6 SERVINGS

Wine Suggestion: A YOUNG BORDEAUX, PREFERABLY FROM MARGAUX OR PAULLIAC

Boneless Roast Loin of Pork with Aromatic Vegetables

Carré de Porc Rôti aux Tomates, Ail, Oignons, et Carottes

. . . .

This is the sort of dish Chef Robuchon likes to make on weekends when the restaurant is closed and his family gathers for a relaxed meal in their Paris apartment. Colorfully appealing and flavorful, it's great for those who love moist and tender pork. As with any recipe that calls for fresh herbs, make an effort to use fresh sage, or substitute fresh rosemary or summer savory. Do not use dried sage, for it has a tendency to turn bitter.

EQUIPMENT: One oval baking dish (about 9 × 13 inches)

12 small plum tomatoes

5 tablespoons unsalted butter

2 large onions, cut crosswise into ½-inch rounds

Sea salt and freshly ground white pepper to taste

2 tablespoons extra-virgin olive oil

5 large carrots, cut diagonally into ½-inch slices

4 plump fresh garlic cloves, halved

Small bunch of fresh sage

2 teaspoons fresh thyme leaves

3 pounds rolled boneless top loin pork roast, trimmed and tied, at room temperature

1. Preheat the oven to 400°F.

2. Prepare the tomatoes: Core the tomatoes. With a vegetable peeler, peel the tomatoes. Halve each tomato lengthwise, and squeeze slightly to remove the seeds. With a small spoon, remove the tomato pulp. (The pulp and seeds may be reserved for preparing a tomato sauce. They will not be needed in this recipe.) Set aside the outer shells of the tomatoes.

3. Cook the onions: In a large skillet, heat 3 tablespoons of the butter over low heat. When hot, add the onions, but do not salt (this allows the onions to brown more easily).

Cook the onions, shaking the pan from time to time, until nicely, evenly browned on one side, about 5 minutes. Turn carefully with a two-pronged fork, and cook on the other side until evenly browned, about 5 minutes more. The onions will have a tendency to fall apart, but try to keep them in a single piece as you turn them. Remove from the heat and season generously with salt and pepper. Drain and set aside.

CRISP AND GOLDEN

VS.

SOFT AND MOIST

. . . .

Do you want ingredients—such as onions or potatoes—sautéed to a golden brown? Or do you want them soft and moist? Here are tips to remember:

1. For crisp, golden coloring, heat the fat first, then add the ingredients, but do not salt. Salt impedes browning.

2. For soft, moist cooking, heat the fat, ingredients, and salt together.

---

4. Cook the tomatoes: In a large skillet, heat the oil over moderately high heat. When hot, add the tomato shells and cook, shaking the pan from time to time, until nicely, evenly browned, about 10 minutes. Remove from the heat and season generously with salt and pepper. Drain and set aside.

5. Cook the carrots: In a large skillet, heat the remaining 2 tablespoons butter over low heat. When hot, add the carrots, seasoning generously with salt and pepper. Cook the carrots, shaking the pan from time to time, until nicely, evenly browned and soft and tender when pierced with a fork, about 15 minutes. Add the garlic and cook for 2 to 3 minutes more. Remove from the heat and season generously with salt and pepper. Drain and set aside.

6. Select an oval baking dish that will hold the pork and vegetables without crowding. With a two-pronged fork, arrange an overlapping layer of onions at one end of the baking dish. Place an overlapping layer of tomatoes alongside the onions. Place an overlapping layer of carrots alongside the tomatoes. Repeat until all the vegetables cover the bottom of the dish in a single layer. Mince half the sage leaves and sprinkle over the vegetables, along with the thyme. Season the pork generously with salt and pepper. Tuck the remaining whole sage leaves beneath the string around the pork. Place the pork, fat side up, on top of the vegetables. Place the baking dish, uncovered, in the center of the oven and roast for 1 hour. Add ½ cup water, cover the pork loosely with aluminum foil, and roast for 15 minutes more. Leaving the foil covering in place, turn

off the oven and leave the door slightly ajar. Let rest a minimum of 15 minutes or up to 1 hour. The pork will continue to cook as it rests.

7. To serve, remove and discard the string. Carve the pork into thick slices and arrange on warmed dinner plates. Serve with the roasted vegetables alongside.

Yield: 6 TO 8 SERVINGS

Wine Suggestion: A YOUNG, FRUITY RED FROM PROVENCE

THICK VEAL CHOP WITH WILD MUSHROOMS AND ASPARAGUS

La Côte de Veau Poêlée aux Champignons et Asperges

, , , , , , , , , , , , , , , ,

Mention veal chops and many of us think of thin, dried-out things, virtually devoid of flavor and personality. Rather than spoiling delicious veal by cutting it too thin, next time try a big, thick, juicy chop, one that's 2 inches thick and plenty for two hungry diners. The accompaniment is an elegant mixture of varied wild mushrooms, baby onions, and asparagus. (If wild mushrooms are not available, substitute 1 pound domestic mushrooms caps, quartered.) I love this dish, and when time is limited I prepare just the extra-thick veal chop and serve sautéed potatoes alongside.

VEGETABLE GARNISH

10 fresh baby onions (or substitute pearl onions)

1 tablespoon sugar

Sea salt

12 small green asparagus, tough ends trimmed

5 ounces horn-of-plenty mushrooms, trimmed and brushed clean

1 tablespoon unsalted butter

1 tablespoon peanut oil

7 ounces chanterelle mushrooms, trimmed and brushed clean

5 ounces oyster mushrooms, trimmed and brushed clean

7 ounces shiitake mushrooms, trimmed and brushed clean

1 tablespoon freshly squeezed lemon juice (for domestic mushrooms)

Sea salt and freshly ground white pepper to taste

VEAL

2 extra-thick veal chops (about 2 inches thick, 1¼ pounds each), trimmings reserved

Sea salt and freshly ground white pepper to taste

1 tablespoon fresh thyme leaves

1 tablespoon unsalted butter

1 tablespoon peanut oil

2 whole heads plump fresh garlic, unpeeled, cut in half horizontally

3 ounces slab bacon, rind removed, finely diced

1. Cook the onions: In a small saucepan, combine the onions, sugar, and a pinch of salt. Add water to cover by half, cover, and cook over moderately low heat until the water has almost completely evaporated, 15 to 20 minutes. Shake the pan from time to time and watch carefully at the end, so the onions do not burn. Remove from the heat, drain, and set aside.

2. Cook the asparagus: Prepare a large bowl of ice water. Bring a large pot of water to a boil over high heat. Add salt and the asparagus. Cook until tender, about 5 minutes. With a slotted spoon, transfer to the ice water to cool thoroughly. Drain the asparagus, cut at an angle into four to five equal pieces, and set aside.

3. Cook the mushrooms: Place the horn-of-plenty mushrooms in a medium skillet (with no added fat) over moderate heat. Salt, cover, and cook for 3 to 4 minutes. Transfer the mushrooms to a colander, and drain the liquid from the skillet. When the mushrooms are cool enough to handle, squeeze out excess liquid with your hands; set aside. In the same skillet, combine the butter and oil over moderate heat. Add the chanterelle, oyster, and shiitake mushrooms. Cook until softened, 3 to 4 minutes. Season to taste. Drain, set aside, and keep warm. (If you are using domestic mushrooms, cook them in the butter, oil, and lemon juice over moderately high heat until golden, about 5 minutes. Season with salt and pepper to taste.)

4. Cube the veal trimmings and set aside.

5. Season the veal chops with salt, pepper, and thyme. In a very large heavy-bottomed skillet, combine the butter and oil over moderately high heat. When hot, add the trimmings, garlic, bacon, and veal chops. Reduce the heat to moderate and cook for 15 to 20 minutes, basting frequently. Turn the chops and cook the other side for 15 to 20 minutes more, basting frequently. The veal should be tender and slightly rare.

6. For each veal chop, and for the trimmings, place one salad plate upside down on top of a dinner plate. When the veal is cooked, season it, and place each chop on an upturned salad plate. Do the same for the trimmings. If desired, reserve the halved heads of garlic to serve with the vegetables. Cover loosely with aluminum foil; set aside and keep warm.

7. Return the skillet to the heat, increase the heat to high, add the 1¼ cups cold water, and deglaze the pan, scraping up any bits that cling to the bottom. Cook until reduced by two thirds, 5 to 7 minutes. Taste for seasoning. Strain the sauce through a fine-mesh sieve into a sauceboat. Set aside and keep warm.

8. To finish, combine the onions, asparagus, and mushrooms in the same skillet, adding any juices that have been released from the veal and trimmings. Warm over moderate heat. Transfer the mixture to a warmed serving bowl. Carve the veal into thick strips and serve immediately, with the vegetables and sauce on the side.

Yield: 4 TO 6 SERVINGS

Wine Suggestion: A RICH AND EARTHY RED BORDEAUX, SUCH AS A GRAVES

NOTE: If unavailable locally, top-quality veal chops can be ordered from Summerfield Farm, HCR 4, Box 195A, Brightwood, VA 22715; tel. 703-948-3100.

AND NOW, TO REST

"Resting" is all about allowing meat and poultry to relax after it has been cooked and before it is sliced or carved. It is essential to good flavor, and once you get the knack of it, it will change the way you cook forever. When red meat cooks, all the juices flow toward the center. If you cut the meat as soon as it is removed from the heat, the interior will be moist, the exterior dry. By allowing the meat to rest, the juices will evenly permeate it.

In Chef Robuchon's kitchen, meats rest at an angle on the edge of a small plate turned upside down on top of a larger plate. This makes for a slightly elevated platform, which allows air to circulate, creating an even circulation of juices. (If you let the meat rest flat on a carving board, the bottom portion will remain warm and the top side will be exposed to the air, and the juices will less evenly permeate the meat.)

PORK LOIN WITH SAGE, LEEKS, AND JUNIPER

Carré de Porc aux Poireaux à la Maraîchère

. . . .

I love even the thought of this dish: wintry roast pork studded with garlic, perfumed with fresh sage and thyme, surrounded by leeks. This is one dish that's delicious the next day: Serve it at room temperature, with the vegetables, along with a drizzle of red wine vinegar and a sprinkling of julienned cornichons. The recipe was offered by Chef Robuchon's longtime friend and colleague from Jean Delaveyne.

EQUIPMENT: One ovenproof casserole large enough to hold the roast, with a tight-fitting lid

3 pounds boneless top-loin pork roast, trimmed and tied	6 medium onions, halved
6 plump fresh garlic cloves, cut in slivers	3 vine-ripened tomatoes, cored, peeled, seeded, and chopped
2 tablespoons coarse sea salt	2 tablespoons sugar
Handful of fresh sage leaves, crumbled	1 tablespoon best-quality red wine vinegar
1 sprig fresh thyme	1 cup white wine, preferably a Chardonnay
24 baby leeks, or 6 medium leeks	
2 tablespoons peanut oil	Freshly ground white pepper to taste
Several pork bones, very coarsely chopped	5 to 6 juniper berries
	2 tablespoons unsalted butter

1. One day before serving, prepare the pork: Stud the pork roast with the garlic slivers. Rub the entire surface of the meat with the salt, half the sage, and half the thyme leaves. Wrap securely in plastic wrap and refrigerate. (Salting the meat ahead will cure it briefly, and will heighten the intensity of the herbs and garlic.)

2. On serving day, remove the roast from the refrigerator, rinse thoroughly, and pat dry. Set aside to bring to room temperature.

3. Prepare the leeks: Prepare a large bowl of hot salted water. Trim the leeks at the root. Trim the bottom section (the white part) to about 6 inches. Cut the greens into

4 sections. Place all the leek sections in the hot salt water to soak for 10 minutes. Remove the leeks and dry thoroughly. Set aside.

4. In the casserole, heat the oil over moderately high heat. When hot, add the roast and the bones and cook, turning frequently, until the meat is thoroughly browned. Add the onions and tomatoes, and continue cooking for 3 to 4 minutes. Dissolve the sugar in the vinegar and add to the pork mixture. Add the wine and stir to blend. Cook to reduce slightly, about 5 minutes. Add the leeks, placing them around the meat and pushing down for a tight fit. Season lightly, and add the remaining sage and the juniper berries. Hold the thyme sprig over the casserole and roll it between your hands to release just the small leaves, which contain all the flavor. Add the butter. Cover, reduce the heat to low, and simmer, stirring occasionally to ensure that the leeks are equally distributed in the cooking liquid, for 1½ hours. (Alternatively, cook in a 325°F oven.)

5. To serve, untie the roast and slice it thinly. Place the pork slices on a warmed serving platter, and arrange the leeks and onions around the meat. Strain the cooking liquid through a fine-mesh sieve into a sauceboat, and serve immediately.

Yield: 6 SERVINGS

Wine Suggestion: A DELICATE, FRUITY RED, SUCH AS A SAVIGNY-LES-BEAUNE, FROM BURGUNDY

Roasted Lamb Shoulder with Spicy Red Pepper Crust

Epaule d'Agneau Rôtie à la Fleur de Poivron Rouge

. . . .

Lamb shoulder is one of the firmest and most gelatinous of lamb cuts, yet it is tender enough for grilling or roasting over high heat. Chef Robuchon serves lamb shoulder topped with a brilliant sunset-orange hot pepper crust—a blend of fresh bread crumbs, butter, garlic, red bell pepper, and ground spicy peppers. (The crust can also be used on other roast meats, fish, or poultry. Try it with a whole roast leg of lamb, chicken, or any rather strongly flavored whole fish, such as turbot or John Dory.) At Jamin, the crust is prepared with *niora,* a small, mildly hot pepper found in markets in Spain and in the south of France. Substitutes include dried ancho chili powder, small New Mexican peppers, or hot pepper flakes. The flavor of *niora* is mildly hot, but far from wimpy. It reminds me of paprika with an extra depth of flavor.

Serve this with potato purée and a mixed green salad.

PEPPER CRUST
1 tablespoon extra-virgin olive oil
½ red bell pepper, finely diced
3 cups finely ground fresh bread crumbs
    (about 11 trimmed slices)
10 tablespoons unsalted butter,
    softened
1 plump fresh garlic clove, finely
    minced

2 tablespoons ground dried chili
    pepper, or 1 to 2 teaspoons hot
    pepper flakes
Pinch of sea salt

1 small lamb shoulder (2 pounds), bone
    in, trimmed of excess fat
Sea salt and freshly ground black
    pepper to taste

1. Prepare the pepper crust: In a small skillet, combine the oil and red bell pepper over moderately high heat. Cook for 2 to 3 minutes (the pepper should retain its crunch). Drain thoroughly and transfer to a large mixing bowl. Add the bread crumbs, butter, garlic, dried hot pepper, and salt. With a wooden spoon, mix until the "dough" is soft and pliable. Form into a ball.

2. Place a piece of waxed paper large enough to generously cover the lamb shoulder on a flat surface. Place the ball of "dough" in the center and cover with another piece of paper. Roll the pastry evenly to form a piece just large enough to place over the lamb. Transfer to a baking sheet and refrigerate until firm, at least 1 hour.

3. Preheat the oven to 450°F.

4. Generously season the lamb with salt and pepper. Place it on a rack in a roasting pan, place in the oven, and roast, uncovered, about 20 minutes (allow 10 minutes per pound). Turn occasionally. Remove the lamb from the oven, and again season generously with salt and pepper. Cover the lamb loosely with aluminum foil. Turn off the oven, and place the lamb in the oven with the door ajar. Let it rest for at least 20 minutes or up to several hours (it will be reheated just before serving time). The lamb will continue to cook as it rests.

5. Preheat the broiler.

6. Place the lamb on a rack in a broiling pan. Remove the pastry from the refrigerator and peel off the top layer of paper. Turn the pastry over onto the lamb, and remove the second layer of paper. Place about 3 inches from the broiler, and broil until the pastry is browned, about 5 minutes.

7. To serve, carve the lamb shoulder, and place a slice of lamb and several spoonfuls of the golden pepper crust on each warmed dinner plate.

Yield: 4 SERVINGS

Wine Suggestion: A RED BORDEAUX, PREFERABLY A PAULLIAC

OLD-FASHIONED SPRING VEGETABLES WITH VEAL STEW

Blanquette de Veau aux Légumes Printaniers

. . . .

This dish is a pure revelation. On one hand, what could be more banal and commonplace than *blanquette de veau*? We think that, because most often what we're served in cafés and restaurants is bland, pale, flavorless. Well, this is the flip coin of that version: delicate, fragrant, flavorful, with an abundance of colorful vegetables, each cooked separately so they retain their natural flavors. Make this on a chilly day when you want to stick around the stove, taking in wonderful aromas, peeling vegetables, straining sauces, gathering friends and family to join in on a veritable feast. If tiny spring "baby" vegetables are not available, trim standard-size vegetables, adding the trimmings to the assortment of aromatic vegetables used for cooking the veal. And don't let the unavailability of one or two of the vegetables—such as wild mushrooms or fresh asparagus—deprive you of the pleasures of this dish.

1 pound veal shoulder, cut into 4-inch cubes

1 pound veal breast, cut into 4-inch cubes

2 tablespoons coarse sea salt

5 whole white peppercorns

AROMATIC VEGETABLES

1 medium onion, studded with 1 whole clove

1 carrot, finely chopped

1 leek, trimmed and well rinsed

Heart of 1 bunch of celery

2 plump fresh garlic cloves, unpeeled, cut in half

Bouquet garni: several parsley stems, celery leaves, and sprigs of thyme, wrapped in the green part of a leek and securely fastened with cotton twine

VEGETABLE GARNISH

8 tiny or 4 medium leeks, white part only, well rinsed

4 tender inner ribs of celery, well rinsed

12 small green asparagus, tough ends trimmed

12 young baby carrots, scrubbed and greens trimmed to 1 inch from base

12 young baby turnips, greens trimmed
    to 1 inch from base
1 small fennel bulb, coarsely chopped
Sea salt to taste
3 ounces young, tender green beans

7 ounces fresh baby onions (or
    substitute pearl onions)
1 tablespoon sugar
Sea salt to taste

7 ounces horn-of-plenty mushrooms,
    trimmed and brushed clean
7 ounces domestic mushrooms, trimmed
    and brushed clean
3 tablespoons unsalted butter
2 tablespoons freshly squeezed lemon
    juice
¾ cup *crème fraîche* (page 339) or
    heavy cream
3 large egg yolks
Freshly grated nutmeg to taste

1. Place the meat in a large saucepan. Add cold water to cover and 1 tablespoon of the salt, and bring to a boil over high heat. Boil for 2 minutes. Remove the meat with a slotted spoon and rinse quickly under cold running water. Discard the cooking liquid. Return the meat to a large, clean saucepan, add cold water to cover, and season with the remaining 1 tablespoon salt and the peppercorns. Bring to a boil over high heat. With a slotted spoon, regularly skim the foam, or impurities, that rise to the surface. When the foam subsides, add the aromatic vegetables: onion, carrot, leek, celery, garlic, and bouquet garni. Cover and simmer gently for 2 hours.

2. Meanwhile, prepare the vegetable garnish: With cotton twine, tie the leeks, celery, and asparagus in individual bundles. Place the leeks, celery, carrots, turnips, and fennel in a large stockpot (or cook them individually, or in twos, in several pots). Add cold water to cover and bring to a boil over high heat. When the water boils, season with salt. Prepare a large bowl of ice water. With a slotted spoon, remove each vegetable as soon as it is cooked and transfer to the ice water to fix the color and stop the cooking. Drain and set aside. (Cooking times for each vegetable will vary according to size. The vegetables should be just cooked through, still crisp and tender.)

3. For the green beans and asparagus: Prepare a large bowl of ice water. Bring a large pot of water to a boil. Salt the water, and add the green beans. Cook until crisp-tender, about 4 minutes. Remove with a slotted spoon and place in the ice water. Drain, and set aside. In the same boiling water, cook the asparagus until tender, 4 to 8 minutes, depending upon their size. Remove with a slotted spoon and place in the ice water. Drain, and set aside.

4. For the onions: In a medium skillet, combine the onions, sugar, and a pinch of salt. Add water to cover by half, cover, and cook over moderately low heat until most

of the water has evaporated and the onions are soft and slightly golden, but not browned, about 20 minutes. Remove from the heat and set aside.

5. For the mushrooms: Place the horn-of-plenty mushrooms in a medium skillet. Add salt to taste, cover, and cook over moderate heat for 3 to 4 minutes. Drain off the liquid and set aside until cool enough to handle. With your hands, squeeze the mushrooms over the sink to extract any remaining liquid, and set aside. If the domestic mushrooms are large, quarter them. In the same skillet, combine 1 tablespoon of the butter, the domestic mushrooms, and the lemon juice. Cover, and cook over moderate heat until tender, about 5 minutes. Remove the mushrooms and set aside; add the mushroom cooking liquid to the simmering meat mixture.

6. With a slotted spoon, transfer the meat to a large clean saucepan. Add the mushrooms and onions. Cover and set aside.

7. Place a piece of moistened cheesecloth over a fine-mesh sieve set over a large clean saucepan. Strain the veal cooking liquid, discarding the vegetables cooked with the veal. Increase the heat to high and reduce the veal broth by half, about 5 minutes.

8. Meanwhile, in a large bowl, combine 1 tablespoon of the *crème fraîche,* the egg yolks, and the nutmeg, and stir to blend. Set aside.

CHEF ROBUCHON'S

TIPS FOR A

GREAT

BLANQUETTE

. . . .

Blanquette de veau is one of the most traditional veal preparations, and one of the best. Contrary to popular belief, the meat should not be soaked before cooking to make it whiter; this washes out the blood and with it the flavor. Rather, blanch the meat—preferably chunks of veal shoulder or of veal breast, which has a slightly stronger flavor—for 2 minutes in boiling water and refresh it quickly under cold running water. This springtime *blanquette* is garnished with a mixture of seasonal baby vegetables, rather than the traditional rice.

9. Once the broth has reduced by half, whisk in the remaining *crème fraîche.* Return to a boil, and reduce by one third, 3 to 4 minutes.

10. Transfer a ladleful of the broth to the egg yolk mixture and whisk thoroughly. Continue whisking, adding another ladleful of broth. Slowly pour the egg yolk mixture

into the broth, reduce the heat, and cook for 5 minutes, stirring constantly to prevent the egg yolks from coagulating. Do not let the mixture boil. The sauce will thicken ever so slightly.

11. Strain the sauce through a fine-mesh sieve over the veal mixture. Heat the mixture over low heat, keeping the liquid just at a simmer.

12. In another large skillet, melt the remaining 2 tablespoons butter over moderate heat. Untie the precooked garnish vegetables—leeks, celery, asparagus, carrots, turnips, fennel, onions, mushrooms, and green beans—add them to the skillet, and cook just to warm through, about 2 minutes. Taste for seasoning.

13. To finish, place the veal mixture in a warmed deep serving platter, arrange the garnish vegetables on top, and serve immediately.

Yield: 6 TO 8 SERVINGS

Wine Suggestion: A LIGHT RED BURGUNDY, SUCH AS A MERCUREY

INDIVIDUAL
LAMB TARTS WITH
EGGPLANT, ZUCCHINI,
AND TOMATOES

Tourtières d'Agneau aux Aubergines, Courgettes, et Tomates

....

With intense Mediterranean spicing (generous seasoning of cumin, curry, and fresh thyme), this is a fragrant and substantial main course that may be prepared as individual tarts for an elegant dinner party or as one large tart (using a springform pan) for a more homey, simple presentation.

EQUIPMENT: Four 4-inch individual tart pans with removable bottoms; 1½-inch round pastry cutter

12 small plum tomatoes

VEGETABLE LINING
2 medium eggplants (about 1¼ pounds total)
4 small zucchini (about 1 pound total)
2 teaspoons fresh thyme leaves
Sea salt and freshly ground black pepper to taste

LAMB AND VEGETABLE FILLING
6 tablespoons extra-virgin olive oil
1 small zucchini (about 4 ounces), finely diced
1 very small eggplant (about 4 ounces), finely diced
1 teaspoon fresh thyme leaves
1 small onion, minced

10 ounces lamb shoulder, trimmed and coarsely ground (ask your butcher to do this for you)
3 tablespoons fresh flat-leaf parsely leaves, snipped with a scissors
1 tablespoon curry powder
1 tablespoon cumin seeds, freshly ground
Sea salt to taste

TOMATO AND RED PEPPER SAUCE
3 tablespoons extra-virgin olive oil
2 small onions, minced
3 plum tomatoes (about 10 ounces) cored, peeled, seeded, and chopped
1 small red bell pepper, peeled and chopped

(continued)

2 plump fresh garlic cloves, minced
Bouquet garni: several parsley stems,
celery leaves, and sprigs of thyme,
wrapped in the green part of a leek
and securely fastened with cotton
twine
1 imported bay leaf
Sea salt and freshly ground black
pepper to taste

3 tablespoons chopped fresh basil
leaves

Unsalted butter, softened, for the tart
pans
Fresh thyme leaves, for garnish
Extra-virgin olive oil, for garnish
Sea salt and freshly ground black
pepper to taste

1. Prepare the tomato disks: Core the tomatoes. With a vegetable peeler, peel the tomatoes. Halve each tomato lengthwise, and squeeze slightly to remove the seeds. Discard the seeds, leaving the outer shell. With a small spoon, remove the tomato pulp. Finely chop the pulp, place in a medium-size bowl, and reserve for the tomato sauce. Carefully flatten each tomato half, and with a round 1½-inch pastry cutter, cut the tomatoes into even disks. Arrange the disks side by side on a baking sheet or platter. You will need 21 tomato disks for each tart. Chop any leftover pieces of tomato and add to the tomato pulp. (The pulp will be reserved for step 9.) Set aside. (The recipe may be prepared to this point several hours in advance. Cover securely with plastic wrap and refrigerate.)

2. Prepare the vegetable lining: With a vegetable peeler, peel the skins of the eggplant and the zucchini into strips at least 1½ inches by 4 inches. You will need about 12 strips per vegetable for each individual tart. Set aside. (Reserve the zucchini pulp for the zucchini disks. The eggplant pulp may be used for another recipe, such as ratatouille, page 229.)

3. Prepare a large bowl of ice water. Bring a large pot of water to a boil.

4. Salt the boiling water, add the zucchini and eggplant strips, and blanch for 10 seconds. With a slotted spoon, transfer the vegetable strips to the bowl of ice water. When cool, drain, and place the strips side by side on a baking sheet or platter.

5. Prepare the zucchini disks: With a sharp knife, slice the zucchini pulp lengthwise into very thin strips, and with a 1½-inch round pastry cutter, cut the zucchini strips into disks. You will need about 20 zucchini disks for each individual tart. Set aside.

6. Prepare the lamb and vegetable filling: In a medium-size skillet, combine 4 tablespoons of the oil, the diced zucchini, and the diced eggplant over moderate heat. Cook until the vegetables are softened, 4 to 5 minutes. Transfer to a small bowl, stir in the thyme, and set aside.

7. In the same skillet, combine the remaining 2 tablespoons oil and the onions over moderate heat. Cook until the onions are soft and translucent, 3 to 4 minutes. Add to the vegetable mixture, stir to blend, and set aside.

8. In a large bowl, combine the lamb, parsley, curry powder, and cumin. Toss to blend thoroughly. Add the cooled vegetable mixture, and toss to blend thoroughly. Taste for seasoning. Cover and refrigerate.

9. Prepare the tomato and red pepper sauce: In a large skillet, combine the oil and onions over moderate heat. Cook until the onions are soft and translucent, 3 to 4 minutes. Add the reserved tomato pulp, the chopped plum tomatoes, red peppers, garlic, bouquet garni, bay leaf, and seasonings. Stir to blend and cook, uncovered, until the sauce thickens, about 15 minutes. Taste for seasoning. Remove from the heat, remove and discard the bouquet garni and the bay leaf, and stir in the basil. Combine the lamb and vegetable filling with the tomato and red pepper sauce. Set aside.

10. Preheat the oven to 375°F.

11. To assemble the lining: With a brush, generously butter the bottom and sides of the tart pans. Line each pan with alternating strips of eggplant and zucchini, pinwheel-style, placing 1 end of each strip in the middle of the pan and allowing some overhang on the edge. Sprinkle the lining with the thyme leaves, and season with salt and pepper. Spoon the filling into the center and smooth out with the back of the spoon. Fold back the overhanging pieces of eggplant and zucchini to enclose the top edges of the filling.

12. To assemble the top: Beginning on the outermost edge and working clockwise, arrange alternating tomato and zucchini disks on top of the filling, overlapping slightly. To fill the center, arrange alternating tomato and zucchini disks counterclockwise, overlapping slightly. Repeat for the remaining 3 tarts. Sprinkle each with thyme, just a few drops of oil, and season with salt and pepper.

13. Place the tarts on a baking sheet in the center of the oven and bake until golden, about 30 minutes.

14. Remove the baking sheet from the oven. To serve, remove the outer ring of the tart pans, slide each tart off the tart bottom to a warmed dinner plate, and serve immediately.

Yield: 4 SERVINGS

Wine Suggestion: A VIBRANT RED FROM THE CÔTES-DU-RHÔNE, SUCH AS A GIGONDAS

SAUTÉED CHICKEN WITH ONION AND TOMATO SAUCE

Poulet Sauté à la Poitevine

. . . .

Although this recipe is slightly more complicated than your basic sautéed chicken, the extra steps pay off in flavor and taste sophistication. Reducing the wine makes for a more complex, flavorful sauce, and the added step of straining the vegetables results in a more elegant presentation. Even in the dead of winter, the onion and tomato sauce offers a lively, summery accent. This dish is very mild but far from bland—typical of the fare (and the people) from the Poitevin, the area surrounding Poitiers. It's even better if prepared one day in advance, allowing the flavors to mellow.

ONION AND TOMATO SAUCE

3 tablespoons extra-virgin olive oil

2 medium onions, halved and thinly
   sliced

10 plum tomatoes, cored, peeled,
   seeded, and chopped

Sea salt and freshly ground black
   pepper to taste

2 cups dry white wine, preferably a
   Chardonnay

1 free-range chicken (3 to 4 pounds), at
   room temperature, well rinsed,
   patted dry, and cut into 8 serving
   pieces

3 tablespoons extra-virgin olive oil

1 tablespoon unsalted butter

2 carrots, diced

2 onions, finely chopped

Bouquet garni: several parsley stems,
   celery leaves, and sprigs of thyme,
   wrapped in the green part of a leek
   and securely fastened with cotton
   twine

1. Prepare the sauce: In a large skillet, heat the oil over high heat. When hot, add the onions and cook until soft and translucent, about 5 minutes. Add the tomatoes, season, and cook until thick, about 10 minutes more. Taste for seasoning, and set aside.

2. In a medium saucepan, bring the wine to a boil over high heat. Cook until reduced by half, 5 to 7 minutes. Set aside.

3. Season the chicken liberally with salt and pepper. In a large skillet, combine the oil and butter over high heat. When hot, add several pieces of chicken and cook on the skin side until it turns an even, golden brown, about 5 minutes. Turn the pieces and brown them on the other side, 5 minutes more. Do not crowd the pan; brown the chicken in several batches. Carefully regulate the heat to avoid scorching the skin. When all the pieces are browned, transfer them to a platter.

4. Discard the fat in the skillet. Add the carrots, onions, bouquet garni, and wine, and bring to a boil over high heat. Reduce the heat to low and add the chicken, burying the pieces in the vegetables and liquid. Cover, and simmer until the chicken is cooked through, about 20 minutes.

5. Transfer the chicken to a platter. Strain the liquid in the skillet through a fine-mesh sieve. Return the chicken to the skillet, and add the strained liquid and the onion and tomato sauce. Cook over moderate heat until heated through, about 5 minutes. Transfer to a warmed platter and serve on warmed dinner plates.

Yield: 4 TO 6 SERVINGS

Wine Suggestion: A FRESH AND FRUITY RED, SUCH AS THE LOIRE VALLEY'S SAUMUR-CHAMPIGNY

GRANDMOTHER'S ROAST CHICKEN

Poulet Rôti "Grand-Maman"

. . . .

Is there anything better than a golden, moist roast chicken? This roasting method is a brilliant one: The chicken is roasted first on one side, then the other. Once it is nicely browned, it's turned breast side up to finish cooking. When a chicken is roasted in this way—as opposed to leaving it breast side up throughout the cooking time—there is less danger of drying out the delicate white meat. Once roasted, the chicken is turned to rest, tail in the air. This makes for a perfectly moist bird, as the flavorful juices flow down through the breast meat.

VARIATION: You've just come home from the market with a plump roasting chicken and you don't want to wait for the oven to warm up: For a very crisp-skinned chicken, try the cold oven method. Simply butter and season the bird as described, place it in the oven, and turn the oven to 425°F. Follow the recipe, allowing about 15 additional minutes' roasting time. Since some ovens heat up more quickly than others, roasting time may vary.

EQUIPMENT: One ovenproof oval baking dish, just slightly larger than the chicken (about 9 × 13 inches)

1 free-range roasting chicken (about 5 pounds), neck reserved
1½ tablespoons unsalted butter, softened
Sea salt and freshly ground white pepper to taste

2 whole heads plump fresh garlic, unpeeled, cut in half horizontally
1 large sprig fresh rosemary
1 large sprig fresh thyme

1. Preheat the oven to 425°F.

2. Rub the skin of the chicken with the butter and season it generously, inside and out, with salt and pepper. Truss (page 153).

3. Place the chicken on its side in the baking dish. Alongside the chicken, scatter the reserved neck, the halved garlic heads (cut side up), the rosemary and thyme. Place

the baking dish in the center of the oven and roast, uncovered, for 20 minutes. Baste the chicken, turn it to the other side, and roast for another 20 minutes. Baste again, turn the chicken breast side up, and roast for 20 minutes more, for a total of 1 hour roasting time. By this time the skin should be a deep golden color. Reduce the heat to 375°F and baste again. Roast until the juices run clear when you pierce a thigh with a skewer, about 15 minutes more.

STRAINING FOR
ELEGANCE

. . . .

My sister, Judy Jones, tested most of the recipes for this volume. When the book was about completed, she made a confession: "Before I began testing these recipes, I didn't even own a strainer. Whenever a recipe called for a sauce to be strained, I just skipped the step. I figured it wasn't worth the bother." Now she's a convert, and I hope you will be too. Straining makes for finer, more elegant, and smoother sauces, an extra step that tranforms an amateur's effort into a professional's. Some sauces need only to be strained through a fine-mesh sieve. Others, particularly shellfish liquors, should be strained through a sieve lined with moistened cheesecloth to ensure that any sandy particles are left behind.

4. Remove the dish from the oven and season the chicken generously with salt and pepper. Transfer the chicken to a platter, and place it at an angle against the edge of an overturned plate, with its head down and tail in the air. (This heightens the flavor by allowing the juices to flow down through the breast meat.) Cover the chicken loosely with foil. Turn off the oven and place the chicken in the oven, with the door ajar. Let it rest for at least 10 minutes or up to 30 minutes. The chicken will continue to cook as it rests.

5. Meanwhile, prepare the sauce: Place the baking dish over moderate heat, scraping up any bits that cling to the bottom. Cook for 2 to 3 minutes, scraping and stirring until the liquid is almost caramelized. Do not let it burn. Spoon off and discard any excess fat. Add several tablespoons cold water to deglaze (hot water would cloud the sauce), and bring to a boil. Reduce the heat to low and simmer until thickened, about 5 minutes.

6. While the sauce is cooking, carve the chicken and arrange it on a warmed platter.

7. Strain the sauce through a fine-mesh sieve, and pour into a sauceboat. Serve immediately with the chicken and the halved heads of garlic.

Yield: 4 TO 6 SERVINGS

Wine Suggestion: A SILKY, FRAGRANT RED, SUCH AS A VOLNAY, FROM BURGUNDY

CHARCOAL-BROILED HALVED CHICKEN WITH HOT MUSTARD

Poulet Grillé en Crapaudine

. . . .

This is one of the quickest methods of cooking a whole chicken, and one of the most flavorful. It's faster than roasting, and as long as you are careful not to overcook it, or to pierce the skin while cooking, you'll have moist, juicy poultry. Note that broiling and grilling require special attention because the food is exposed to very intense and drying heat. The surface is seared quickly, keeping the interior meat very moist, with concentrated juices. Poultry takes particularly well to this kind of cooking, making for crispy brown skin and juicy meat, with the white and dark portions evenly cooked. *En craupadine,* by the way, is the French name given to any bird that is split in half and flattened to look like a toad, or *crapaud.* I like to serve this with golden and crispy sautéed potatoes (page 211).

1 free-range roasting chicken (about 3 pounds)	Sea salt and freshly ground black pepper to taste
⅓ cup freshly squeezed lemon juice	2 tablespoons imported Dijon mustard
3 tablespoons extra-virgin olive oil	

1. Prepare the chicken: Place the chicken, breast side down, on a flat surface. With a pair of poultry shears, split the bird lengthwise along the backbone. Open it flat, and press down with the heel of your hand to flatten completely. With a sharp knife, make slits in the skin near the tail, and tuck the wing tips in to secure them. The bird should be as flat as possible, to ensure even cooking.

2. Place the chicken in a deep dish, and add the lemon juice and oil. Cover, and marinate at room temperature for at least 2 hours.

3. Preheat the broiler for about 15 minutes. (Or prepare a wood or charcoal fire. The fire is ready when the coals glow red and are covered with ash.)

4. Season the chicken generously with salt and pepper. With the skin side toward the heat, place the chicken beneath the broiler or on the grill, about 5 inches from the heat so that the poultry cooks evenly without burning. Cook until the skin is evenly browned, basting occasionally, about 15 minutes. Using tongs so you do not pierce the meat, turn and cook the other side, basting occasionally, about 15 minutes more. To test for doneness, pierce the thigh with a skewer. The chicken is done when the juices run clear.

5. Remove the chicken from the heat and coat the skin side with the mustard. Season again with salt and pepper. Return it to the heat to brown, 1 to 2 minutes more.

6. To serve, quarter the chicken and slice the breast meat, arranging it on a serving platter.

Yield: 4 TO 6 SERVINGS

Wine Suggestion: A YOUNG AND FRUITY RED, SUCH AS A RICH BEAUJOLAIS CRU MORGON

NOTE: If you broil the chicken, you can prepare a sauce with the drippings: Place the broiler pan over moderate heat, scraping up any bits that cling to the bottom. Cook for several minutes, continuing to scrape and stir until the liquid is almost caramelized but not burned. Spoon off any excess fat, and deglaze with several tablespoons of cold water (hot water would cloud the sauce). Bring to a boil. Reduce the heat and simmer until thickened, about 5 minutes. Strain the sauce through a fine-mesh sieve and transfer to a sauceboat. Serve immediately with the chicken.

ENDLESS VARIATIONS

While this mustard-coated version of broiled or grilled chicken is a classic, the variations are unlimited: Marinate the poultry with plenty of lemon juice, olive oil, and freshly ground black pepper; or with a blend of olive oil, garlic, lemon juice, and fresh herbs. For a bit of spice, mix cayenne pepper in with the mustard before coating. Or rather than coating with mustard after broiling, combine herbs, grated Parmesan, and butter, and coat the chicken for a final warm-up.

BEEF TENDERLOIN ROASTED IN AN HERB-INFUSED SALT CRUST

Rôti de Filet de Boeuf en Croûte de Sel aux Herbes

. . . .

Beef tenderloin—known in France as *filet de boeuf*—is one of the finest, juciest, and leanest cuts of meat. And this is a marvelous way to cook it, for the *filet* is seared at high heat to seal in the juices, then roasted at moderate temperature to ensure meat that is rare and juicy, and perfectly and evenly pink. As the roasted beef rests in the salt crust it continues to cook, and the herbs and salt are drawn into the meat. Since beef tenderloin is naturally tender, it does not need a long cooking time. Tenderloin should always be served rare or medium-rare—never well done, which would toughen the meat, undoing the very advantage of the cut. When roasted in this manner, the beef cooks evenly, slices evenly and easily, and shrinks less, and there's no waste. It's a great dish for entertaining, for all the work is done ahead of time.

In general I advise using unrefined sea salt for cooking, preferably *sel de Guérande* from Brittany. But here the salt is simply used as a cooking vessel and won't be consumed, so refined sea salt or kosher salt, both of which are far less expensive, is suggested.

SALT CRUST
2 cups kosher salt
4 tablespoons fresh thyme leaves
1 tablespoon minced fresh rosemary
   leaves
2 large egg whites
⅔ cup water
2 to 3 cups all-purpose flour

1 boneless beef tenderloin (about 2
   pounds, 4 inches wide, 5 inches
   thick), at room temperature
1 tablespoon unsalted butter
1 tablespoon extra-virgin olive oil
1 large egg yolk
1 teaspoon fresh thyme leaves
2 tablespoons coarse sea salt
Freshly ground black pepper to taste

1. At least 3½ hours before serving, prepare the salt crust: In the bowl of a heavy-duty electric mixer fitted with a paddle, combine the salt and herbs and mix to blend. Add the egg whites and ⅔ cup water, and mix until thoroughly blended. Add 2 cups of the flour, a little at a time, and knead until the mixture forms a firm, homogeneous dough, 2 to 3 minutes. (You may not need all of the flour.) The dough should be firm, not too moist or sticky, or the beef will steam, not roast. If necessary, knead in additional flour or water for a firm dough. Cover with plastic wrap and let rest at room temperature for a minimum of 2 hours, or up to 24 hours. (This resting period will make the dough less sticky and easier to roll out.)

2. Preheat the oven to 375°F.

3. Prepare the beef: Pat the meat dry with paper towels. (Do not salt the meat at this point, or flavorful juices will be drawn from the meat and it will not brown evenly.) In a large skillet, combine the butter and oil over moderately high heat. When hot, add the beef and sear well on all sides, 2 to 3 minutes per side. Place a salad plate upside down on a large platter. Transfer the seared beef to rest on the salad plate, placing it at an angle. This will allow air to circulate evenly around the beef as it continues to cook while resting, making for meat that is evenly cooked and tender. Let rest for 5 minutes.

4. Meanwhile, on a lightly floured surface, roll the dough out to form a 10 × 15-inch rectangle, or one large enough to easily enclose the beef without stretching the dough.

5. In a small bowl, combine the egg yolk and ½ teaspoon water to make a glaze. Set aside.

TESTING FOR DONENESS

. . . .

There are many ways to test meat for doneness. For beef, insert an instant-reading meat thermometer into the center of the meat, away from the bones, and leave it there for 30 seconds. Remove the thermometer to check the interior temperature of the meat: 140°F for rare, 150°F for medium-rare, 160°F for medium, 170°F for well done. If you do not have a meat thermometer, do as many chefs do: Place a metal skewer into the thickest part of the meat and wait 30 seconds. Remove the skewer and touch it to your bottom lip: If the skewer is cold, the meat is underdone; if the skewer is warm, the meat is rare; if the skewer is hot, the meat is well done.

6. Sprinkle the beef with the thyme. Completely wrap the beef in the salt crust, pressing all the seams together. Be sure that all the seams are well sealed. (Wrap the beef just before roasting. If you wrap it in advance, the meat and the salt crust will turn soggy.) Transfer the wrapped beef to a baking sheet. With a brush, coat the entire surface of the crust with the glaze. Sprinkle the crust with the sea salt.

THE WAITING TIME

All meat—particularly this beef tenderloin roasted in a salt crust—should rest once it has been removed from the oven. The resting time allows the juices to be reabsorbed into the meat, making the meat tender and easier to cut. (If you slice it right away, all the flavorful juices will flow out, leaving tougher, less flavorful meat.) Cut across the grain in thick, even slices, so that the pieces are easy to chew. The more tender the meat, the more thickly it may be sliced.

7. Place the baking sheet in the center of the oven and roast for 15 minutes per pound for rare meat (or until the interior registers 125°F when measured with a meat thermometer). For medium rare, roast an additional 3 to 4 minutes per pound. The crust should be a light, golden brown. Let the beef rest in the crust on the baking sheet at room temperature for 1 hour before serving. (The beef will remain warm.)

8. To serve, slice off the crust at one end, remove the beef, and discard the crust. Season the beef with pepper. Cut on the diagonal into thick slices and arrange on a warmed serving platter. Serve immediately.

Yield: 6 TO 8 SERVINGS

Wine Suggestion: A FIRM AND ELEGANT RED BURGUNDY, SUCH AS A POMMARD

SIMPLY OUT OF THE ORDINARY

. . . .

Shrimp sautéed in butter and veal stew with spring vegetables may sound like somewhat ordinary fare. But with that Robuchon touch they enter the realm of the extraordinary. For dessert, plan a fresh plum tart flavored with almond cream. The wine lineup might read like this: A Rhône Valley Condrieu to start, a light red Burgundy (such as a Mercurey) with the veal, then a slightly sweet white wine with the tart, such as a Monbazillac from France's southwest.

. . . .

FRESH SHRIMP SAUTÉED IN BUTTER
CREVETTES SAUTÉE AU BEURRE

OLD-FASHIONED VEAL STEW WITH SPRING VEGETABLES
BLANQUETTE DE VEAU AUX LÉGUMES PRINTANIERS

FRESH PLUM TART WITH FRAGRANT ALMOND CREAM
TARTE AUX PRUNES, CRÈME D'AMANDES

VEGETABLES, SIDE DISHES, AND PASTA

....

Legumes, Garnitures, et Pâtes

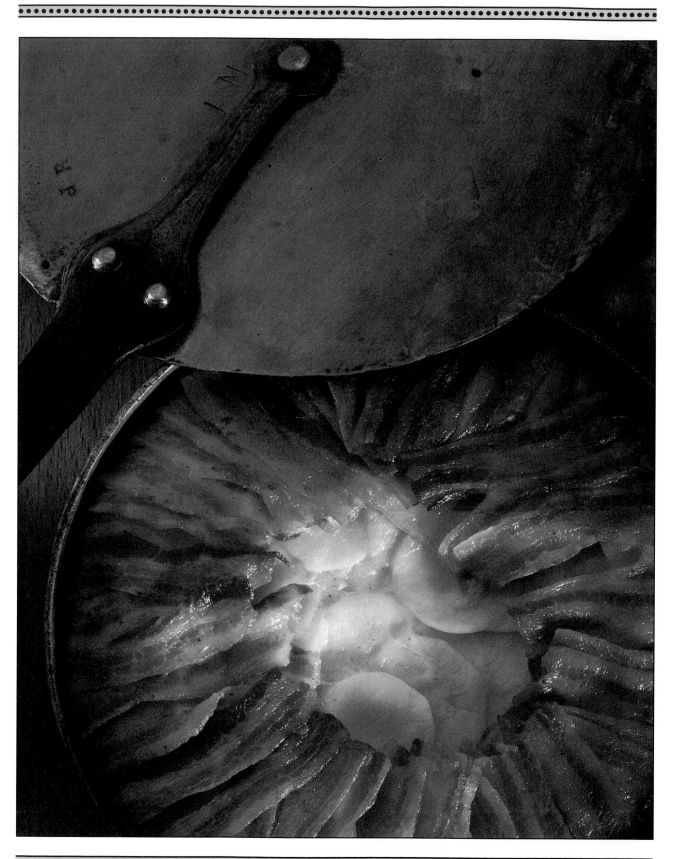

CHEESE AND BACON POTATO CAKE

Pommes des Vendangeurs

. . . .

This is a rich, delicious potato dish that cries out for a green salad and a glass of tannic red wine. Since the potatoes are baked without cream, milk, or eggs, you end up with a very pure potato flavor, enriched by the bacon and a touch of cheese.

EQUIPMENT: One ovenproof 9-inch round baking pan, preferably nonstick

1 tablespoon clarified butter (page 326)
6 ounces slab bacon, rind removed, fat trimmed, and thinly sliced
2½ pounds baking potatoes, such as Idaho Russets

1¼ cups freshly grated imported Gruyère cheese
Freshly ground black pepper to taste

1. Preheat the oven to 425°F.

2. Butter the bottom and sides of the pan. Arrange the bacon slices, spiral fashion, on the bottom and sides of the pan. Allow the bacon to drape over the edge. Set aside.

3. Peel the potatoes, rinse under cold running water, and pat dry. Slice into thin rounds, rinse again, and dry thoroughly in a thick towel.

4. Arrange one third of the potato slices on top of the bacon, and sprinkle with one third of the cheese. Repeat, creating two additional layers of potatoes and cheese. Fold the overhanging bacon onto the potatoes.

5. Bake, uncovered, until the potatoes offer no resistance when pierced with a knife, 40 to 50 minutes.

6. Remove the pan from the oven and transfer it to a rack. Let it rest, still covered, for 15 minutes, so that the potatoes will unmold easily. Unmold the potatoes onto a warmed serving platter, season generously with freshly ground black pepper, and serve, cutting into wedges.

Yield: 6 TO 8 SERVINGS

POTATO PURÉE

Purée de Pommes de Terre

. . . .

Ever homey, ever elegant, ever irresistible, this is the dish that helped make chef Robuchon's reputation. Clever man that he is, he realized early on that if you give people potatoes, potatoes, and more potatoes, they'll be eternally grateful, forever fulfilled. These are, of course, no ordinary mashed potatoes, but a purée that is softened with an avalanche of butter and mellowed with bubbly boiling milk. The quantity of butter and milk needed for a successfully silken and satiny purée will vary according to the potatoes and the season. Early-season potatoes will be firmer, demanding more butter and milk for a perfectly soft, almost fluffy purée.

The keys here are potatoes of uniform size (so they are uniformly cooked), and a strong arm for drying the potatoes with a flat wooden spatula. Be sure that the butter is well chilled, for it will help make a finer, smoother purée. Also follow the proportions of salt to water when cooking the potatoes: You won't be able to make up for it with additional salt at the end. I agree, this is a lot of work for a simple potato purée. But once you taste the results, you'll agree that your labor has been pleasantly rewarded. For exceptionally rich potatoes, the quantity of butter may be doubled.

EQUIPMENT: A food mill; a flat fine-mesh (drum) sieve

2 pounds baking potatoes, such as Idaho Russets
¾ to 1¼ cups whole milk

About 16 tablespoons (1 cup) unsalted butter, chilled, cut into pieces
Sea salt to taste

1. Scrub the potatoes, but do not peel them. Place the potatoes in a large pot, add salted water (1 tablespoon salt per quart of water) to cover by at least 1 inch. Simmer, uncovered, over moderate heat until a knife inserted into a potato comes away easily, 20 to 30 minutes. Drain the potatoes as soon as they are cooked. (If they are allowed to cool in the water, the potatoes will end up tasting reheated.)

2. Meanwhile, in a large saucepan, bring the milk just to a boil over high heat. Set aside.

3. As soon as the potatoes are cool enough to handle, peel them. Pass the potatoes

through the finest grid of a food mill into a large heavy-bottomed saucepan set over low heat. With a wooden spatula, stir the potatoes vigorously to dry them, 4 to 5 minutes. Now begin adding about 12 tablespoons of the butter, little by little, stirring vigorously until each batch of butter is thoroughly incorporated; the mixture should be fluffy and light. Then slowly add about three fourths of the hot milk in a thin stream, stirring vigorously until the milk is thoroughly incorpoated.

4. Pass the mixture though a flat fine-mesh (drum) sieve (see box, below) into another heavy-bottomed saucepan. Stir vigorously, and if the purée seems a bit heavy and stiff, add additional butter and milk, stirring all the while. Taste for seasoning. (The purée may be made up to 1 hour in advance. Place in the top of a double boiler, uncovered, over simmering water. Stir occasionally to keep smooth.)

Yield: 6 TO 8 SERVINGS

FOR PERFECT PURÉES

. . . .

One of the more miraculous and effective of kitchen tools is the drum sieve or *tamis,* a round, wooden-edged fine-mesh sieve shaped like a drum or embroidery hoop. Its fine, flat metal screen is easier to work with than a round-bottomed sieve: It allows you to press or force solids such as mashed potatoes through the screen with a pastry scraper. The drum sieve is also practical for adding a touch of refinement to pastry creams or when preparing vanilla butter.

THE "UPPER CRUST" POTATO GRATIN

Le Gratin des Gratins

. . . .

I am sure that if you polled a hundred Frenchmen, each one would have a strong opinion on the "best" potato gratin. Well, for me the "best" is the last great gratin I sampled. This recipe brings up the ever-present question of "to wash or not to wash." There are those who believe that all potatoes should be rinsed of starch, which on its own does not have a pleasing flavor. Others enjoy the earthiness the starch imparts. Since you're the cook, you can have it your way. Or try the recipe both ways and see which is closer to your own taste.

EQUIPMENT: One oval baking dish (about 9 × 13 inches)

3 pounds baking potatoes, such as
    Idaho Russets
1 quart whole milk
Bouquet garni: several parsley stems,
    celery leaves, and sprigs of thyme,
    wrapped in the green part of a leek
    and securely fastened with cotton
    twine
Freshly grated nutmeg to taste

Sea salt to taste
2 tablespoons unsalted butter
1 cup heavy cream
2 cups freshly grated imported Gruyère
    cheese
Freshly ground white pepper to taste
1 plump fresh garlic clove, halved
    lengthwise

1. Preheat the oven to 375°F.

2. Peel and thinly slice the potatoes. If desired, rinse the potatoes to rid them of starch. Dry thoroughly in a thick towel.

3. In a large saucepan, combine the potatoes, milk, bouquet garni, nutmeg, salt, and 1 tablespoon of the butter, and bring to a boil over moderately high heat. Stir occasionally to prevent the potatoes from sticking to the bottom of the pan. Reduce the heat to moderate and cook, stirring occasionally, until the potatoes are tender but not falling apart, about 10 minutes.

4. Prepare the topping: In a medium-size bowl, combine ½ cup of the cream and 1 cup of the cheese, and stir to blend. Set aside.

5. Rub the bottom of the baking dish with the garlic and the remaining 1 tablespoon butter. With a slotted spoon, transfer half the potatoes to the baking dish. Sprinkle with additional nutmeg, pepper, the remaining ½ cup cream, and the remaining 1 cup cheese. Cover with the remaining potatoes and sprinkle again with nutmeg and pepper. Cover with the reserved topping. Discard the milk and the bouquet garni.

6. Place the baking dish in the center of the oven and bake until the potatoes are crisp and golden on top, about 1 hour. Serve immediately.

Yield: 6 TO 8 SERVINGS

A TOUCH OF GARLIC

. . . .

To some cooks, the idea of rubbing a baking dish with a halved clove of garlic, then discarding the garlic, seems like a waste of time. The trick is to rub the bottom of the dish vigorously and thoroughly, so that the clove of garlic all but falls apart and seems to disappear, totally impregnating the baking dish with its essence. As the gratin bakes, the garlic gently flavors the potatoes and milk, adding that essential touch of extra seasoning.

GOLDEN HAM AND CHIVE POTATO CAKE

Gâteau de Pommes de Terre Duchesse

. . . .

The colors of this hearty potato cake—golden and green, laced with a touch of mahogany-hued ham—remind me of springtime. This is a great one-dish meal that simply needs a tossed green salad and a sip of dry white wine to complete the picture. Be sure to taste the ham before preparing the potato cake: If it is exceptionally salty, reduce the amount of salt you add to other ingredients.

EQUIPMENT: One 9-inch round nonstick cake pan

Unsalted butter, softened (for the pan)
2 pounds boiling potatoes, such as
    round whites from Maine or Long
    Island
1 heaping tablespoon coarse sea salt
4 tablespoons unsalted butter, softened
1 medium onion, finely chopped
Sea salt and freshly ground black
    pepper to taste

Freshly grated nutmeg to taste
4 large egg yolks
4 ounces unsmoked salt-cured ham,
    such as prosciutto, coarsely chopped
¼ cup fresh chives, snipped with a
    scissors

1. Preheat the oven to 300°F. Coat the bottom and sides of the cake pan with butter. Set aside.

2. Peel and rinse the potatoes. Place in a saucepan, and cover generously with cold water. Add the salt and cook over moderate heat—do not boil—until a skewer inserted in a potato comes away easily, about 20 minutes.

3. Meanwhile, in a medium skillet, combine 1 tablespoon of the butter and the onions over moderate heat. Season lightly, and cook until the onions are soft and translucent, 3 to 4 minutes. Set aside.

4. As soon as the potatoes are cooked, drain them well. Pass them through the fine

grid of a food mill into a large mixing bowl. (If the potatoes are large, you may want to halve or quarter them before passing through the mill.) With a wooden spoon, stir in the nutmeg, the remaining 3 tablespoons butter, and the egg yolks, one at a time. Continue stirring vigorously until the butter and egg yolks are thoroughly incorporated. The mixture will be thick and slippery.

5. Fold the onions, ham, and chives into the potato mixture. Transfer the mixture to the cake pan, and smooth it out with the back of a spoon. Place it in the center of the oven and bake, uncovered, until the potato cake is firm and the top is browned, 45 to 50 minutes.

6. Remove the potato cake from the oven and transfer it, browned-side up (for the golden top side is the prettier), to a large platter. Slice into wedges and serve warm or at room temperature.

Yield: 6 TO 8 SERVINGS

VARIATION: For very pretty individual potato cakes, bake these in nonstick muffin tins. Alternatively, bake the cake in a single 10½-inch round porcelain baking dish.

SAUTÉ ADVICE

As cooks, we all seem to have an instinctive desire to shuffle pans around on the stove—maybe it makes us feel that we're being efficient. However, it's often better to leave well enough alone when sautéing. Potatoes, for example, should completely color on one side before they are turned. In this way they will cook evenly and thoroughly.

CRISPY SAUTÉED POTATOES

Pommes de Terre Sautées à Cru

. . . .

I first sampled these potatoes at a lunch in the Poitou region, at the home of Joël Robuchon's cousin, who raises lambs and goats on a lovely little farm not far from Poitiers. We lunched on homemade quiche, salad from the garden, a rustic *civet* (game stew), and these golden potatoes. At first I thought they'd been deep fried, they tasted so rich and crunchy. But this method offers terrific flavor and considerably fewer calories. In this recipe, the potatoes should be peeled, rinsed, quartered, then rinsed again, so that the starch is eliminated; the final rinsing will prevent the potatoes from sticking to the pan. The ideal fat for cooking potatoes in this manner is goose or duck fat. Lacking that, use clarified butter. And be sure not to season the potatoes until they are thoroughly browned, or they will become soggy. Although the potatoes are cooked in only 1 tablespoon of fat, the resulting flavor is deliciously rich. Select small potatoes of equal size, so that they will cook quickly and evenly.

1 pound small round red-skinned potatoes

1 tablespoon goose fat (or clarified butter, page 326)

1 plump fresh garlic clove, minced

Sea salt to taste

1. Peel, rinse, and quarter the potatoes. Rinse again in several changes of cold water, and dry thoroughly with a thick towel. Set aside.

2. In a large skillet, heat the fat over moderately high heat. When hot, add the potatoes and brown thoroughly on one side before tossing to brown another side. Be patient and resist the urge to intervene. Cook until the potatoes are thoroughly browned and offer no resistance when pierced with a fork, about 15 minutes in all. Add the garlic and cook for 1 minute more, but do not allow it to burn. Transfer the potatoes to a serving bowl, season with salt, and serve immediately.

Yield: 4 SERVINGS

POTATOES "CHANTEDUC"

Pommes "Chanteduc"

. . . .

One weekend in the country, Chef Robuchon set about preparing this dish in my kitchen. I worked as sous-chef (well, to be more exact, as dishwasher) as he went about preparing several dishes for the evening meal. This potato gratin is typically Robuchonesque in its attention to details. The few extra moments of effort pay off in depth and complexity of flavor.

EQUIPMENT: One oval baking dish (about 9 × 13 inches); 1½-inch round pastry cutter (optional)

ONION AND TOMATO SAUCE

4 tablespoons extra-virgin olive oil

2 medium onions, halved and thinly sliced

Sea salt and freshly ground white pepper to taste

3 plump fresh garlic cloves, minced

5 medium vine-ripened tomatoes, cored, peeled, seeded, and chopped

1 tablespoon sugar

3 pounds baking potatoes, such as Idaho Russets

1 plump fresh garlic clove, halved

2 tablespoons unsalted butter, melted

1½ cups chicken stock (page 334)

½ cup fresh flat-leaf parsley leaves, snipped with a scissors

2 teaspoons fresh thyme

1. Preheat the oven to 425°F.

2. Prepare the sauce: In a large skillet, heat 2 tablespoons of the oil over high heat. When hot, reduce the heat to moderate and add the onions. Cook until soft and translucent, about 5 minutes. Season and set aside.

3. In another large skillet, heat the remaining 2 tablespoons oil over moderately high heat. When hot, add the garlic and cook until just tender and slightly brown, 2 to 3 minutes. Add the tomatoes and cook until the mixture thickens, about 10 minutes. Add the sugar, and season.

4. Combine the onions and tomatoes, and continue cooking to thicken, about 10 minutes more. Taste for seasoning.

5. Meanwhile, prepare the potatoes: Peel, wash, and cut the potatoes into very thin slices. Wash again and dry thoroughly. In a small bowl, set aside about one quarter of the potatoes, which will be used as the topping. (For a particularly elegant presentation, trim the reserved potatoes into perfectly even rounds with a 1½-inch pastry cutter.)

6. Rub the bottom of the baking dish with the garlic and 1 tablespoon of the butter.

7. In a large bowl, combine the remaining potatoes with the sauce, and with your hands, toss to blend. Transfer the mixture to the baking dish, smoothing it out with the back of the spoon. Add enough chicken stock to cover.

8. In a medium-size bowl, combine the reserved topping potatoes, the remaining 1 tablespoon butter, and the parsley. Toss to coat evenly. Beginning at one end of the dish, place the buttered potatoes, one by one, in slightly overlapping rows on top of the tomato-coated potatoes, until the entire dish is covered with an even potato layer. Sprinkle with the thyme.

ON SLICING ONIONS

. . . .

To obtain thin half-moon slices that separate easily, first peel the onion and trim both ends. Cut the onion in half lengthwise. Place the flat side against a cutting board, and cut into paper-thin half-round slices.

POTATOES AND ACID

. . . .

Acid prevents potatoes from cooking fully, so it's best not to prepare a gratin with white wine, which is acidic. And though tomatoes may be added for color and flavor, add a touch of sugar at the same time to reduce the acidity.

9. Place the dish in the center of the oven and bake until the potatoes are soft, most of the liquid has been absorbed, and the top is golden, about 1½ hours. Serve immediately.

Yield: 6 TO 8 SERVINGS

CONFIT OF FRESH CHESTNUTS, WALNUTS, FENNEL, AND ONIONS

Confit de Châtaignes, Noix, Fenouil, et Oignons

With its warming winter flavors and deep aromas, this savory side dish, or *garniture*, is so delicious and satisfying that I could see serving it as a main course, with a salad to follow. But this tender combination of chestnuts, walnuts, fennel, and baby onions is quite rich, so a little goes a long way. When it's made with really fresh ingredients, you'll swear that the vegetables are bathed in fresh walnut oil. This is an excellent accompaniment to any kind of roast game or fowl. Toss a few spoonfuls of the pan juices into the *confit* just before serving.

1 pound unpeeled fresh chestnuts, or about 1½ cups peeled fresh chestnuts

1 quart peanut oil, for deep frying

Sea salt to taste

20 fresh baby onions (or substitute pearl onions), peeled

1 tablespoon sugar

5 tablespoons unsalted butter

1 cup chicken stock (page 334)

Bouquet garni: several parsley stems, celery leaves, and sprigs of thyme, wrapped in the green part of a leek and securely fastened with cotton twine

1 fennel bulb, cut into fine julienne, fronds reserved

4 shallots, each bulb cut lengthwise into eighths

½ cup freshly cracked walnut halves

Several tablespoons poultry cooking juices (optional)

Freshly ground white pepper to taste

1. Peel the chestnuts: With a small sharp knife, make a long cut—actually a tear—along both rounded sides of the chestnut, cutting through the tough outer shell and into the brown skin underneath. This will make the chestnut easier to peel. Pour the oil into a heavy 2-quart saucepan or a deep-fat fryer. Heat the oil to 320°F. Fry the chestnuts in batches of five or six for about 3 minutes, or until the shells curl away from the meat. Drain thoroughly. When they are cool, peel the chestnuts, removing both the tough outer

shell and thin brown inner skin. (The chestnuts may be prepared 1 day in advance. Cover securely and refrigerate. Bring to room temperature before cooking.)

2. Cook the onions: Bring a large pot of water to a boil. Salt the water and add the onions. Cook for 2 minutes to blanch. Drain and set aside. In a large saucepan with a tight-fitting lid, combine the onions, sugar, and 1 tablespoon of the butter over low heat. Season, and cover. Cook until the onions are moist and tender, about 20 minutes. Watch carefully, and shake the pan occasionally to prevent the onions from browning. Drain and set aside.

3. Preheat the oven to 400°F.

4. In a large ovenproof skillet, melt the remaining 4 tablespoons butter over moderately high heat. When hot, add the chestnuts and cook, shaking the pan, until the chestnuts are evenly golden (but not deep brown) and are fork-tender, about 15 minutes. Watch carefully so the chestnuts do not burn. Add the chicken stock and the bouquet garni, and bring to a boil over high heat.

5. Transfer the skillet with the chestnuts to the oven, and braise, uncovered, until almost all the liquid has been absorbed, 15 to 20 minutes. Do not allow the chestnuts to dry out. If necessary, spoon the liquid over the chestnuts so they remain moist.

6. Meanwhile, return the onions to low heat. Stir in the fennel julienne and shallots, and cook until softened, about 5 to 10 minutes. Add the walnuts and cook just until heated through, 1 to 2 minutes more. Remove the bouquet garni.

7. When the chestnuts have absorbed most of the liquid, add the onion mixture. Add poultry juices if available, stir, and taste for seasoning. Transfer to a large warmed serving bowl. Garnish with fennel fronds, and serve.

Yield: 8 TO 10 SIDE-DISH SERVINGS

LAYERS OF FLAVORS

Here is an example of Chef Robuchon's ability to layer flavor upon flavor, reinforcing a dish with both a cooked and a raw version of the ingredient. The fresh fennel bulb is cooked with the chestnuts, and then the fragrant fennel fronds are sprinkled on top, as an encore of flavor. If you cannot find fennel bulbs with lots of fronds still intact, use the little "sprouts" of fronds you'll find inside the bulb when you cut it open.

TAGLIATELLE WITH MUSHROOMS AND BELL PEPPERS

Pâtes Fraîches aux Champignons et aux Poivrons

. . . .

A marvelously full-flavored pasta dish, this is one that everyone seems to love. The dash of vinegar and the touch of butter at the end make for a delicious and different flavor. For dinner, I like to serve it as a first course, followed by a roast chicken or leg of lamb. For lunch it can stand all on its own.

4 large domestic mushrooms, rinsed
    and patted dry
2 tablespoons freshly squeezed lemon
    juice
2 tablespoons extra-virgin olive oil
1 medium onion, minced into tiny
    cubes
Sea salt and freshly ground white
    pepper to taste
1 large red bell pepper, minced into
    tiny cubes
1 large green bell pepper, minced into
    tiny cubes

2 tablespoons best-quality sherry wine
    vinegar

PASTA
¼ cup table salt, or ½ cup coarse sea
    salt
¼ cup olive oil
12 ounces fresh tagliatelle or fettuccine

3 tablespoons unsalted butter, cut into
    pieces

1. Mince the mushrooms into tiny cubes and place in a small bowl. Add the lemon juice and toss to coat evenly (to prevent discoloring). Set aside.

2. In a large skillet, heat the oil over moderate heat. When hot, add the onions and season to taste. Cook until softened, about 2 minutes. Add the red and green peppers, and continue cooking for another 5 minutes. Add the mushrooms and juice and continue cooking for another 3 minutes. Taste for seasoning. Do not overcook the vegetables; the mixture should neither brown nor stick to the pan.

ON SALT AND WATER

. . . .

Unsalted water will come to a boil faster than salted water, so when cooking pasta or vegetables in boiling water, it is most practical to salt just before adding the ingredients. Make this a habit and you'll avoid the common problem of trying to remember whether or not you salted at the beginning. In general, 2 tablespoons of table salt, or 4 tablespoons of coarse salt, for each 3 quarts of water make for perfectly salted pasta and blanched vegetables.

DRAINING PASTA

. . . .

When draining pasta, it is always better to transfer the pasta from the pot into a colander with tongs or a slotted spoon. In this way you avoid pouring the starch—which doesn't have a particularly pleasant flavor—back over the pasta.

3. Remove from the heat and add the vinegar. Stir to blend, and set aside.

4. Meanwhile, prepare the pasta: In a large pot, bring 6 quarts water to a boil over high heat. Add the salt and the oil. Add the pasta, and cook just until tender. With tongs or a slotted spoon, transfer the pasta to a colander to drain. Toss well to eliminate as much water as possible.

5. To finish: In a large shallow bowl, combine the pasta and the pepper mixture. Add the butter, toss well, and taste for seasoning. Serve immediately.

Yield: 4 SERVINGS

Wine Suggestion: A FRESH AND FRUITY ROSÉ, PREFERABLY A CÔTES DE PROVENCE

WHITE VS. BLACK PEPPER

. . . .

The debate goes on over the taste superiority of black pepper over white. Many people prefer the more aromatic, assertive flavor of black peppercorns (picked unripe, then dried in the sun) to that of white peppercorns (produced from ripe berries that have been washed clean of the outer layer before they are set out to dry in the sun). In most cases, the differences between the two are highly subtle, with white peppercorns coming off as slightly milder. Chef Robuchon uses freshly ground white pepper exclusively, more for appearance than anything, for he does not want black pepper to fleck light-colored dishes. Now, after years of working with freshly ground white pepper, I prefer its subtlety for most dishes, reserving black pepper for seasoning grilled steaks, mussels, or full-flavored smoked foods.

GLAZED SPRING VEGETABLES

Printanière de Légumes Glacés

. . . .

As fragrant and beautiful as it is flavorful, this mélange of all the freshest and crispiest of spring vegetables is the sort of dish that attracts *oohs* and *aahs* even from those who may be nonchalant about vegetables. Serve this with a leg of lamb, roast beef, or a simple roast chicken. If one or the other vegetable is missing from the market, don't worry. And if you can't find baby varieties, trim full-size vegetables down to size. It's the suggestion of variety and color that's important, as well as the cooking method. While this is the assortment served at Jamin, I've sometimes varied the mixture by adding baby corn, tiny crisp zucchini, little leeks, and spring scallions. Cooking times and quantities will vary according to the size of each vegetable. The vegetables may be precooked several hours in advance, then reheated at serving time.

5 ounces baby carrots, scrubbed and greens trimmed to 1 inch from base

About 4 tablespoons sugar

About 8 tablespoons unsalted butter

Sea salt to taste

5 ounces baby turnips, scrubbed and greens trimmed to 1 inch from base

1 celery heart, root end and leaves trimmed, ribs separated

7 ounces fresh baby onions (or substitute pearl onions)

3 ounces young, tender green beans, trimmed

3 ounces shelled fresh peas

3 ounces shelled tender fava beans

3 ounces snow peas, ends trimmed and strings removed

1 pound small green asparagus, tough ends trimmed, tied in a bundle with cotton twine

3 ounces fresh chanterelle mushrooms, trimmed and brushed clean (or substitute domestic mushroom caps, trimmed, brushed clean, and quartered)

1 tablespoon freshly squeezed lemon juice (for domestic mushrooms)

Freshly ground white pepper to taste

1. Prepare the root vegetables: In a small saucepan with a tight-fitting lid, combine the carrots, 1 tablespoon of the sugar, and 1 tablespoon of the butter over moderate

heat. Season, add cold water to just cover, and cover. Cook until the carrots are tender and much of the water has evaporated, 15 to 20 minutes. Drain and set aside.

2. Repeat for all the remaining root vegetables (turnips, celery, onions), cooking each without the addition of water, but in the same manner, with 1 tablespoon of the butter and 1 tablespoon of the sugar. Drain and set aside.

3. Prepare the green vegetables: Prepare a large bowl of ice water. Bring a large pot of water to a boil, adding 1 tablespoon salt for each quart of water. Add the green beans. Cook until crisp-tender, about 4 minutes. Remove the beans with a slotted spoon and immediately plunge them into the ice water, so they cool down as quickly as possible. Drain the beans and set aside. Repeat for the peas, fava beans, and snow peas (baby corn and zucchini as well), changing the cooking water for each vegetable.

5. Prepare the asparagus: Bring a small deep saucepan of water to a boil. Add salt and the asparagus, standing up, and cook just until the lower portions are crisp-tender, about 4 minutes. Add boiling water to cover the tips, and continue cooking for 3 to 5 minutes. Remove with a slotted spoon and place in the ice water. Drain, and set aside, removing the twine.

6. Prepare the mushrooms: In a medium skillet, combine the mushrooms and 1 tablespoon of the butter over moderate heat. (If you are using domestic mushrooms, add the lemon juice along with the butter.) Season, and cook until tender, about 5 minutes.

7. At serving time, prepare a large pot of boiling water. Add salt, place the green beans, peas, fava beans, and snow peas in a strainer, and immerse in the water for 1 minute to warm. Drain thoroughly.

8. In a large skillet, combine all the vegetables with the remaining 3 tablespoons butter over moderately low heat. Cook just to warm through, stirring gently, about 2 minutes. Taste for seasoning. Transfer to a warmed serving bowl and serve immediately.

Yield: 6 SERVINGS

Madame Lucienne le Comte, in the village of Pierrelaye, northwest of Paris, where from September to March her family greenhouses produce asparagus for Joël Robuchon and other French chefs

WHEN SUMMER
TURNS TO FALL

. . . .

Prepare this menu while you can still find great fresh tomatoes in the market, but just as the signs of fall put you in the mood for a soothing potato purée and roasted beef tenderloin. Begin with a chilled Pouilly-Fumé from the Loire Valley. With the beef, uncork one of your best red Burgundies. For dessert, search around in your cellar or at your wine shop for a sweet dessert wine, a Spanish Málaga if possible.

. . . .

SAVORY TOMATO AND BASIL TARTS
TARTES FRIANDES AUX TOMATES, POIVRONS, ET BASILIC

BEEF TENDERLOIN ROASTED IN AN
HERB-INFUSED SALT CRUST
RÔTI DE BOEUF EN CROÛTE DE SEL AUX HERBES

POTATO PURÉE
PURÉE DE POMMES DE TERRE

BITTERSWEET CHOCOLATE TART
TARTE AU CHOCOLAT AMER

FRIED ZUCCHINI

Courgettes Frites

. . . .

A wonderful summertime snack, this dish is ideal for gardeners who run out of ideas for prolific zucchini. These deep-fried slices are beautiful when served in a wicker basket, where they resemble rich, golden nuggets. A tip from Chef Robuchon: Zucchini blossoms may be deep fried in the same manner. But cook them at a lower temperature, for they're delicate.

About 1 pound large fresh zucchini	Sea salt to taste
½ cup superfine flour (such as Wondra)	1½ cups fresh bread crumbs
2 large eggs	2½ quarts peanut oil, for deep frying
2 tablespoons peanut oil	

1. Peel the zucchini and slice diagonally into ¼-inch-thick slices. Set aside.

2. Prepare the coating: Prepare three shallow bowls. Place the flour in the first bowl. In the second, whisk together the eggs and 2 tablespoons oil, and season generously. Place the bread crumbs in the third.

3. Pour the oil into a heavy 3-quart saucepan, or use a deep-fat fryer. Heat the oil to 360°F.

4. Meanwhile, prepare the zucchini: Dip each slice first into the flour, turning to coat evenly, and shake off the excess. Then dip into the egg mixture, turning to coat evenly, and shake off the excess. Finally dip into the bread crumbs, turning to coat evenly, and shake off the excess. Place the coated slices side by side on paper towels. Be sure to prepare all the slices before you begin frying.

FRIED HERB GARNISHES

. . . .

As a garnish—for fish in particular—whole fried leaves of basil, parsley, sage, or celery are beautiful and delicious. Follow the same procedure as for the fried zucchini, but heat the oil only to 285°F.

5. Fry the zucchini in batches (about six slices at a time), until deep golden, 2 to 3 minutes per batch. With a flat mesh skimmer, transfer to paper towels to drain. Sprinkle immediately with salt, and serve warm. (*Note:* A combination of zucchini and zucchini blossoms may be served together. Follow the same procedure for the zucchini blossoms, but cook them in oil heated to 285°F, so that they remain bright and golden.)

Yield: 4 TO 6 SERVINGS

BRAISED ENDIVES

Endives "Meunière"

....

I admit that until I began preparing it this way, I was not much of a fan of cooked endive, even though I love this popular winter vegetable raw in salads. Traditionally endive is cooked with butter, some water, a touch of lemon juice, and a pinch of salt—a method that can result in a very brown and bitter vegetable. Here, the endive cooks first in sweetened well-acidulated water, then is finished off with a touch of butter and sugar, making for a vegetable that's golden, sweet, and almost caramelized. This is delicious as a side vegetable and perfect as a base for roasting duck or pheasant (page 151).

8 Belgian endives
3 tablespoons freshly squeezed lemon
 juice
3 tablespoons sugar

Sea salt and freshly ground white
 pepper to taste
2 tablespoons butter

1. Rinse and dry the endives, and remove any leaves that have darkened. Trim the ends slightly and using a small knife, remove the bitter cone at the base of each head. Bring a large pot of water to a boil. Salt the water, add the lemon juice, 1 tablespoon of the sugar, and the endives, and cook until soft, about 30 minutes. Drain thoroughly and place in a single layer on a platter. Sprinkle with 1 tablespoon sugar, salt, and pepper, and set aside until cool enough to handle. Do not be concerned if the endives brown a bit—they will be browned later in butter. (The recipe may be prepared to this point several hours in advance. Cover until needed.)

2. With your hands, gently but firmly squeeze each endive to extract the bitter liquid.

3. In a large skillet, melt the butter over moderately high heat. When hot, add the endives in a single layer and brown evenly on each side, about 3 minutes per side. Remove and drain well. Transfer the endives to a warmed serving bowl, toss with the remaining 1 tablespoon sugar, and season to taste with salt and pepper. Serve immediately.

Yield: 4 SERVINGS

PROVENÇAL VEGETABLES
Ratatouille

. . . .

Here is a recipe where that extra touch, extra attention to detail, makes all the difference. Straining the juice from tomatoes that have been peeled, cored, and seeded makes for a richer, more flavorful sauce. The thought of cutting the vegetables into little matchsticks may seem like busy work—until you sample the results. The vegetables have more flavor, and though it would be a mistake to think of ratatouille as an "elegant" dish, the smaller pieces make for a more refined ratatouille in the end. Chef Robuchon is opposed to disgorging vegetables, such as eggplant, with salt, a practice that makes for soggy vegetables. The tomato paste and saffron are optional boosters, to add according to taste and to season.

10 medium vine-ripened tomatoes (about 2 pounds)

2 medium onions, finely chopped

1 cup extra-virgin olive oil

Sea salt to taste

1 green bell pepper, peeled and thinly sliced

1 red bell pepper, peeled and thinly sliced

Bouquet garni: several parsley stems, celery leaves, and sprigs of thyme, wrapped in the green part of a leek

and securely fastened with cotton twine

4 garlic cloves, minced

Freshly ground white pepper to taste

1 teaspoon tomato paste (optional)

6 to 7 small zucchini (about 1¼ pounds), scrubbed, trimmed, and cut into matchsticks

2 teaspoons fresh thyme leaves

3 small eggplants (about 1½ pounds), peeled and cut into matchsticks

Pinch of saffron threads (optional)

1. Prepare the tomatoes: Core, peel, and seed the tomatoes. Recuperate as much tomato juice as possible, and strain. (If the strained juice does not measure 1 cup, add enough water to make up the difference.) Finely chop the tomatoes. Set aside.

2. In a large skillet, combine the onions, ¼ cup of the oil, and a pinch of salt. Cook over low heat until soft and translucent, about 5 minutes. Add the peppers and a pinch of salt. Cover and continue cooking for about 5 minutes more. Then add the chopped tomatoes, stir, and continue cooking for another 5 minutes.

3. Stir in the tomato juice, bouquet garni, and garlic, and taste for seasoning. Cover

and simmer gently for about 30 minutes. Do not overcook: The vegetables should be cooked through but not mushy. If the tomatoes lack flavor, add the tomato paste.

4. Meanwhile, in another skillet heat ½ cup of the oil over moderate heat. When hot, add the zucchini and cook until lightly colored, about 5 minutes. (Do not salt the zucchini before cooking or flavorful liquids will be lost.) Transfer to a colander to drain any excess oil. Season with thyme and salt. Set aside.

5. In the same skillet, heat the remaining ¼ cup oil over moderate heat. When hot, add the eggplant and cook until lightly colored, about 5 minutes. Transfer to a colander to drain any excess oil. Add the eggplant and zucchini to the tomato mixture. Taste for seasoning. If desired, add a pinch of saffron. Cover and simmer gently for 30 minutes.

6. Serve warm or at room temperature, as a vegetable side dish. Ratatouille will keep fresh, covered and refrigerated, for several days.

Yield: 8 TO 10 SERVINGS

TOMATO TRUCS

A quick way to peel tomatoes without the bother of bringing a large pot of water to a boil: Core the tomato, then pierce it with a large two-pronged fork and hold it directly over a gas flame. Turn just until the skin begins to crack, about 1 minute. Do not overcook, or the tomato will become mushy. This method is preferable to boiling the tomatoes in water to ease the removal of the peel, a method that makes the tomatoes watery.

A second method: Core the tomato and peel the skin with a vegetable peeler, using a back and forth "sawing" motion.

When halving tomatoes that will be seeded, always halve them horizontally so that you can easily remove all the seeds.

FRICASSEE OF WILD MUSHROOMS
Fricassée de Champignons Sauvages

. . . .

This is a brilliant and uncomplicated method for capturing the maxium flavor from any assortment of wild or domestic mushrooms. Each variety is cooked on its own with a touch of olive oil over high heat, a method that helps the mushrooms maintain their delicate texture. At the last moment they are "finished off" when they're tossed together with a whisper of butter to fix the flavors. Even if you try this recipe with only two or three varieties of wild mushroom (and add one portion of domestic mushrooms to fill in the blanks), you'll be amazed at the depth of flavors.

In all, you will need approximately 1 pound of assorted fresh mushrooms for four servings as a side dish. Should you have any leftover mushrooms, toss them in a vinaigrette with some finely chopped tarragon, or tuck them inside an omelet. Recommended varieties include small cèpe or boletus, horn-of-plenty mushrooms, chanterelles, and all members of the russula group. Cultivated mushrooms, such as shiitake or golden oak, oyster mushrooms, and little brown cremini, are also excellent in this fall mixture.

Serve this as a side dish to any roast meat or poultry.

1 pound mixed wild and domestic
   mushrooms
4 tablespoons extra-virgin olive oil
Sea salt to taste
2 tablespoons unsalted butter
1 shallot, finely minced

1 tablespoon flat-leaf parsley leaves,
   snipped with a scissors
1 tablespoon fresh chives, snipped with
   a scissors
1 tablespoon fresh chervil leaves,
   snipped with a scissors (optional)

1. Prepare the mushrooms: Trim off the stems and clean all the mushrooms; simply brush them if they are very clean. If they must be washed, rinse very quickly under cold running water and dry quickly with paper towels or, for firm varieties, in a salad spinner. If the mushrooms are small, leave them whole. If large, quarter lengthwise.

2. Cook each variety separately (except horn-of-plenty mushrooms; see below) in this manner: For 4 ounces of cleaned mushrooms, heat 1 tablespoon of the oil in a small

skillet over high heat. When hot, add a single variety of mushroom and cook, shaking the pan, for about 2 minutes. Drain and season with salt. Set aside. Repeat for the remaining mushrooms, adding fresh oil for each batch.

For horn-of-plenty mushrooms: These must disgorge their water or they will make the final dish soggy. Place them in a small skillet (with no fat) and sprinkle with salt. Cover the skillet, and over high heat, wilt the mushrooms to release their liquid, about 1 minute. Drain, and season with salt. Set aside.

3. In a large nonstick skillet, melt the butter over moderate heat. Add the shallots, a pinch of salt, and all the mushrooms—except for horn-of-plenty mushrooms, if you are using them (they would become dry if cooked with the others). Cook, tossing occasionally, just until the mushrooms are warmed through. Add the horn-of-plenty mushrooms, and taste for seasoning. Arrange on 4 small warmed plates, garnish with the herbs, and serve immediately.

Yield: 4 SERVINGS

Mushrooms, both domestic and wild, are extremely delicate. Do not bother with anything other than quality fresh mushrooms, for they are not only expensive but also time-consuming to clean carefully. Mushrooms should be eaten as soon as possible after picking or purchasing. If you must store them for a day or so, do not wrap them in a plastic bag, or they will begin to spoil. Store them in a cool spot in an open basket or well-ventilated box. When selecting wild mushrooms, carefully examine the stem end: If it is ringed with holes, reject it, for it is likely to be worm-eaten.

A Fireside Festival

· · · · · · · · · · · · · · · · ·

*This is, in fact, a menu Chef Robuchon and I prepared
one cold wintry night in Provence. We moved the table
right in front of the fire and feasted on the following fare.
Select a red Bordeaux to start, a late-vintage
Gewürztraminer to finish.*

· · · · · · · · · · · · · · · · ·

ROAST LEG OF LAMB WITH PARSLEY CRUST
GIGOT D'AGNEAU RÔTI ET PERSILLÉ

POTATOES "CHANTEDUC"
POMMES "CHANTEDUC"

RUSTIC WHEAT AND RYE BREAD
PAIN DE CAMPAGNE

PEAR, VANILLA, AND STAR ANISE CLAFOUTIS
CLAFOUTIS AUX POIRES, VANILLE, ET ANIS ÉTOILÉ

PROVENCAL ROAST TOMATOES

Tomates à la Provençale

. . . .

A classic, wonderfully fragrant, and flavorful dish, these tomatoes are a perfect accompaniment to a roast chicken or beef. They're also great on their own, or as part of a vegetable buffet. Searing the tomatoes in advance gives them a deeper, richer tomato flavor. Since they're so easy, this is an ideal dish for a large summertime gathering.

EQUIPMENT: One oval baking dish large enough to hold all the tomatoes in a single layer
(about 10 × 16 inches)

¼ cup extra-virgin olive oil
8 firm medium-size vine-ripened
    tomatoes, cored and halved
    horizontally
Sea salt to taste

¼ cup fresh flat-leaf parsley leaves,
    snipped with a scissors
2 teaspoons fresh thyme
4 plump fresh garlic cloves, minced
¼ cup freshly made bread crumbs

1. Preheat the oven to 400°F.

2. In a very large skillet, heat the oil over moderately high heat. When hot, add as many tomatoes as will easily fit in the skillet, cut side down. Sear the tomatoes, without moving them until they are dark and almost caramelized, 3 to 4 minutes. Transfer the tomatoes, cooked side up, to the baking dish. Continue until all the tomatoes are cooked. Pour the cooking juices over the tomatoes, and season lightly with salt. Sprinkle the tomatoes with the herbs, garlic, and bread crumbs.

3. Place the baking dish in the center of the oven and bake, uncovered, until the topping has browned and the tomatoes are sizzling, about 30 minutes. Serve immediately.

Yield: 8 SERVINGS

TAGLIATELLE WITH BABY CLAMS

Tagliatelles aux Coques

. . . .

This is a double-your-money recipe, for you profit from not just the flavor of the sweet, succulent clams but also the flavorful clam juices. Chef Robuchon reduces the clam broth until it is intensely flavorful, then blends that reduction with cream and a touch of butter. The pasta then absorbs the sauce, with its distinctive clam flavor. And don't bother with dried thyme—insist on fresh.

2 pounds small fresh littleneck or Manila clams	8 ounces fresh tagliatelle
Freshly ground white pepper	¾ cup heavy cream
1 cup water	3 tablespoons unsalted butter, chilled, cut into pieces
2 tablespoons sea salt	1 tablespoon fresh thyme leaves

1. If necessary, purge the clams (see box, page 237). Scrub the clams thoroughly with a stiff brush under cold running water. Discard any with broken shells or shells that do not close when tapped. Transfer the clams to a steamer basket, and season generously with freshly ground pepper.

2. Prepare a large steamer: Place 1 cup water in the bottom portion and bring to a boil. Place the steamer basket on top and steam, removing the clams one by one as they open. The entire process should take less than 10 minutes. Discard any that do not open. Leave the cooking liquor in the steamer. Remove the clams from their shells and place in a small bowl. Line a strainer with a double thickness of moistened cheesecloth, and strain the clam liquor through the cheesecloth directly over the clams. Rinse the clams in the clam liquor to help remove any recalcitrant sand and to plump the clams in their own juices. With a slotted spoon, transfer the clams to another small bowl, and cover so they do not dry out. Strain the clam liquor through a double thickness of moistened cheesecloth into a large saucepan. Set aside.

3. Cook the pasta: In a large pot, bring 3 quarts of water to a boil, and add the salt. Add the pasta, and cook just until tender but still firm to the bite, 2 to 3 minutes. With a slotted spoon, transfer the pasta to a colander to drain. Toss well to eliminate as much water as possible.

4. Place the saucepan over high heat, and reduce the clam liquor to ⅓ cup, 6 to 7 minutes. Whisk in the cream and, still over high heat, reduce until the sauce is thick and unctuous, 2 to 3 minutes. Remove the pan from the heat and whisk in the butter, a few pieces at a time, working on and off the heat so that the butter melts gently to thicken the sauce. Add the drained pasta and toss. Cover and warm gently over very low heat, allowing the pasta to absorb the sauce, 1 to 2 minutes. Taste for seasoning. Add the clams and toss. Transfer to warmed individual shallow bowls, sprinkle with the thyme, and serve immediately.

Yield: 4 SERVINGS

Wine Suggestion: A SUBTLE WHITE WITH A LINGERING RICHNESS, SUCH AS A PULIGNY-MONTRACHET OR A MEURSAULT-CHARMES, BOTH FROM BURGUNDY

FOR CLEANER CLAMS

· · · · · · · · · · · · · · · · ·

Since most clams grow in sandy areas, they tend to be sandy themselves. Nothing is more unpleasant than biting into a tender little clam, only to find a mouthful of grit. To test if your clams are sandy, steam a few open and taste them. If they're gritty, purge the remaining clams in salt water: Scrub the shells under cold running water, then purge in salt water (dissolving 1 tablespoon salt per 1 quart of cold water) for 3 hours at room temperature. Once purged, remove the clams with your fingers, leaving behind the grit and sand. You will be amazed at the amount of sand they give up.

A Winter Feast

....

*Elegant rolls of smoked salmon garnished with salmon
roe, thick meaty veal chops with mushrooms and
asparagus, and a warm pineapple dessert fragrant with
vanilla butter: Is there a better menu for perking up a cold
wintry day? Begin with a Loire Valley Savennières, move
on to a good red Graves, then finish off the celebration
with a Rhône Valley Beaumes-de-Venise.*

....

SMOKED SALMON ROLLS WITH FRESH SALMON "CAVIAR"
FRIVOLITÉS DE SAUMON FUMÉ AUX OEUFS DE SAUMON

THICK VEAL CHOP WITH WILD MUSHROOMS
AND ASPARAGUS
CÔTE DE VEAU POÊLÉE AUX CHAMPIGNONS
ET ASPERGES

WARM CARAMELIZED PINEAPPLE WITH
VANILLA BUTTER SAUCE
ANANAS CARAMÉLISÉ, BEURRE DE VANILLE

DESSERTS

. . . .

Desserts

THE ULTIMATE STRAWBERRY SHORTCAKE

Le Fraisalia

∙∙∙∙∙∙∙∙∙∙∙∙∙∙∙∙∙∙

Elegant and beautiful, this is an ideal cake for those who love fussing with desserts. It is also remarkably light, not too sweet, and full of fresh berry goodness. Be sure to use very ripe and flavorful berries, for unripe and/or flavorless berries simply won't be worth the effort. If you have berries that are not quite ripe, you can heighten the flavor of those used in the interior by dusting them with sugar and letting them sit for a few minutes.

With the leftovers—crumbs from the sponge cake, bits of berries, and the Chantilly left in the bowl—you can make a fruit pudding. Simply mix the trio of ingredients and press them into individual ramekins for an extra dessert.

EQUIPMENT: A piping bag with a small star tip; two pieces of cardboard or two tart pan bottoms

One 8-inch sponge cake (page 342)
¹⁄₃ cup granulated sugar
1 tablespoon kirsch (cherry eau-de-vie)

CHANTILLY
1 plump moist vanilla bean

2 cups heavy cream, chilled (see Note)
½ cup confectioners' sugar

1¹⁄₄ pounds small ripe strawberries, hulled
¹⁄₄ cup strawberry or red currant jelly

1. Prepare 2 cardboard circles the diameter of the sponge cake, or use the removable bottoms of 2 tart pans. Place 1 under the cake to support it while you are handling it, and reserve the other to help replace the top layer when reassembling. (If you used a springform pan for the cake, only 1 cardboard circle is needed.)

2. Prepare the syrup: In a small saucepan, combine the granulated sugar with ³⁄₄ cup water over moderately high heat. Stir to dissolve the sugar, and boil gently for 5 minutes. Skim any foam that may rise to the surface. Transfer 3 tablespoons of the syrup to a bowl, and stir in the kirsch. Set aside to cool. Discard the unflavored syrup.

3. Prepare the cake shell: With a large serrated bread knife, carefully slice off the top third of the cake, taking care not to break the top layer. Set the top layer aside. With a small pointed knife, preferably serrated, cut around the center section of the cake base, leaving a ½-inch wall around the sides and bottom. With a long, thin pointed knife, begin removing the center section by cutting out slices, as if you were cutting a whole cake. Use your hands to gently pull away this inside section. (This part will be turned into crumbs, so the pieces do not have to come out intact.) Take care not to damage the side or bottom of the cake shell. Set it aside.

4. In a food processor, process the pieces from the center section to obtain crumbs. Set aside.

5. Prepare the Chantilly: Flatten the vanilla bean, cut it in half lengthwise, and scrape out the seeds with the aid of a small spoon. Place the seeds in the chilled bowl of an electric mixer. (The pod itself may be used to prepare vanilla sugar, page 341.) Add the cream, and whip until it holds soft peaks. With the beaters running, gradually add the confectioners' sugar. Beat until the Chantilly holds stiff peaks, 3 to 4 minutes. Refrigerate until needed.

6. To assemble: With a brush, moisten the bottom of the cake shell with the syrup. Use any remaining syrup to moisten the inside of the top layer. Do not soak the top layer, however, or it may break when reassembled.

7. Spread a thin, even layer of Chantilly on the bottom and sides of the cake shell. Set aside the most attractive strawberries for the top of the cake (to get an accurate count of how many you'll need, arrange the berries in the cake pan as if it were the top of the cake). Arrange the remaining strawberries side by side, tops in the air, on top of the Chantilly, fitting in as many as possible. They do not have to be perfectly arranged, but they must not be taller than the sides of the cake shell. If necessary, lay some flat, or trim or cut in half. The center must be well filled with berries, or the finished cake will sag. Cover with Chantilly to fill just to the top, and carefully replace the top cake layer.

8. With a thin metal spatula, spread a thin, even layer of Chantilly over the top and sides of the cake. Trim the wide ends of the reserved strawberries so they lie flat, making sure that they will all be about the same height. Evenly arrange the strawberries on top of the cake, beginning around the outside edge and spiraling in. Refrigerate. (The recipe may be prepared to this point several hours in advance. Refrigerate until needed.)

9. Prepare the glaze: Place the jelly in a small saucepan over low heat. Cook just until the jelly melts, 2 to 3 minutes. If necessary, add 1 teaspoon water to thin. Cool slightly before coating.

10. To finish: Remove the cake from the refrigerator. With a brush, coat the tips of the strawberries with the glaze. Lift the cake up in one hand, and with the other, coat the sides with an even layer of the cake crumbs. Place the remaining Chantilly in a pastry bag fitted with a small star tip, and pipe a row of rosettes around the upper edge and between the strawberries. Serve immediately, or freeze for up to 2 hours before serving.

Yield: 8 TO 12 SERVINGS

NOTE: For a very tangy Chantilly, use *crème fraîche* (page 339), or mix 1 part whole milk with 3 parts thick *crème fraîche,* instead of the heavy cream.

READING THE RECIPE

Much of the success or failure of a recipe depends upon the cook's ability to focus on matters at hand. No matter how simple a recipe may appear, reward yourself by following these four tips:

1. Read the recipe completely, even before shopping for ingredients.

2. As you read it, visualize the recipe, step by step.

3. Measure, weigh, cut, and dice before you begin. This is the reason I include even water as an ingredient, so when you need it, it's there, all measured out, at the proper temperature. At home, I arrange all of the necessary ingredients for each dish on a separate tray, so there is no confusion.

4. Relax! If you've followed the first three steps, you're more than halfway there.

GOLDEN SUNBURST APPLE TART

Tarte Fine aux Pommes

....

I love this delicious golden tart. It's a cinch to make, and the layers of apple, like a sunburst or the petals on a daisy, make for a very elegant presentation. You don't have to tell people how easy it is! The thin layer of compote adds a smooth and vibrant touch, a nice contrast to the crispness of the apples. Serve it warm, if you can, with a dollop of cinnamon ice cream (page 306).

For best results, try to select apples of equal size. Although at Jamin the tart is often prepared with Golden Delicious apples, you'll find even better flavor with a top-quality baking apple such as Jonagold, Gala, Gravenstein, or Cortland.

EQUIPMENT: An apple corer

One 10½-inch partially rimless puff
  pastry shell (page 344)

3 tablespoons vanilla sugar (page 341)
1 tablespoon unsalted butter

APPLE COMPOTE
2 plump moist vanilla beans
2 baking apples
3 tablespoons water

3 baking apples
2 tablespoons unsalted butter, melted
2 tablespoons vanilla sugar (page 341)
Confectioners' sugar, for garnish

1. Prepare the apple compote: With the side of a knife, flatten the vanilla beans, cut them in half lengthwise, and scrape out the seeds with the aid of a small spoon. Place the seeds in a small bowl and set aside. (The bean itself may be used to prepare vanilla sugar.) Peel and core the apples and cut into small cubes. In a medium saucepan, combine the apple cubes, the 3 tablespoons water, sugar, and vanilla seeds over moderate heat. Cook, covered, until the apples are very soft, about 10 minutes. Watch carefully so they do not scorch. Remove from the heat, add the butter, and stir to blend. Purée in a food processor and set aside. You should have about ⅔ cup apple compote.

2. Preheat the oven to 425°F.

3. Once the apple compote has cooled, spoon it onto the cooled pastry and spread it out evenly with a thin, flexible spatula.

4. Prepare the apples: Peel and carefully core the apples. Using a mandoline, electric slicer, or sharp knife, slice the apples horizontally, as thin as possible. With a round cookie cutter, cut out one 2-inch circle to decorate the center of the tart.

5. Arrange the apple slices: Beginning with the outside row, arrange a ring of overlapping slices so that the hole in the center of each slice is covered. When the first row is completed, brush with melted butter. Continue with the second row, slightly overlapping the apples in the outside row as well as the apples in this row. Brush this row with melted butter. Place 2 or 3 overlapping slices in the center, again covering the hole in the center of the slices. Place the round decorative slice of apple in the center, and brush with melted butter. Dust evenly with the vanilla sugar.

6. Place the tart in the center of the oven and bake until the apples are lightly golden, 20 to 25 minutes. Remove the tart from the oven, and while still hot, sprinkle it evenly and generously with confectioners' sugar. Preheat the broiler and place the tart beneath it until golden brown, 1 to 2 minutes. Watch carefully so the sugar does not burn. Serve warm.

Yield: 8 SERVINGS

Wine Suggestion: A YOUNG SAUTERNES

CARAMELIZED PEAR NAPOLEONS WITH VANILLA ANISE SAUCE

Croquant aux Poires

. . . .

Once you've mastered this dessert, you'll feel you deserve your Ph.D. in pastry-making! I admit I was daunted at first, thinking of conquering pastry cream, caramelized puff pastry, trying to get mine to look as spectacular as pastry chef Philippe Gobet's version. In the end, however, I found that the pieces of the puzzle aren't all that complicated, and the taste reward is well worth it. Note that all the ingredients (except the puff pastry) can be prepared a day in advance. The puff pastry can be baked several hours in advance, so all you have to do is to assemble the desserts at the last moment.

A LABOR-SAVING VARIATION: When pears are in full season and time is of the essence, simply prepare the pear *coulis* enriched with vanilla anise syrup and serve it, warm, with the rich caramelized pears.

VANILLA ANISE SYRUP
1 plump moist vanilla bean
1⅓ cups water
½ cup granulated sugar
4 whole star anise

PASTRY CREAM
1 plump moist vanilla bean
1 cup whole milk
2 large egg yolks
⅓ cup granulated sugar
1 tablespoon all-purpose flour
1 tablespoon cornstarch

CARAMELIZED PEARS
3 tablespoons clarified butter (page 326)
2 Bartlett pears, peeled, cored, and quartered

PEAR COULIS
1 plump moist vanilla bean
2 Bartlett pears, peeled, cored, and cubed
4 tablespoons freshly squeezed lemon juice
1 tablespoon Poire Williams (pear eau-de-vie)

CARAMELIZED PUFF PASTRY
8 ounces puff pastry (page 344)
Confectioners' sugar, for garnish

Mint leaves, for garnish

1. Prepare the vanilla anise syrup: With the side of a knife, flatten the vanilla bean, cut it in half lengthwise, and scrape out the seeds with the aid of a small spoon. Place the seeds in a small bowl, and set aside. (The bean itself may be used to prepare vanilla sugar, page 341.) In a large saucepan over high heat, bring the 1⅓ cups water and the sugar to a boil. Remove from the heat, add the star anise and vanilla seeds, and cover. Set aside to infuse for 20 minutes. (Do not let it infuse longer, or the syrup will taste "woody.") Strain the syrup, discarding the vanilla seeds and star anise. Set aside.

2. Prepare the pastry cream: Remove the seeds from the vanilla bean as described in step 1. Rinse a medium-size saucepan with cold water (to prevent the milk from sticking to it when cooked). In the saucepan, combine the milk and the vanilla seeds and bring to a boil over high heat. Meanwhile, in a large bowl, whisk together the egg yolks and sugar until thick and lemon-colored. Whisk in the flour and cornstarch just to combine (overmixing encourages development of the gluten in the flour). As soon as the milk boils, pour one third of it into the egg yolk mixture and whisk to blend thoroughly. Return the saucepan to high heat, and whisk in the egg yolk and milk mixture. Whisk constantly until the mixture just begins to boil, about 1 minute. The pastry cream should be thick and spreadable. Remove the pan from the heat, and transfer the pastry cream to a bowl. Cover with plastic wrap, placing it directly on top of the cream, to prevent a film from forming.

3. Caramelize the pears: In a large skillet, heat the clarified butter over high heat until hot and sizzling. Reduce the heat to moderately high, add the pears, and sauté until evenly golden brown, about 5 minutes. Deglaze the pan with ½ cup of the reserved vanilla-anise syrup, and continue cooking, stirring until the liquid is thick and almost caramelized, constantly spooning the juice up and over the pears to moisten and flavor them. Transfer to a bowl and set aside. (The pears may be prepared 1 day in advance. Store in the refrigerator, in a sealed container. Bring to room temperature to serve.)

4. Prepare the pear *coulis:* Remove the seeds from the vanilla bean as described in step 1. Set aside. In a medium saucepan, combine the pears and lemon juice. Cover with 1 cup of the reserved vanilla-anise syrup, and bring to a boil over high heat. Cook, stirring from time to time, until the pears are very soft, about 15 minutes. Add the

vanilla seeds and stir to blend. Transfer to a food processor and purée. Stir in the Poire Williams and set aside. (The pear *coulis* may be prepared 1 day in advance. Store in the refrigerator, in a sealed container. Bring to room temperature to serve.)

5. Prepare the caramelized puff pastry: Divide the dough into 2 equal portions. On a lightly floured surface, carefully roll out each portion of dough as thin as possible, forming a 5 × 20-inch rectangle. Using a long serrated knife, cut each rectangle in half crosswise, to form two 5 × 10-inch rectangles. Continue with the remaining portion of dough, until you have 4 rectangles. Dust off any excess flour. Neatly trim each rectangle. Place the rectangles side by side on two large baking sheets. Generously prick the dough, and refrigerate for at least 30 minutes.

6. Preheat the oven to 425°F.

7. Remove the baking sheets from the refrigerator. Cover each sheet with another baking sheet, to weight them down so the dough does not puff up too much. Place in the center of the oven and immediately reduce the temperature to 400°F. Bake just until the pastry begins to brown, 5 to 10 minutes. (Baking time will vary from oven to oven.) Remove the top baking sheets and bake, uncovered, until evenly golden brown, about 5 minutes more.

8. Remove the pastry from the oven, and while it is still hot, quarter each rectangle, trimming to approximately 2 × 4 inches, for a total of 16 rectangles. Dust each pastry evenly and generously with confectioners' sugar (this is best done by sifting the sugar over the pastry). Heat the broiler and place the dusted pastry beneath it until golden brown, 1 to 2 minutes. Watch carefully so the sugar does not burn. (The pastry may be baked several hours in advance. Store at room temperature in an airtight container.)

9. Assemble the individual pastries: On each dessert plate, arrange one pastry rectangle, caramelized side up. Spread a spoonful of pastry cream on each rectangle. Arrange a caramelized pear quarter in the center, and cover with another pastry rectangle, caramelized side up. Dust the top of the pastry with confectioners' sugar. Spoon the pear *coulis* all around. Garnish with several mint leaves, and serve immediately.

Yield: 8 SERVINGS

Wine Suggestion: A HIGHLY FLAVORED MUSCAT DESSERT WINE, SUCH AS A MUSCAT DE BEAUMES DE VENISE

INDIVIDUAL VANILLA CUSTARDS

Petits Pots de Crème à la Vanille

. . . .

A rich, simple, and inexpensive make-ahead dessert, *pots de crème* are among my favorite foods to serve for a crowd. People enjoy individual desserts, and these are especially lovely when served with warm honey madeleines (page 262). The recipe can easily be doubled.

EQUIPMENT: Eight ½-cup ovenproof ramekins, custard cups, or *petits pots*

1⅔ cups whole milk
2 plump moist vanilla beans, split
   lengthwise

4 large egg yolks
⅓ cup sugar
Boiling water

1. Preheat the oven to 325°F.

2. Cut 3 slits in a piece of sulfurized or waxed paper, and use it to line a baking pan large enough to hold the ramekins. Place the ramekins in the pan, on top of the paper, and set aside. (The paper will prevent the water from boiling and splashing up on the custards.)

3. In a medium-size saucepan, combine the milk and vanilla beans over high heat. Bring to a boil and remove from the heat. Cover, and set aside to infuse for 15 minutes.

4. In the bowl of an electric mixer, whisk the egg yolks and sugar until thick and lemon-colored. Set aside.

5. Bring the vanilla-infused milk back to a boil, and very gradually add to the yolk mixture in a thin stream, whisking constantly. Strain into a bowl through a fine-mesh sieve or several layers of cheesecloth. Let stand for 2 to 3 minutes, then remove any foam that has risen to the top.

6. Divide the cream evenly among the individual ramekins. Pour enough boiling water into the pan to reach about halfway up the side of the ramekins. Cover the pan loosely

with aluminum foil, to prevent a skin from forming on the custards. Place in the center of the oven, and bake until the custard is just set at the edges but still trembling in the center, 30 to 35 minutes.

7. Remove the pan from the oven and carefully remove the ramekins from the water. Refrigerate, loosely covered, for at least 2 hours or up to 24 hours. Serve the *pots de crème* well chilled, without unmolding.

Yield: 8 SERVINGS

Wine Suggestion: A FORTIFIED SWEET RED WINE, SUCH AS A VIEUX BANYULS, OR A PORT

INDIVIDUAL CHOCOLATE CREAMS

Petits Crèmes au Chocolat

. . . .

Rich, easy, pretty, and delicious, these little chocolate creams are a wonderful dessert for entertaining, for they can be prepared a day in advance. For added elegance, bake them in decorative ovenproof cups, *petits pots,* or small bowls. Serve the chocolate creams with warm toasted brioche, or with chocolate or lemon madeleines (pages 266 or 264).

EQUIPMENT: Six ½-cup ovenproof ramekins, custard cups, or *petits pots*

½ cup whole milk

3 ounces bittersweet chocolate, preferably Lindt Excellence, finely chopped

¾ cup heavy cream

3 large egg yolks

⅓ cup sugar

Boiling water

1. Cut 3 slits in a piece of sulfurized or waxed paper, and use it to line a baking pan large enough to hold the ramekins. Place the ramekins in the pan, on top of the paper, and set aside. (The paper will prevent the water from boiling and splashing up on the custards.)

2. In a medium saucepan, scald the milk over high heat. Stir in the chocolate. Remove from the heat and add the cream; stir to blend. Set aside to cool.

3. In a medium-size bowl, gently combine the egg yolks and sugar. Do not let the mixture foam. Slowly pour the chocolate mixture into the egg yolk mixture, stirring constantly. Strain through a fine-mesh sieve. Let rest, uncovered, at room temperature, for 1 hour.

4. Preheat the oven to 325°F.

5. Spoon off any foam that may have risen to the surface of the chocolate cream. Divide the cream evenly among the individual ramekins. Pour enough boiling water into the pan to reach about halfway up the side of the ramekins. Cover the pan loosely with

aluminum foil, to prevent a skin from forming on the creams. Place in the center of the oven and bake until the creams are just set at the edges but still trembling in the center, 30 to 35 minutes.

6. Remove the pan from the oven and carefully remove the ramekins from the water. Refrigerate, loosely covered, for at least 2 hours or up to 24 hours. Serve the *pots de crème* well chilled, without unmolding.

Yield: 6 SERVINGS

Wine Suggestion: A FORTIFIED SWEET RED WINE, SUCH AS A VIEUX MAURY, OR A PORT

A Cheery
April Feast

. . . .

*The month of April always makes me think of fresh
salmon and springy green beans, and I love to plan a
menu around this whole grilled side of salmon. With the
salmon select a Volnay, slightly chilled. If cherries are in
the market, prepare a cherry-mint soup for dessert.*

. . . .

WHOLE GRILLED SALMON FILLET
WITH RED SHALLOT SAUCE
SAUMON GRILLÉ AU BEURRE ROUGE

GREEN BEAN SALAD WITH TOMATOES, GARLIC,
AND SHALLOTS
HARICOTS VERTS AUX TOMATES, À L'AIL,
ET AUX ÉCHALOTES

CRISPY SAUTÉED POTATOES
POMMES DE TERRE SAUTÉES À CRU

COOL CHERRY SOUP WITH FRESH MINT
SOUPE DE CERISES À LA MENTHE

WARM CARAMELIZED PINEAPPLE WITH VANILLA BUTTER SAUCE

Ananas Caramélisé, Beurre de Vanille

. . . .

Hot and cold, sweet and acid, this stunningly simple dish has all the elements of a winning winter dessert: It warms your heart, makes your lips pucker, and transports you to a sunny tropical climate. I love the complex blending of flavors, including the sweetness of pineapple, the sharpness of vinegar, a lightly heady touch of rum, and the rich, fragrant blend of butter and vanilla. Top it off with a dollop of coconut ice cream and you're at the threshold of gastronomic heaven. This dessert will mellow with "age," so make it several hours ahead and then reheat at serving time. (At Jamin, the dessert is served with a single slice of pineapple. At home, feel free to serve 2 or more.)

EQUIPMENT: A candy thermometer

VANILLA BUTTER
3 plump moist vanilla beans
3 tablespoons unsalted butter

SYRUP
¾ cup sugar
¾ cup warm water

1 ripe fresh pineapple
3 tablespoons clarified butter
  (page 326)
2 to 3 tablespoons best-quality cider
  vinegar
3 tablespoons dark rum

1 recipe coconut ice cream (page 307)

1. Prepare the vanilla butter: Flatten the vanilla beans and cut them in half lengthwise. With a small spoon, scrape out the seeds and place them in a small bowl. (The beans may be used to prepare vanilla sugar, page 341.) With a fork, mash the seeds with the butter. With a pastry scraper, press the mixture through a fine-mesh sieve. Set aside.

2. Prepare the sugar syrup: Combine the sugar and ¾ cup warm water in a large saucepan (the syrup will boil over in a small pan). Let the mixture sit for 10 minutes,

to help the sugar dissolve. Place the pan over low heat and stir to dissolve thoroughly. Dip a pastry brush in warm water and brush down any grains of sugar that have collected along the sides of the pan. When the sugar has dissolved completely (the liquid will be clear), increase the heat to high and bring to a rolling boil. Boil the syrup for 6 minutes, or until a candy thermometer immersed in the center of the syrup reads 215°F. Pour into a small bowl and set aside to cool.

3. Prepare the pineapple: Cut off both ends, saving several interior leaves for decoration. With a large sharp knife, carefully and evenly cut away the rind. Slice the pineapple horizontally into 12 equal slices. With a knife or a round pastry cutter, remove the tough inner core from each slice, and discard.

4. In a large heavy-bottomed skillet, heat the clarified butter over high heat until it begins to smoke. Add a single layer of pineapple slices, and cook until well browned, about 2 to 3 minutes on each side. (You will have to do this in several batches.) Transfer the cooked pineapple slices to a plate.

5. Discard the butter in the skillet. Return the pineapple to the skillet in layers if necessary, and add 2 tablespoons of the vinegar to deglaze. Add the rum and the syrup, and cook over moderate heat, turning occasionally, for 10 minutes.

6. With a spatula or slotted spoon, transfer the pineapple slices to another skillet. Remove the skillet containing the sauce from the heat, and stir in the vanilla butter, swirling the pan until the butter has melted. Taste the sauce and add, to taste, up to 1 tablespoon vinegar.

7. Strain the sauce through a fine-mesh sieve over the pineapple in the second skillet. (The recipe may be prepared to this point several hours in advance. Cover and set aside at room temperature.) Reheat lightly, but do not boil, or the butter will separate from the sauce.

8. To serve: Arrange 2 slices of pineapple on each warmed dessert plate.

REINFORCING FLAVORS

As I worked with Chef Robuchon in Jamin's kitchen, I noticed time and again the reinforcement of flavors, a Robuchon trademark and a habit we should all adopt. Here, for instance, the vinegar used in the original sauce is reintroduced at the end, offering an intensified layer of flavors and that extra, final, tasteful punch.

Spoon the sauce around and on top of the pineapple. Place a scoop of coconut ice cream in the center and decorate with a small trimmed pineapple leaf and candied orange peel, if desired. Serve immediately.

Yield: 6 SERVINGS

Wine Suggestion: A MUSCAT DE BEAUMES DE VENISE, WITH ITS AROMA OF EXOTIC FRUITS

FIVE-FLAVORED MADELEINES

Les Madeleines
aux Cinq Parfums

. . . .

I call this a madeleine festival! For those who love the golden shell-shaped French cookies known as madeleines, these are a dream come true. They are moist on the inside, crisp on the outside, and delicious anytime, particularly when served just slightly warm from the oven. The basic recipe will yield 24 madeleines, and each batch may be flavored according to taste—chocolate, lemon, pistachio, and hazelnut and of course the "plain" honey-flavored version, the true classic.

After years of making madeleines, I've decided that it's a cold, cold batter that makes for the delightful little "bump" on top of the cookies, so don't be afraid to let the batter rest in the refrigerator an hour or so before baking. For more evenly sized madeleines, spoon the batter into the pans and then chill. Note that madeleine tins come in different sizes; the classic tin, used here, yields twelve 3-inch madeleines. If you have only one madeleine tin, chill the batter in the mixing bowl, then bake the madeleines in several batches.

STICKY PROBLEMS

. . . .

There is nothing more discouraging than to make perfect cakes or madeleines only to have them stick to the pan when they're unmolded. As extra insurance, always butter baking pans, then very lightly dust them with flour, so that the batter won't adhere to the spots where the butter inevitably leaves gaps.

HONEY MADELEINES

Madeleines au Miel

. . . .

I like to vary the flavor of these madeleines with the exotic honeys found in the markets of Provence. I confess a weakness for the robust and virile *châtaigne*, or chestnut honey, which even honey producers find a bit strong for cooking. Try making several batches and experimenting with different honeys. One friend noted after making these: "They'll be part of my repertoire forever!"

EQUIPMENT: Tins for about twenty-four 3-inch madeleines

Unsalted butter, softened, and all-purpose flour, for the tins

13 tablespoons unsalted butter

1²/₃ cups confectioners' sugar

½ cup plus 1 tablespoon all-purpose flour

½ cup finely ground unblanched almonds

6 large egg whites

1 tablespoon strong-flavored honey, such as chestnut

1. With a brush, evenly coat the madeleine molds with butter, making sure you get into the indentations, and dust lightly with flour. Shake out the excess flour. Set aside.

2. Prepare the brown butter: In a large saucepan, heat the butter over moderately high heat. The butter will go through several stages, from a foamy white liquid to one that's almost clear and golden, with big airy bubbles. When the butter begins to brown and gives off a nutty aroma (about 5 minutes), transfer it to a medium-size metal or ceramic bowl to stop the cooking. Set aside to cool.

3. Sift the sugar and flour into a medium-size bowl. Stir in the ground almonds, and set aside.

4. In the bowl of an electric mixer, whisk the egg whites until frothy. Add the almond mixture and whisk until thoroughly combined. Whisk in the brown butter and the honey.

5. Spoon the batter into the prepared molds, filling them almost to the top. Refrigerate for 1 hour to firm up the batter.

6. Preheat the oven to 375°F.

7. Place the tins in the oven and bake until the madeleines are light golden and springy to the touch, 12 to 15 minutes. Remove from the oven. Sharply rap the tins against a flat surface to loosen the madeleines. Unmold immediately, using the tip of a sharp knife if necessary, and transfer to a rack to cool. Serve slightly warm or at room temperature. When completely cooled, the madeleines may be stored for several days in an airtight container.

Yield: ABOUT 24 MADELEINES

LEMON MADELEINES
Madeleines au Citron

. . . .

Shall it be lemon or chocolate? For me it's always a toss-up. These are incredibly delicate madeleines, mildly perfumed with lemon zest and enriched with honey. Although Proustians won't be able to resist dipping these in a freshly brewed infusion of *tilleul,* or linden blossoms, I'd vie for a more fragrant drink such as *verveine,* or lemon verbena herbal tea.

EQUIPMENT: Tins for about thirty 3-inch madeleines

Unsalted butter, softened, and all-purpose flour, for the tins
13 tablespoons unsalted butter
1²/₃ cups confectioners' sugar
½ cup plus 1 tablespoon all-purpose flour
½ cup finely ground unblanched almonds

6 large egg whites
1 tablespoon mild-flavored honey, such as lavender
Grated zest (yellow peel) of 2 lemons
¼ cup freshly squeezed lemon juice

1. With a brush, evenly coat the madeleine molds with butter, making sure you get into the indentations, and dust lightly with flour. Shake out the excess flour. Set aside.

2. Prepare the brown butter: In a large saucepan, heat the butter over moderately high heat. The butter will go through several stages, from a foamy white liquid to one that's almost clear and golden, with big airy bubbles. When the butter begins to brown and gives off a nutty aroma (about 5 minutes), transfer it to a medium-size metal or ceramic bowl to stop the cooking. Set aside to cool.

3. Sift the sugar and flour into a medium-size bowl. Stir in the ground almonds, and set aside.

4. In the bowl of an electric mixer, whisk the egg whites until frothy. Add the almond mixture and whisk until thoroughly combined. Add the brown butter, honey, lemon zest, and lemon juice, and whisk to blend.

5. Spoon the batter into the prepared molds, filling them almost to the top. Refrigerate for 1 hour to firm up the batter.

6. Preheat the oven to 375°F.

7. Place the tins in the oven and bake until the madeleines are light golden and springy to the touch, 12 to 15 minutes. Remove from the oven. Sharply rap the tins against a flat surface to loosen the madeleines. Unmold immediately, using the tip of a sharp knife if necessary, and transfer to a rack to cool. Serve slightly warm or at room temperature. Once completely cooled, the madeleines may be stored for several days in an airtight container.

Yield: ABOUT 30 MADELEINES

CHOCOLATE MADELEINES

Madeleines au Chocolat

. . . .

These are undeniably my favorite of all the madeleines. They're like individual chocolate cakes, with their proud domes, firm exterior, and meltingly moist interior. Serve these at your next party along with bittersweet chocolate sorbet (page 287). You'll love the applause.

EQUIPMENT: Tins for about thirty 3-inch madeleines

Unsalted butter, softened, and all-purpose flour, for the tins

13 tablespoons unsalted butter

5 ounces bittersweet chocolate, preferably Lindt Excellence, finely grated or chopped

1⅔ cups confectioners' sugar

½ cup plus 1 tablespoon all-purpose flour

½ cup finely ground unblanched almonds

6 large egg whites

1 tablespoon mild honey, such as lavender

1. With a brush, evenly coat the madeleine molds with butter, making sure you get into the indentations, and dust lightly with flour. Shake out the excess flour. Set aside.

2. Prepare the brown butter: In a large saucepan, heat the butter over moderately high heat. The butter will go through several stages, from a foamy white liquid to one that's almost clear and golden, with big airy bubbles. When the butter begins to brown and gives off a nutty aroma (about 5 minutes), transfer it to a medium-size metal or ceramic bowl to stop the cooking. Set aside to cool.

3. Melt the chocolate: Place the chocolate in the top of a double boiler set over gently simmering water. (The top container should not touch the water, or the chocolate will melt too quickly. Also, do not cover the pan, or drops of water will drip into the chocolate and alter its texture.) Stir frequently, and remove from the heat before all the pieces have melted. The residual heat will melt the remaining pieces. Set aside to cool.

4. Sift the sugar and flour into a medium-size bowl. Stir in the ground almonds, and set aside.

5. In the bowl of an electric mixer, whisk the egg whites until frothy. Add the almond mixture and whisk until thoroughly combined. Whisk in the brown butter and the honey. Add the melted chocolate, and whisk to blend.

6. Spoon the batter into the prepared molds, filling them almost to the top. Refrigerate for about 50 minutes to firm up the batter.

7. Preheat the oven to 375°F.

8. Place the tins in the oven and bake until the madeleines are evenly dark brown and springy to the touch, 12 to 15 minutes. Remove from the oven. Sharply rap the tins against a flat surface to loosen the madeleines. Unmold immediately, using the tip of a sharp knife if necessary, and transfer to a rack to cool. Serve slightly warm or at room temperature. When completely cooled, the madeleines may be stored for several days in an airtight container.

Yield: ABOUT 30 MADELEINES

PISTACHIO MADELEINES
Madeleines aux Pistaches

. . . .

These are truly exotic madeleines for the pistachio-lovers in the crowd. For flavoring, use ground unsalted pistachio nuts plus pistachio extract; or if pistachio nuts are difficult to find, simply add a touch of pistachio extract or almond extract, making for almond-flavored madeleines. If desired, add a touch of green food coloring to distinguish these from the other madeleines.

EQUIPMENT: Tins for about twenty-four 3-inch madeleines

Unsalted butter, softened, and all-
   purpose flour, for the tins
13 tablespoons unsalted butter
1²/₃ cups confectioners' sugar
½ cup plus 1 tablespoon all-purpose
   flour
½ cup shelled unsalted pistachio nuts,
   finely ground (or substitute finely
   ground unblanched almonds)

6 large egg whites
1 tablespoon mild honey, such as
   lavender
1 teaspoon pistachio or almond extract
Several drops green food coloring
   (optional)

1. With a brush, evenly coat the madeleine molds with butter, making sure you get into the indentations, and dust lightly with flour. Shake out the excess flour. Set aside.

2. Prepare the brown butter: In a large saucepan, heat the butter over moderately high heat. The butter will go through several stages, from a foamy white liquid to one that's almost clear and golden, with big airy bubbles. When the butter begins to brown and gives off a nutty aroma (about 5 minutes), transfer it to a medium-size metal or ceramic bowl to stop the cooking. Set aside to cool.

3. Sift the sugar and flour into a medium-size bowl. Stir in the nuts, and set aside.

4. In the bowl of an electric mixer, whisk the egg whites until frothy. Add the nut mixture and whisk until thoroughly combined. Add the brown butter and the honey, and whisk to blend. Add the pistachio extract and food coloring (if using), and whisk to blend.

5. Spoon the batter into the prepared molds, filling them almost to the top. Refrigerate for 1 hour to firm up the batter.

6. Preheat the oven to 375°F.

7. Place the tins in the oven and bake until the madeleines are evenly colored and springy to the touch, 12 to 15 minutes. Remove from the oven. Sharply rap the tins against a flat surface to loosen the madeleines. Unmold immediately, using the tip of a sharp knife if necessary, and transfer to a rack to cool. Serve slightly warm or at room temperature. Once completely cooled, the madeleines may be stored for several days in an airtight container.

Yield: ABOUT 24 MADELEINES

HAZELNUT MADELEINES

Madeleines aux Noisettes

. . . .

For some reason hazelnuts always remind me of winter, and I can just imagine sitting around the kitchen table, chatting with friends on a snowy day, as these fragrant madeleines come from the oven. These are particularly delicious with a little bowl of vanilla ice cream (quite conveniently, the madeleines require 6 egg whites, the ice cream, page 308, 6 egg yolks).

EQUIPMENT: Tins for about twenty-four 3-inch madeleines

Unsalted butter, softened, and all-purpose flour, for the tins

13 tablespoons unsalted butter

8 ounces hazelnut-flavored milk chocolate candy bar, broken into pieces

¾ cup confectioners' sugar

½ cup plus 1 tablespoon all-purpose flour

½ cup finely ground hazelnuts

6 large egg whites

1. With a brush, evenly coat the madeleine molds with butter, making sure you get into the indentations, and dust lightly with flour. Shake out the excess flour. Set aside.

2. Prepare the brown butter: In a large saucepan, heat the butter over moderately high heat. The butter will go through several stages, from a foamy white liquid to one that's almost clear and golden, with big airy bubbles. When the butter begins to brown and gives off a nutty aroma (about 5 minutes), transfer it to a medium-size metal or ceramic bowl to stop the cooking. Set aside to cool.

3. Melt the chocolate bar: Place in the top of a double boiler set over gently simmering water. (The top container should not touch the water, or the chocolate will melt too quickly. Do not cover the pan, or drops of water will drip into the chocolate and alter its texture.) Stir frequently, and remove from the heat before all the pieces have melted. The residual heat will melt the remaining pieces. Set aside to cool.

4. Sift the sugar and flour into a medium-size bowl. Stir in the ground hazelnuts, and set aside.

5. In the bowl of an electric mixer, whisk the egg whites until frothy. Add the hazel-nut mixture and whisk until thoroughly combined. Add the brown butter, and whisk to blend. Add the melted chocolate bar, and whisk to blend.

6. Spoon the batter into the prepared molds, filling them almost to the top. Refrigerate for 1 hour to firm up the batter.

7. Preheat the oven to 375°F.

8. Place the tins in the oven and bake until the madeleines are evenly brown and springy to the touch, 12 to 15 minutes. Remove from the oven. Sharply rap the tins against a flat surface to loosen the madeleines. Unmold immediately, using the tip of a sharp knife if necessary, and transfer to a rack to cool. Serve slightly warm or at room temperature. Once completely cooled, the madeleines may be stored for several days in an airtight container.

Yield: ABOUT 24 MADELEINES

CHERRY CLAFOUTIS
Clafoutis Aux Cerises

. . . .

Leave it to Chef Robuchon to come up with a truly stunning, original version of the most classic of all French *clafoutis* (see box, page 276). Cherries—one of the few truly seasonal fruits left in the world—are delicious but problematical. Their juiciness often gets in the way when cooking, causing tarts and desserts to turn soggy or to overflow. In Jamin's kitchens, the problem is solved in two ways. First, the pitted cherries are baked with a touch of kirsch and sugar, as a way of reducing and thus harnessing the rich flavors of the juice. Then before baking, the cherries are sprinkled with fine crumbs prepared from the trimmed sweet pastry. As with most recipes, this is a simple blueprint. For a more rustic (and traditional) *clafoutis,* the dessert may be baked in a porcelain baking dish, without the pastry. Also, cherries are not pitted in the traditional cherry *clafoutis,* so you may choose to follow suit.

Serve this with whipped cream flavored with a touch of kirsch or the cherry cooking juices, or with vanilla ice cream (page 308).

EQUIPMENT: An ovenproof dish

1 pound fresh sweet cherries, pitted
2 tablespoons kirsch (cherry eau-de-vie)
2 tablespoons granulated sugar

BATTER
2 large eggs
½ cup granulated sugar
6 tablespoons *crème fraîche* (page 339) or
  heavy cream
6 tablespoons whole milk

One 9-inch partially baked sweet pastry
  shell, cooled (page 350; see Note)
2 tablespoons pastry crumbs (reserved
  from pastry trimmings)
Confectioners' sugar, for garnish

WHY NOT

CHERRY VINEGAR?

. . . .

I love to have a variety of flavored vinegars around the house, to perk up vinaigrettes or to sprinkle on varied raw vegetables. For a deliciously flavored cherry vinegar, simply strain the leftover cooking juices from the *clafoutis* and add to a bottle of best-quality red wine vinegar.

1. Preheat the oven to 425°F.

2. In an ovenproof dish, combine the cherries, 1 tablespoon of the kirsch, and the 2 tablespoons sugar. Stir to dissolve the sugar. Place the dish in the center of the oven and bake until the cherries are hot and steaming, about 5 minutes. Remove, and drain the cherries. (The liquid will not be used in this recipe, but may be reserved to flavor whipped cream or to flavor red wine vinegar.) Set aside to cool, about 5 minutes.

3. Reduce the oven temperature to 350°F.

4. Prepare the batter: In the bowl of an electric mixer, whisk the eggs until frothy, 1 to 2 minutes. Add the sugar and whisk until well blended, 1 to 2 minutes more. Add the *crème fraîche*, milk, and remaining 1 tablespoon kirsch. Whisk until well blended, and set aside.

5. Place the prebaked pastry shell on a baking sheet. Transfer the cherries to the shell, and arrange them in a single layer. Sprinkle with the pastry crumbs. Carefully pour the batter over the cherries. (You may have an excess of batter. If so, fill to the top, bake the *clafoutis* for 5 minutes, and then add the remaining batter.)

6. Place the baking sheet in the center of the oven and bake until the *clafoutis* is golden and firm, 35 to 40 minutes. Leaving it on the baking sheet, transfer to a rack to cool.

7. Preheat the broiler.

8. When the *clafoutis* is cool, sprinkle the top evenly and generously with confectioners' sugar. Place the baking sheet under the broiler, about 1 inch from the heat. Broil until the sugar is caramelized and golden, about 1 minute. Transfer to a rack to cool. Serve at room temperature.

Yield: 8 SERVINGS

Wine Suggestion: A FRESH AND FESTIVE APERITIF, SUCH AS A CHAMPAGNE ROSÉ

NOTE: When prebaking the pastry, be sure to reserve the trimmed edges. Allow them to cool, then process into fine crumbs in a food processor.

PEAR, VANILLA, AND STAR ANISE CLAFOUTIS

Clafoutis aux Poires, Vanille, et Anis Étoilé

. . . .

I have a passion for *clafoutis*, the name now rather generically applied to any homey custard-based fruit tart. This version was inspired by a conversation with Chef Robuchon after I'd served him a very basic pear *clafoutis*. He suggested that star anise and pear were wonderful together. We got to talking, and agreed that a good dose of vanilla would be a nice addition as well. So I went back to the drawing board to create this fragrant dessert, one that's all the more welcome on a cold winter's day when the aroma of star anise fills the kitchen with warming, exotic scents. (Note: The star anise may be ground in a small coffee or spice grinder.) If star anise is not available, substitute 1½ teaspoons of freshly ground anise seed.

EQUIPMENT: One 10½-inch round baking dish

2 teaspoons unsalted butter and 2
   teaspoons vanilla sugar (page 341) or
   granulated sugar, for the baking dish
1 plump moist vanilla bean
3 large eggs, at room temperature
¾ cup vanilla sugar (page 341)
6 tablespoons all-purpose flour, sifted
Pinch of salt

¾ cup *crème fraîche* (page 339) or
   heavy cream
¾ cup whole milk
3 whole star anise, finely ground
1 tablespoon Poire Williams (pear eau-
   de-vie)
3 to 4 firm Bartlett pears (about 1½
   pounds)

1. Preheat the oven to 400°F.

2. Butter and sugar the baking dish. Set aside.

3. Prepare the vanilla bean: Flatten the bean and cut it in half lengthwise. With a small spoon, scrape out the seeds and place them in a small bowl. (The pod may be used to prepare vanilla sugar, page 341.)

4. In the bowl of an electric mixer, blend the eggs until frothy. Add the vanilla seeds,

vanilla sugar, flour, salt, *crème fraîche,* milk, star anise, and Poire Williams. Mix until well blended, 2 to 3 minutes. Set aside for 10 minutes.

5. Meanwhile, prepare the pears: Peel, quarter, and core the pears. Cut each quarter lengthwise into 4 equal slices. Arrange the slices in a spiral in the prepared baking dish.

6. Pour the batter over the pears. Place the baking dish in the center of the oven, and bake until the batter puffs up around the pears and turns a deep golden brown, about 40 minutes. Transfer to a rack to cool. Serve warm or at room temperature, but not chilled.

Yield: 8 SERVINGS

Wine Suggestion: A PERFUMED, SPICY WHITE, SUCH AS A LATE-VINTAGE GEWÜRZ-TRAMINER

CLAFOUTIS

· · · · · · · · · · · · · · · · ·

The "original" *clafoutis* comes from the Limousin region of central France, where cooks prepare a sweet and uncomplicated baked dessert consisting of black cherries arranged in a baking dish and covered with a thin batter. The Académie Française—guardians of the French language—once took it upon themselves to define a *clafoutis* as a "sort of fruit flan." The proud inhabitants of the Limousin protested, and the Académie changed the definition to a "cake with black cherries." Today, black cherries are less common, and so red cherries and other fruits (including pears and apples) are generally substituted. The word *clafoutis* comes from the provincial dialect word *clafir,* meaning "to fill."

A Fall
Extravaganza

....

*When wild mushrooms are in the market, you must "seize
the moment" and pounce on every one you can find. Short
of that, prepare a mixed sauté of domestically grown
mushrooms as a spectacular first course or accompaniment
to grilled poultry or meats. A fine fall menu might begin
with the mushroom sauté, continue with the spectacular
dish of rabbit with mustard, then end with a French
version of apple crumble, the apple and currant tart. Wine
suggestions include a light red Burgundy with the
mushrooms and the rabbit, a Sauternes with the apple tart.*

....

FRICASSEE OF WILD MUSHROOMS
FRICASSÉE DE CHAMPIGNONS SAUVAGES

RABBIT WITH MUSTARD, FAVA BEANS, AND BABY
ONIONS
LAPIN SAUTÉ AUX FÈVES ET AUX PETITS OIGNONS

GOLDEN APPLE AND CURRANT TART
TARTE AUX POMMES

BITTERSWEET
CHOCOLATE TART

Tarte au Chocolat Amer

. . . .

Smooth, creamy, ethereal, this exquisitely elegant tart is an instant favorite of any chocolate-lover—and also a cinch to make. At Jamin the tart is prepared at the very last minute and served warm, simply dusted with cocoa powder or accompanied by a scoop of vanilla-scented ice cream (page 308). Offer slender slices, for it's very rich.

¾ cup heavy cream
⅓ cup whole milk
7 ounces bittersweet chocolate,
  preferably Lindt Excellence, grated
  or finely chopped
1 large egg, slightly beaten

One 9-inch partially baked shortbread
  or sweet pastry shell, cooled (pages
  353 or 350)
Unsweetened cocoa, preferably Dutch
  process, for garnish (optional)

1. Preheat the oven to 375°F.

2. In a medium saucepan, combine the cream and milk and bring to a simmer over moderate heat. Remove the pan from the heat, add the chocolate, and stir until the chocolate is thoroughly melted and the mixture is well blended. Set aside to cool to lukewarm.

3. When cooled, add the egg, and whisk until thoroughly blended.

4. Pour the batter into the prepared pastry shell. Place in the center of the oven and bake until the filling is slightly firm but still trembling in the center, 12 to 15 minutes. Watch carefully—ovens vary tremendously, and baking times may differ slightly. Remove from the oven and place on a rack to cool. If desired, dust with unsweetened cocoa powder. Serve warm or at room temperature.

Yield: 8 SERVINGS

Wine Suggestion: A DISTINCTIVE SWEET DESSERT WINE, SUCH AS A WELL-AGED SPANISH MÁLAGA

PEACHES AND STRAWBERRIES IN PINK CHAMPAGNE

Salade de Pêches et Fraises au Champagne Rosé

....

A superbly festive dessert, this dish sings of summer and the sun. The combination of peaches, strawberries, and pink Champagne is elegant, colorful, and rich. Of course you won't want to use your best vintage Champagne here, but don't skimp either.

3¼ cups sugar
1 quart water
8 ounces strawberries, hulled
3 peaches

3 tablespoons freshly squeezed lemon
    juice
1 bottle pink Champagne, chilled
Fresh mint leaves, for garnish

1. Prepare the syrup: In a saucepan, combine the sugar with the 1 quart water and bring to a boil over high heat. Whisk constantly until boiling. Boil without whisking for 1 minute. Set aside to cool.

2. Prepare the fruit: Quarter the strawberries lengthwise and place them in a large bowl. Peel the peaches and cut in half. Remove and discard the pit, and cut each half into 4 equal slices. Place the peaches in the bowl with the strawberries, add the lemon juice and syrup, and toss gently to combine. Cover and place in the refrigerator for 1 hour to allow the flavors to blend.

3. To finish, remove the peach and strawberry mixture from the refrigerator. With a slotted spoon, divide the fruit among 6 large shallow Champagne coupes, allowing about 1 tablespoon of syrup in each glass.

4. Just before serving, uncork the Champagne and pour enough into each glass to just cover the fruit. Garnish with mint and serve.

Yield: 6 SERVINGS

Wine Suggestion: A FRESH AND FESTIVE APERITIF, SUCH AS A CHAMPAGNE ROSÉ

GOLDEN APPLE AND CURRANT TART

Tarte aux Pommes

....

This is pastry chef Philippe Gobet's version of apple crumble, but in a rather sophisticated incarnation. The apples are cooked without sugar until golden and soft, and are flavored with a touch of Calvados. Then they're topped with black currants and a sweet almond and sugar mixture that turns a rich golden brown as it bakes. Add a little scoop of homemade vanilla or cinnamon ice cream (pages 308 or 306), and you're halfway to heaven. Note that unlike most French tarts, in which the pastry is prebaked, here the pastry and the topping are baked together, since the pastry is particularly fine and fragile.

TOPPING

6 tablespoons all-purpose flour, sifted

6 tablespoons dark brown sugar, firmly packed

6 tablespoons finely ground blanched almonds

3 tablespoons unsalted butter, softened

APPLE FILLING

3 tablespoons clarified butter (page 326)

6 large Golden Delicious apples, peeled, cored, quartered, and cut into 1-inch cubes

¼ cup Calvados (apple eau-de-vie)

1 recipe rimless flaky pastry tart base, prepared through step 6 (page 348)

1 cup black currants

1. Prepare the topping: In a large bowl, combine the flour, brown sugar, and ground almonds, and work the mixture together with your fingers. Add the butter and continue working the mixture for several minutes, until it is very crumbly and the butter is thoroughly blended. Set aside to rest for 20 minutes, to firm up.

2. Preheat the oven to 375°F.

3. Prepare the filling: In a large skillet, heat the clarified butter over high heat. When hot, add the apples and cook until soft, about 15 minutes. Stir often to ensure an even golden color. Remove from the heat. Pour the Calvados into a small saucepan over low

heat. Warm the Calvados, then ignite with a match. Add the flaming Calvados to the apples, and stir to mix. The apple mixture should be moist but not soupy. If there is too much liquid, transfer the mixture to a fine-mesh sieve to drain off the excess.

4. Place the tart pan on a baking sheet. Arrange the apples evenly on top of the pastry, and level them with the back of a spoon. Sprinkle the currants over the apples. Then sprinkle with the topping, pressing down gently with your fingers or with a spatula to shape a perfectly even layer.

5. Place the tart in the center of the oven and bake until golden brown, 20 to 30 minutes. Sprinkle with confectioners' sugar, if desired. Serve warm.

Yield: 8 SERVINGS

Wine Suggestion: A GOLDEN SWEET WINE, SUCH AS A SAUTERNES

INDIVIDUAL CHOCOLATE ALMOND CAKES

Palets Moelleux au Chocolat

. . . .

I f you're like me, you're always on the lookout for another chocolate recipe. This one is simple and satisfying, and lovely for a dinner party, for each diner is served an individual cake. I like this accompanied by bittersweet chocolate sorbet (page 287), but you may also want to serve it with a coffee-flavored vanilla cream (page 308).

EQUIPMENT: Six 3½-inch savarin molds, tart tins, or ramekins

Unsalted butter, softened, for the
    molds
6 tablespoons unsalted butter
3 ounces bittersweet chocolate,
    preferably Lindt Excellence, finely
    grated or chopped

¾ cup confectioners' sugar, sifted
⅓ cup all-purpose flour, sifted
½ cup ground almonds
3 large egg whites, lightly beaten
1 tablespoon mild honey

1. Generously butter the bottom and sides of the molds and set aside.

2. Prepare the brown butter: In a small saucepan, heat the butter over moderately high heat. The butter will go through several stages, from a foamy white liquid to one that's almost clear and golden, with big, airy bubbles. When the butter begins to brown and gives off a nutty aroma (3 to 4 minutes), transfer it to a medium-size metal or ceramic bowl to stop the cooking. Set aside to cool.

3. Melt the chocolate: Place the chocolate in the top of a double boiler set over gently simmering water. (The top container should not touch the water, or the chocolate will melt too quickly. Also, do not cover the pan, or drops of water will drip into the chocolate and alter its texture.) Stir frequently and remove from the heat before all the pieces have melted. The residual heat will melt the remaining pieces. Set aside to cool.

4. In the bowl of a heavy-duty electric mixer fitted with a paddle, mix the confectioners' sugar, flour, and almonds until thoroughly blended. Slowly add the chocolate and

mix to blend. Add the egg whites and honey, and mix again. Add the brown butter and mix to blend.

5. Pour the batter into the prepared molds, place them on a baking sheet, cover, and refrigerate for 30 minutes to firm up the batter.

6. Preheat the oven to 350°F.

7. Place the baking sheet in the center of the oven and bake for 15 minutes if using savarin molds or tart tins, 20 minutes if using ramekins. The cakes should still be slightly undercooked in the center. Transfer to a rack to cool.

8. Once they have cooled, unmold the cakes onto individual dessert plates, and serve.

Yield: 6 SERVINGS

Wine Suggestion: A SWEET FORTIFIED WINE, SUCH AS A VIEUX BANYULS, OR A PORT

BITTERSWEET CHOCOLATE SORBET

Sorbet au Chocolat Amer

. . . .

A chocolate-lover's delight, bittersweet chocolate sorbet is one of my earliest taste memories of Paris. And Chef Robuchon's dark and glossy version even lives up to fantasy-filled memories. This is a super-easy recipe, requiring only a few minutes of your time. Just be sure to melt the chocolate carefully, and allow the chocolate and the syrup to chill thoroughly before blending, or the sorbet will be grainy.

EQUIPMENT: One 1-quart capacity ice cream maker

7 ounces bittersweet chocolate, preferably Lindt Excellence, finely chopped	2 cups water 1 cup sugar

1. Place the chocolate in the top of a double boiler set over gently simmering water. (The top container should not touch the water, or the chocolate will melt too quickly. Also, do not cover the pan, or droplets of water will drip into the chocolate and alter its texture.) Stir frequently, and remove from the heat before all the pieces have melted. The heat of the bowl will be sufficient to melt the remaining chunks. Set aside to cool completely.

2. Prepare the sugar syrup: In a medium-size saucepan, combine the 2 cups water and the sugar over moderate heat. Stir to combine, and cook until all the sugar has dissolved. Set aside to cool completely.

3. When both mixtures are cool, combine them in a large mixing bowl. Refrigerate until thoroughly chilled (the sorbet mixture should feel cold to the touch). When chilled, pour into the compartment of an ice cream maker and freeze according to the manufacturer's instructions.

Yield: 3 CUPS SORBET

LEMON-LOVER'S FRESH LEMON TART

Tarte au Citron

. . . .

This is a lemon-lover's dream. I have to admit, it's a recipe made for those who have a steady hand and volumes of patience. But as with so many good things, the work pays off in the end, with applause and requests for seconds.

EQUIPMENT: Two cooling racks, each set over a roasting pan

LEMON CREAM

6 tablespoons freshly squeezed lemon juice (1 to 2 lemons)

½ cup granulated sugar

5 tablespoons unsalted butter, cut into pieces

Grated zest (yellow peel) of 1 large lemon

2 large eggs

Zest (yellow peel) of 3 large lemons, cut in julienne (reserve the lemons)

¼ cup grenadine syrup

1¼ cups granulated sugar

8 large lemons

One 9-inch hand-trimmed, prebaked sweet pastry shell, cooled (page 350)

⅓ cup apricot preserves, strained

Confectioners' sugar, for garnish

1. Prepare the lemon cream: In a medium-size saucepan, combine the lemon juice and sugar, and stir to dissolve. Place the pan over high heat, and add the butter and grated lemon zest. Bring to a boil, whisking constantly, and cook until the mixture thickens, about 5 minutes. Remove the pan from the heat and whisk in the eggs, beating until thoroughly incorporated. To remove any impurities, pass the lemon mixture through a fine-mesh sieve into a clean saucepan. Return the saucepan to low heat and cook, whisking constantly, until the mixture thickens, about 15 minutes. Transfer to a small bowl, cover, and refrigerate until needed.

2. Prepare the candied zest: In a small saucepan, combine the julienned lemon zest with cold water to cover. Bring to a boil over high heat. As soon as the water boils, drain the zest in a strainer. In another small saucepan, combine the blanched zest and the grenadine over moderately low heat. When the liquid boils, reduce the heat and cook for 15 minutes, or until the zest is bright red. Drain thoroughly. With a sharp

knife, mince the zest as fine as possible. Set aside. (The tart may be prepared to this point several hours in advance.)

3. Prepare the syrup: In a medium-size saucepan, combine the sugar with 1 cup water over moderately high heat. Stir gently to dissolve the sugar. Moisten a brush and wipe down the sides of the pan to prevent the sugar from burning. Simmer gently for 5 minutes. Set aside.

4. Prepare the lemon sections: Cut both ends off 1 lemon. Place the lemon, cut end down, on a work surface. With a small sharp knife, cutting downward, slice off a strip of peel, following the curve of the lemon. All of the pith (the white part) should be removed, leaving only the fruit. Continue cutting away strips of peel with the pith until it is completely removed. To separate and lift out each lemon section, begin by slicing between the membrane and the fruit of 1 section, and carefully lift it out. Move to the next lemon section, and slice between the membrane and fruit. Use the knife to gently ease the fruit away from the other membrane (the one that was attached to the first section removed), taking care to keep the section intact. Do not remove the seeds right away; it will be easier to do that after the sections are candied. Transfer the lemon sections to a rack. Continue with the remaining lemons (including the lemons used for the julienned zest) until all of the sections have been removed.

5. Return the syrup to a gentle boil. With a slotted spoon, gently transfer a small batch of lemon sections to the syrup. Cook until the syrup returns to a gentle boil, 2 to 3 minutes. With a slotted spoon, remove the lemon sections and transfer to a rack to drain and cool. Repeat, working in small batches, until all the lemon sections are candied. Set aside.

6. With a thin metal spatula, spread a thin, even layer of lemon cream over the tart shell. Remove any seeds from the candied lemon sections, and arrange them over the lemon cream, beginning from the outside edge and working in. The sections should overlap slightly. Set aside.

7. In a small saucepan, heat the preserves over low heat to thin them slightly. With a brush, gently coat the surface of the tart with a thin layer of preserves. Sprinkle with the minced zest.

8. To finish, dust only the edges of the crust with confectioners' sugar (to protect the lemons, hold a pastry scraper over the center while dusting). Serve at room temperature.

Yield: 8 TO 10 SERVINGS

INDIVIDUAL RASPBERRY GRATINS

Gratins de Framboises

. . . .

There's a complex, creamy elegance about these individual raspberry gratins. I love the sensation of the hot and golden gratin against the chilled, sweet raspberries. This dish must be made ahead of time, so it is ideal for entertaining.

EQUIPMENT: Eight 3½-inch tart rings or ramekins

Unsalted butter, softened, for the
  molds
1 cup granulated sugar
4 teaspoons powdered gelatin
½ cup freshly squeezed lemon juice
½ cup heavy cream
2 tablespoons cornstarch

8 large egg yolks
5 large egg whites
1 pound fresh raspberries (4 to 5 cups)
Confectioners' sugar, for garnish
2 cups fresh raspberry sauce
  (page 293)

1. With a brush, generously butter the molds. Set aside.

2. Prepare a sugar syrup: In a large saucepan, combine ¾ cup of the sugar and 6 tablespoons water over high heat. Bring to a boil and stir, without splashing the sides of the pan, until the sugar has dissolved. Moisten a brush and wipe down the sides of the pan to prevent any sugar splattered on the sides from burning. Continue cooking until the syrup reaches 248°F, or the hard ball stage. (To test without a candy thermometer, let a drop of syrup fall from a spoon into a glass of cold water: The sugar should form a ball and hold its shape on the bottom of the glass.) The whole process should take about 5 minutes. Remove from the heat and set aside.

3. Combine the gelatin with ¼ cup cold water in a small bowl. Stir to dissolve. Set aside.

4. In a large saucepan, combine the lemon juice, cream, and cornstarch over high heat. Whisk continuously until the mixture boils. Remove from the heat, and slowly whisk in the egg yolks until thoroughly incorporated. The mixture should resemble a

thick pastry cream. Return to the heat and cook until very thick, about 2 minutes. Remove from the heat and add the gelatin mixture, whisking until thoroughly incorporated. Set aside.

5. In the bowl of an electric mixer, combine the egg whites and the remaining ¼ cup sugar, and beat until stiff but not dry. With the machine still running, gradually pour the sugar syrup into the egg whites.

6. Add several tablespoons of the egg whites to the egg yolk mixture, whisking constantly. With a spatula, gently fold the rest of the egg whites into the egg yolk mixture. Do this slowly and patiently. Do not overmix, but be certain that the mixture is evenly blended.

7. Prepare the pans: For the rings, line a baking sheet with baking parchment and arrange the rings side by side on the parchment. For the ramekins, arrange them side by side on a baking sheet. Carefully spoon a layer of batter into the rings or ramekins. Arrange the raspberries in a single layer on top of the batter, and cover with another layer of batter. Cover loosely with aluminum foil and refrigerate for at least 2 hours to firm.

8. Preheat the broiler.

9. Remove the gratins from the refrigerator, and sprinkle them evenly and generously with confectioners' sugar. Place under the broiler, about 1 inch from the heat. Broil until the sugar is caramelized and golden, about 20 seconds. If using rings, transfer each gratin to a dessert plate, run a knife around the gratin, and remove the rings. If using ramekins, run a knife around the inside of each gratin, and carefully transfer it, right side up, to a dessert plate. Spoon the raspberry sauce all around. Serve immediately. (The top will be warm, the interior cold.)

Yield: 8 SERVINGS

Wine Suggestion: A BUBBLING PINK CHAMPAGNE ROSÉ

FRESH RASPBERRY SAUCE

Coulis de Framboise

. . . .

8 ounces fresh raspberries (about 2
   cups)
1 tablespoon confectioners' sugar

2 tablespoons freshly squeezed lemon
   juice

In a food processor, combine the raspberries, sugar, and lemon juice. Process to blend.
Strain through a fine-mesh sieve to remove the seeds. Transfer to a sealed container.
The sauce may be refrigerated for 2 to 3 days, or frozen for up to 1 month.

Yield: ABOUT 1 CUP

MARBLEIZED CHOCOLATE WAFERS AND CINNAMON-CHOCOLATE MOUSSE

Feuillantines au Chocolat, Mousse au Chocolat à la Cannelle

....

We all dream of those picture-perfect desserts that draw *oohs, aahs,* and applause. At last, here's one that is easier than it looks. If you have a steady hand and even a minimal amount of patience, you're sure to succeed. For each serving, you layer wafers of marbleized chocolate, sandwich style, and fill them with a stunning cinnamon-flavored chocolate mousse. One word of caution: Don't attempt this on a hot, humid day, for the chocolate will melt as soon as you remove it from the refrigerator. The wafers may be prepared several days in advance. The chocolate mousse, however, must be prepared at the last minute, for if it's made ahead, it will become unworkably thick. At Jamin, this dessert is served with a rich pistachio-flavored custard sauce, but I love it as well with the classic vanilla-flavored version.

EQUIPMENT: A pastry bag with piping tip (optional)

CHOCOLATE WAFERS

3½ ounces best-quality white chocolate, preferably Tobler Narcisse, finely chopped or grated

3½ ounces bittersweet chocolate, preferably Lindt Excellence, finely chopped or grated

CINNAMON-CHOCOLATE MOUSSE

7 ounces bittersweet chocolate, preferably Lindt Excellence, chopped or grated

1¼ cups heavy cream

½ teaspoon freshly ground cinnamon

1 tablespoon unsweetened cocoa, preferably Dutch process

3 cups vanilla custard sauce (page 340)

GARNISH

4 candied cherries (optional)

Fresh mint leaves

1. Prepare 4 strips of aluminum foil, each about 5 inches wide and long enough to wrap over the edges of a baking sheet. Place 2 strips of the foil on a baking sheet and crimp the edges to obtain an even, flat work surface. Repeat with a second baking sheet. Set aside.

2. Make room for the 2 baking sheets in the refrigerator.

3. Melt the chocolates: Place the white chocolate in the top of a double boiler set over gently simmering water. (The top container should not touch the water, or the chocolate will melt too quickly. Also, do not cover the pan, or droplets of water will drip into the chocolate and alter its texture.) Stir frequently, and remove from the heat before all the pieces have melted. The residual heat will melt the remaining pieces. Set aside. In another bowl, repeat the melting process with the bittersweet chocolate.

4. Prepare the wafers: With a spoon, dribble about one fourth of the melted white chocolate—abstract art style—on each strip of foil. Repeat with the melted bittersweet chocolate, dribbling it on top of the white chocolate. With a spatula, smooth out the chocolates to form a thin, even, marbleized layer. With a 3-inch round pastry or cookie cutter, or a very fine glass, mark 12 round indentations in the chocolate. Do not remove the cutouts. Place the baking sheets in the refrigerator to allow the chocolate to harden. (This precutting and chilling will facilitate removal of the delicate wafers.) Refrigerate until the chocolate begins to harden, about 10 minutes.

5. Remove the baking sheets from the refrigerator. With the same cutter, again cut the chocolate rounds where you had previously marked the indentations. Return to the refrigerator to allow the chocolate to harden completely, about 1 hour more.

6. Remove the baking sheets from the refrigerator. Lift up the foil and turn it over onto a clean surface. With a spatula, peel off the excess chocolate around the wafers, and carefully remove each wafer. The side facing the foil will be shinier and should be more marbleized. (The wafers may be prepared several hours in advance. Store them carefully between layers of waxed paper in an airtight container, and refrigerate.)

7. Prepare the mousse: Place the chocolate in a medium-size mixing bowl. In a small saucepan, bring 6 tablespoons of the cream to a boil over moderate heat. Remove from the heat and add to the chocolate. Whisk until thoroughly blended. Add the cinnamon and whisk to blend. Set aside.

8. In the bowl of an electric mixer, beat the remaining cream until it holds stiff peaks. Add to the chocolate mixture and stir with a wooden spoon until thoroughly blended. Add the cocoa powder and stir until thoroughly blended. Set aside.

9. To assemble: Fill a pastry bag with the chocolate mousse. (Alternatively, the mousse may simply be spooned onto the chocolate wafers.) Place a chocolate wafer, shiny side up, in the center of a dessert plate. Pipe or spoon a thick, even layer of mousse onto the center of the wafer. Cover with a second chocolate wafer, shiny side up. Add a second layer of mousse. Cover with a third and final wafer, shiny side up. Spoon the vanilla sauce all around the dessert. Garnish each dessert with several mint leaves, and with a candied cherry if desired. Serve immediately.

Yield: 4 SERVINGS

Wine Suggestion: A FORTIFIED SWEET RED WINE, SUCH AS A BANYULS

V A R I A T I O N : Try this same dessert with wafers made of pure bittersweet chocolate, and between the layers place a dollop of whipped cream and a single layer of fresh raspberries. Serve with fresh raspberry sauce.

ON THE FRAGILITY

OF CHOCOLATE

. . . .

Chocolate is fragile, and the ideal environment for working with all chocolates is a cool (65° to 70°F), dry, and draft-free area. If chocolate is heated to too high a temperature, it will become grainy and the flavor will be altered. To help the chocolate melt quickly and evenly, chop or grate it very fine, using either a large chef's knife or a food processor.

LEMON CAKE WITH DOUBLE CHOCOLATE ICING

Marbré au Citron Glacé aux Deux Chocolats

. . . .

A dessert that promises a festival of flavors, this classic French cake delivers the delicate scent of lemon topped with a swirl of dark and white chocolates. It's the offering of Jamin's pastry chef, Philippe Gobet, who created it in memory of the *fabuleux goûters d'enfance passés à la campagne*—the fabulous after-school snacks that recalled his childhood in the center of the Beaujolais region. Serve it with tangerine marmalade (page 300) which will nicely enhance the lemon, sipping hot tea, hot chocolate, or chilled white wine.

EQUIPMENT: One 9 × 5 × 3-inch loaf pan

CAKE
**Unsalted butter, softened, and all-
   purpose flour, for the pan**
5 large eggs
1³/₄ cups sugar
Pinch of sea salt
2 cups all-purpose flour
1 tablespoon baking powder
²/₃ cup heavy cream

6 tablespoons unsalted butter, melted
Grated zest (yellow peel) of 3 lemons
2 tablespoons dark rum

ICING
**3¹/₂ ounces best-quality white chocolate,
   preferably Tobler's Narcisse**
**3¹/₂ ounces bittersweet chocolate,
   preferably Lindt Excellence**

1. Preheat the oven to 375°F.

2. Coat the bottom and sides of the pan with butter. Dust the pan with flour, tapping the sides to distribute it evenly. Shake out the excess and set aside.

3. In the bowl of an electric mixer, combine the eggs, sugar, and salt, and beat until thick and lemon-colored.

4. Sift together the flour and baking powder. With a wooden spoon, fold the flour

mixture into the egg mixture and blend thoroughly. Stir in the cream, butter, and lemon zest, and mix to blend.

5. Pour the batter into the prepared pan, and place it in the center of the oven. Bake until just golden brown around the edges, 40 to 45 minutes. The center of the cake should cave in slightly during cooking.

6. Remove the cake from the oven, unmold it onto a cake rack, and then carefully turn it right side up. Generously prick the top of the cake with a fork. Slowly pour the rum into the holes, and set aside to cool.

7. When the cake is thoroughly cooled, melt the chocolates: Place the white chocolate in the top of a double boiler set over gently simmering water. (The top container should not touch the water or the chocolate will melt too quickly. Also, do not cover the pan, or drops of water will drip into the chocolate and alter the texture.) Stir frequently and remove from the heat before all the pieces have melted. The residual heat will melt the remaining pieces. Repeat with the bittersweet chocolate.

8. Ice the cake: Alternating white and dark, pour the warm chocolates over the top and sides of the cake, blending just slightly with a metal spatula for a marbled effect. Set aside to harden (at least 30 minutes).

9. To serve, cut the cake into thick slices, and serve with warm marmalade and mugs of tea or hot chocolate.

Yield: 12 TO 16 SERVINGS

Wine Suggestion: A YOUNG SAUTERNES, WITH A FLORAL BOUQUET WITH DELICATE ORANGE FLAVORS

TANGERINE MARMALADE

Confiture d'Oranges Sanguines

. . . .

Warm tangerine marmalade, a cake of lemon and chocolate, a cup of simmering chocolate—not bad for an afternoon snack! The marmalade—prepared either with European blood oranges, called *sanguines,* or with tangerines, called *clémentines*—is just as delicious for breakfast, spread on warm toast. The marmalade is quick and easy to make; precooking the whole orange prevents the peel from toughening when it is cooked with the sugar.

EQUIPMENT: Three ½-pint jelly jars, sterilized

MARMALADE
1 pound oranges, blood oranges, or
   tangerines, thoroughly scrubbed
1 pound sugar cubes

1. Place the whole oranges in a large flat-bottomed pot, and add cold water to cover. Cover and bring to a boil over high heat. Reduce the heat and simmer gently until a knife inserted in an orange easily pierces the fruit, about 30 minutes. Drain thoroughly, and set aside to cool.

2. Without peeling them, cut the oranges crosswise into very fine slices. Remove and discard any seeds. In a large flat-bottomed pot, combine the orange slices and the sugar cubes over low heat. Cook, stirring, until the sugar cubes dissolve. Increase the heat to high and bring to a hard boil, stirring to prevent scorching, and cook until the syrup reaches 200°F, the orange slices are translucent, and the marmalade is beginning to

A NOTE OF REFINEMENT

. . . .

Why use sugar cubes rather than standard granulated sugar when preparing jams or marmalades? Because cubed sugar is the most refined and most pure of all sugars, making for purer, clearer, more refined preserves.

thicken, about 5 minutes. (To test by hand: Dip a cool metal spoon into the boiling mixture. When two drops form together and break from the spoon in a sheet, the jelly is done.) Remove the pot from the heat, and skim off any foam. Transfer the marmalade to sterilized jars, and cool. The marmalade may be stored up to 1 month, refrigerated, in a sealed container.

Yield: ABOUT 3 CUPS MARMALADE

APPLE, PINEAPPLE, AND CINNAMON MOLDS

Turbans de Pommes à la Cannelle

. . . .

This is a wonderful warm winter dessert, sort of sweet and sour and golden, rich with vanilla, fruits, and cinnamon ice cream. Don't be put off by the seeming complexity of the recipe—it's much less daunting than it looks. The only trick here is getting the apples evenly and thinly sliced, and arranging them evenly in the molds. Once that's accomplished, the rest is child's play. If you are using nonstick molds, you can prepare this dessert a day or two in advance, for the apples will not interact with the molds.

EQUIPMENT: Six 3½-inch savarin or ring molds, preferably nonstick; a large steamer

CARAMELIZED APPLES

4 tablespoons unsalted butter, melted

3 to 4 cooking apples

½ cup sugar

1½ tablespoons best-quality cider vinegar

1 teaspoon honey

½ teaspoon freshly ground cinnamon

VANILLA BUTTER

4 plump moist vanilla beans

6 tablespoons unsalted butter, softened

SAUCE

3 tablespoons unsalted butter

¼ cup sugar

¼ cup best-quality cider vinegar

FRUIT FILLING

7 ounces fresh pineapple, cut into ½-inch cubes

3 tablespoons clarified butter (page 326)

1 quart cinnamon ice cream (page 306)

1. Preheat the broiler.

2. Prepare the caramelized apples: Brush a baking sheet with some of the melted butter. Core and peel the apples, but leave them whole. Trim off about one fourth of the apple at both ends so that the slices will be uniform. Reserve the trimmed ends for

the fruit filling. Cut the apples in half vertically, cutting through the hole. With a very sharp knife, an electric slicer, or a mandoline, cut the halves into very thin, even half-moon slices. You will need 15 slices per mold.

3. Arrange the apple slices side by side, but not touching, on the buttered baking sheet. With a brush, coat each apple slice with melted butter. Sprinkle generously with sugar. Tip the baking sheet to remove excess sugar.

4. Place the baking sheet about 2 inches from the heat, and broil until the apples are golden and caramelized, 2 to 3 minutes. Transfer the apples to a rack to cool slightly, but do not cool completely or they will harden. Repeat with the remaining apple slices.

5. As soon as the apples are cool enough to handle, line each mold with slightly overlapping caramelized apple slices. Center each slice to allow a slight overhang on the inside and outside edges of the mold. Set aside.

6. Prepare the vanilla butter: Flatten the vanilla beans, cut them in half lengthwise, and scrape out the seeds with the aid of a small spoon. Place the seeds in a small bowl. (The bean may be used to prepare vanilla sugar, page 341.) Using a fork, mash together the seeds and the butter. With a pastry scraper, press the mixture through a flat fine-mesh sieve. Divide the vanilla butter in half. Set aside.

7. Prepare the fruit filling: Place the cubed pineapple in a sieve set over a bowl, and press to release the juice. Reserve 2 tablespoons of the juice for the sauce. Cut the reserved trimmed ends of the apples into ½-inch cubes. You will need about 2 cups (about 7 ounces) of apples for the filling.

8. In a medium-size skillet, heat the clarified butter over moderately high heat. When the butter begins to smoke, add the pineapple and cook, shaking the pan from time to time, until the fruit begins to brown, 4 to 5 minutes. Add the apples and toss to blend. Continue to cook, shaking the pan occasionally, until the apples begin to brown, 4 to 5 minutes more. Add the vinegar, honey, and cinnamon, and stir to blend. Add half the vanilla butter, and stir to blend. Remove from the heat. Transfer the filling to a fine-mesh sieve to drain, and set aside.

9. With a small spoon, fill each mold generously with the fruit filling, pressing down with the back of the spoon to even it out. Turn the overhanging apple slices over to enclose the filling. Wrap tightly in plastic wrap and set aside. (The recipe may be prepared to this point 2 days in advance. Refrigerate until needed.)

10. Prepare the sauce: Just before serving, melt the butter in a medium-size saucepan over moderate heat. Whisk in the sugar, and continue whisking to dissolve. Bring just to a boil, and then whisk in the vinegar. Bring back to a boil, and boil for 2 minutes. Add the reserved 2 tablespoons pineapple juice and continue cooking until reduced by half, about 4 minutes. Remove from the heat and whisk in the remaining vanilla butter. Strain through a fine-mesh sieve. Transfer to the top of a double boiler to keep warm.

11. To finish: Bring water to a boil in the bottom of a steam cooker. Place the apple molds, still wrapped in plastic wrap, in a single layer on the steamer tray. Steam until warmed through, about 10 minutes.

12. To serve: Carefully unwrap each mold and turn it out onto a warmed dessert plate. Whisk the sauce, and spoon it around the mold and in the center. Pipe or scoop cinnamon ice cream in the center. Serve immediately.

Yield: 6 SERVINGS

Wine Suggestion: A GRAND SAUTERNES

CINNAMON ICE CREAM
Glace à la Cannelle

. . . .

Cinnamon ice cream is a perfect accompaniment to any apple- or pear-flavored dessert. At Jamin, it's served with the elegant wintry apple, pineapple, and cinnamon molds (page 303).

EQUIPMENT: One 1-quart capacity ice cream maker

1²/₃ cups whole milk
1 tablespoon freshly grated cinnamon
5 large egg yolks

²/₃ cup sugar
³/₄ cup heavy cream

1. In a heavy saucepan, combine the milk and cinnamon over high heat. Bring just to a boil, and remove from the heat. Cover, and set aside to infuse for 15 minutes.

2. In the bowl of an electric mixer, whisk the egg yolks and sugar until thick and lemon-colored. Set aside.

3. Return the milk mixture to high heat and return to a boil. Pour one third of the boiling milk into the egg yolk mixture, whisking constantly. Return this milk and egg yolk mixture to the milk in the saucepan. Reduce the heat to low and cook, stirring constantly, until the mixture thickens to a creamy consistency. Do not let it boil. To test, run your finger down the back of a wooden spoon: If the mixture is sufficiently cooked, the mark will hold. The whole process should take about 5 minutes.

4. Remove the pan from the heat and immediately stir in the cream to stop the cooking. Pass the mixture through a fine-mesh sieve, and cool completely. (To speed cooling, transfer the cream to a large chilled bowl. Place that bowl inside a slightly larger bowl filled with ice cubes and water. Stir occasionally. To test the temperature, dip your fingers into the mixture: The cream should feel cold to the touch. The process should take about 30 minutes.)

5. When the mixture is thoroughly cooled, transfer it to an ice cream maker and freeze according to the manufacturer's instructions.

Yield: 1 QUART ICE CREAM

COCONUT ICE CREAM

Glace à la Noix de Coco

. . . .

A simple dessert that offers extraordinary results—isn't that the cook's dream? Well here it is, a recipe in which you open a can and a carton of milk, and create a deliciously rich and fragrant dessert. It's designed to accompany warm caramelized pineapple (page 257) but is great all on its own. At Jamin, the ice cream is prepared with Coco López brand *crème de noix de coco*.

EQUIPMENT: One 1-quart capacity ice cream maker

2 cups whole milk
1½ cups sweetened coconut milk
1 teaspoon rum

1. In a large saucepan, bring the milk to a boil over high heat. Stir in the coconut milk.

2. Pass the mixture through a fine-mesh sieve into a bowl, and stir in the rum. Cool completely before transferring the mixture to an ice cream maker. (To speed cooling, transfer the cream to a large chilled bowl. Place that bowl inside a slightly larger bowl filled with ice cubes and water. Stir occasionally. To test the temperature, dip a finger into the mixture. The cream should feel cold to the touch. The process should take about 30 minutes.)

3. When thoroughly cooled, transfer to an ice cream maker and freeze according to the manufacturer's instructions.

Yield: 3 CUPS ICE CREAM

VANILLA-RICH ICE CREAM
Crème Glacée à la Vanille

. . . .

This is the *crème de la crème* of vanilla ice creams. Don't balk at the number of vanilla beans: They're necessary for a truly vanilla-rich cream. The touch of coffee gives the ice cream that extra layer of flavor. The cooled ice cream mixture may be chilled for several days before freezing, making for an even richer vanilla flavor.

EQUIPMENT: One 1-quart capacity ice cream maker

4 plump moist vanilla beans	6 large egg yolks
2 cups whole milk	¾ cup sugar
3 whole coffee beans, crushed with the back of a knife	1 cup heavy cream

1. Flatten the vanilla beans and cut them in half lengthwise. With a small spoon, scrape out the seeds and place them in a bowl. Reserve the pods.

2. In a large saucepan, combine the milk, vanilla pods, and coffee beans over high heat. Bring just to a boil, and remove from the heat. Cover, and set aside to infuse for 15 minutes.

3. In the bowl of an electric mixer, whisk the vanilla seeds, egg yolks, and sugar until thick and lemon-colored. Set aside.

4. Strain the milk through a fine-mesh sieve into a large saucepan. Bring just to a boil over high heat. Pour one third of the boiling milk into the egg yolk mixture, whisking constantly. Return this milk and egg yolk mixture to the saucepan. Reduce the heat to low and cook, stirring constantly, until the mixture thickens to a creamy consistency. Do not let it boil. To test, run your finger down the back of a wooden spoon: If the mixture is sufficiently cooked, the mark will hold. The whole process should take about 5 minutes.

5. Remove the pan from the heat and immediately stir in the cream to stop the cooking. Pass the mixture through a fine-mesh sieve, and cool completely before placing the mixture in an ice cream maker. (To speed cooling, transfer the cream to a large

chilled bowl. Place that bowl inside a slightly larger bowl filled with ice cubes and water. Stir occasionally. To test the temperature, dip your fingers into the mixture: The cream should feel cold to the touch. The process should take about 30 minutes.)

For a richer vanilla flavor, prepare the mixture several days in advance, and store, refrigerated, in a sealed container.

6. When thoroughly cooled, transfer to an ice cream maker and freeze according to the manufacturer's instructions.

Yield: 1 QUART ICE CREAM

THE PERFUME OF

VANILLA

Vanilla has become such a common flavoring that we barely acknowledge its exotic, extraordinary qualities. Plump, moist, supple black beans (the best come from Madagascar, Tahiti, and Réunion) are as precious as a great bottle of Champagne or Cognac. All the flavor of a vanilla bean comes from the moist film that coats the seeds inside. While the exterior pod offers little flavor on its own, it still manages to emit a gentle perfume, particularly when buried in a tightly sealed jar of sugar (page 341). Yes, good beans are costly, but they're well worth it. Don't waste money on dried and shriveled beans, for they harbor no magic.

Fresh Plum Tart with Fragrant Almond Cream

Tarte aux Prunes, Crème d'Amandes

. . . .

At Jamin the tart is prepared in the fall with greengage plums, but it's also nice with apricots, purple plums, or nectarines. A tip from Chef Robuchon: When baking plums or any thick-skinned juicy fruit, place them skin side down, cut side up, so that the liquid does not make the pastry shell soggy.

ALMOND CREAM
Scant ½ cup whole blanched almonds
4 tablespoons unsalted butter, softened
⅓ cup granulated sugar
1 large egg, at room temperature
1 large egg white, at room temperature

One 9-inch partially baked puff pastry, shortbread pastry, or sweet pastry shell (pages 344, 353, or 350)
About 20 purple plums (1¾ pounds), cut in half (or substitute greengage plums, apricots, or nectarines)
Confectioners' sugar, for garnish

1. Preheat the oven to 350°F.

2. Prepare the almond cream: In a food processor, process the almonds to a fine powder. Add the butter and sugar, and process until blended. Add the egg and egg white, and process until blended.

3. Pour the almond cream into the prepared shell. Arrange the fruit, cut side up, on top of the cream.

4. Place the tart in the center of the oven, and bake until the almond cream is golden brown and mounds up around the fruit, about 30 minutes.

5. Transfer to a rack to cool. When cool, sprinkle with confectioners' sugar. Serve at room temperature.

Yield: 6 SERVINGS

BITTERSWEET CHOCOLATE MOUSSE

Mousse au Chocolat Amer

. . . .

Now *this* is chocolate mousse. Dip a spoon into this ethereal dessert and you'll understand immediately what the word *mousse* is all about. True to form, Robuchon's version has an extra note—a touch of freshly whipped cream—that takes it beyond the realm of the ordinary.

5 ounces bittersweet chocolate,
    preferably Lindt Excellence, finely
    grated or chopped
2 tablespoons unsalted butter, softened

4 large eggs, separated
1 tablespoon vanilla sugar (page 341)
¼ cup heavy cream, chilled
6 tablespoons confectioners' sugar

1. Melt the chocolate: Place the chocolate in the top of a double boiler set over gently simmering water. (The top container should not touch the water, or the chocolate will melt too quickly. Do not cover the pan, or drops of water will drip into the chocolate and alter its texture.) Add the butter. Stir frequently, and remove from the heat before all the chocolate pieces have melted. The residual heat will melt the remaining pieces. Transfer to a large mixing bowl and set aside to cool.

2. In the bowl of an electric mixer, beat the egg yolks and vanilla sugar until thick and lemon-colored. Whisk this into the cooled chocolate mixture until thoroughly blended.

CHOCOLATE AND

REFRIGERATOR ODORS

. . . .

Chocolate is one ingredient that has a tendency to absorb odors, so always store it well covered, either in its original wrapper or in a sealed container. When storing or refrigerating any dish containing chocolate for more than an hour, be sure to cover it securely—or you're likely to wind up with pickle-flavored chocolate mousse!

3. In the bowl of an electric mixer, whip the cream until stiff. With a rubber spatula, fold the whipped cream into the chocolate mixture until thoroughly blended. Set aside.

4. In the bowl of an electric mixer, combine the egg whites and confectioners' sugar, and whisk until stiff but not dry. Whisk one third of the egg whites into the chocolate mixture and combine thoroughly. With a rubber spatula, gently fold in the remaining whites. Do this slowly and patiently. Do not overmix, but be sure that the mixture is well blended and that no streaks of white remain. Transfer to a 1-quart serving bowl, cover, and refrigerate for at least 1 hour before serving.

Yield: 6 TO 8 SERVINGS

COOL CHERRY SOUP WITH FRESH MINT

Soupe de Cerises à la Menthe

. . . .

Reminding me of sunny days in late May, this dessert soup sings a song of spring-time, when the orchards hang heavy with fat, shiny, vermilion cherries. This recipe convinced me that cornstarch, when used sparingly, can turn an otherwise thin, amateur-ish soup into a velvety, elegant liquid. The combination of mint and whole fresh cherries is bright and refreshing, and looks particularly beautiful when served in white porcelain bowls. Do not try to make the soup more than a few hours in advance, for the delicate freshness of the cherries will fade. Warm honey madeleines (page 262) would be a welcome accompaniment.

1 bottle best-quality tannic red wine,
  such as a Côtes-du-Rhône
¾ cup confectioners' sugar
2 teaspoons cornstarch dissolved in 1
  tablespoon water
2 pounds fresh sweet cherries, pitted
  but left whole

24 small fresh mint leaves with stems,
  tied in a bundle
8 small fresh mint leaves, snipped with
  a scissors, for garnish

1. In a very large saucepan, bring the wine to a boil over high heat. Boil until reduced by half, about 5 minutes. Stir in the sugar and dissolved cornstarch. Cook for just 30 seconds, stirring to thicken. Add the cherries and return just to a boil.

2. Carefully transfer the mixture to a large soup tureen. Add the mint bundle, cover, and set aside to infuse for 30 minutes.

3. Remove and discard the mint bundle, and ladle the soup into shallow soup bowls. Garnish with the snipped fresh mint, and serve.

Yield: 6 TO 8 SERVINGS

BASIC RECIPES

....

Préparations de Base

INDIVIDUAL DINNER ROLLS

Petits Pains Parisiens

. . . .

These crusty, wheaty, golden rolls are baked twice daily at Jamin, where the average diner consumes three per meal. The *petits pains* should be consumed the day they are baked, preferably within two to three hours, since there is no oil in the dough to maintain freshness.

EQUIPMENT: A heavy-duty electric mixer; a baking stone

1 package (about 2 teaspoons) active
    dry yeast, or one 0.6-ounce cake
    fresh yeast, crumbled
1 teaspoon sugar

$1\frac{1}{4}$ cups lukewarm water
2 teaspoons fine sea salt
About $3\frac{3}{4}$ cups unbleached all-purpose
    flour, at room temperature

1. Proof the yeast: In the bowl of a heavy-duty electric mixer fitted with a dough hook or paddle, combine the yeast, sugar, and 1 cup of the lukewarm water. Mix to blend. Cover the bowl with a clean cloth and set aside to proof for 15 minutes.

2. Meanwhile, combine $\frac{1}{4}$ cup lukewarm water and the salt in a small bowl. Stir to blend, and set aside.

3. Knead the proofed yeast on low speed, and slowly pour in the salt water. When thoroughly incorporated, add the flour, little by little, until well blended, 2 to 3 minutes. The dough should come away from the sides of the bowl. Depending upon the humidity, you may not need all the flour. Continue kneading at low speed for 12 minutes more. The dough should be firm, smooth, and just slightly sticky.

4. Transfer the dough to a lightly floured surface, and knead it gently by hand for 1 minute. Cover with a damp cloth and let rise for 40 minutes. The dough should rise slightly.

5. Cut the dough into four equal pieces. Roll each piece into a small sausage-shaped roll about 8 inches long. Cut each roll into four equal pieces, each weighing about

1½ ounces. Form each piece into a ball by rolling it between the work surface and the palm of your hand, slightly cupped, bringing the edges under to form a "seam" on the bottom. Place the balls on a baking sheet, about 2 inches apart. (You may need two baking sheets.) Cover with a damp cloth and let rise for 1 hour. The dough should rise slightly.

6. About 40 minutes before baking the bread, place a baking stone in the oven and preheat the oven to 475°F.

7. Just before baking, spray the baking stone with water (a plant mister is ideal). The steam will help the rolls form a good crust. Place the baking sheet in the oven, on top of the baking stone. Bake until the rolls are golden brown, 12 to 15 minutes. (Since most ovens heat rather unevenly, watch carefully and turn the baking sheet if some of the rolls seem to be browning too quickly.) Transfer the rolls to a rack to cool—preferably one that allows air to circulate around the bread—to ensure a firm, crispy crust. Serve still warm from the oven, if possible.

Yield: 16 ROLLS

RUSTIC WHEAT AND RYE BREAD

Pain de Campagne

. . . .

This is the base for the country bread and for the currant and walnut bread that are served with the cheese course at Jamin. These loaves are baked twice daily in the restaurant's kitchen. Because the dough contains a high percentage of rye flour—which has very little gluten—it will not rise as much as dough made only with wheat flour. The bread will also be more dense. The times given for resting and rising are the minimum needed to obtain a nice, firm texture, and are the times used by Jamin's pastry chef and baker, Philippe Gobet.

VARIATIONS

DRIED APRICOT BREAD: With a scissors, cut 1½ cups dried apricots into julienne strips. Add to the dough at the end of the kneading period, kneading for 1 minute more. This bread is particularly delicious with fresh goat cheese.

CURRANT WALNUT BREAD: Add 1 cup black currants and 1 cup walnut halves to the dough at the end of the kneading period, and knead for 1 minute more.

EQUIPMENT: A heavy-duty electric mixer; a baking stone

1 package (about 2 teaspoons) active dry yeast; or one 0.6-ounce cake fresh yeast, crumbled
1 teaspoon sugar
2 cups lukewarm water

About 3¾ cups unbleached all-purpose flour, at room temperature
2 cups rye flour, at room temperature
1 tablespoon fine sea salt
1 tablespoon honey

1. Prepare the starter: In the bowl of a heavy-duty electric mixer fitted with a dough hook or paddle, combine the yeast, sugar, and 1 cup lukewarm water. Mix to blend. Set aside to proof for 15 minutes.

2. Once the yeast has proofed, gradually add 2 cups of the all-purpose flour and 1 cup of the rye flour, and knead at low speed until thoroughly blended, 2 to 3 minutes. The starter will be rather soft and very sticky. Cover the bowl with plastic wrap or with a damp cloth, and let rest at room temperature for at least 30 minutes.

3. Prepare the final dough: In a measuring cup, combine 1 cup of the lukewarm water and the salt, and stir to dissolve the salt. Slowly add the salt water to the starter, along with the remaining 1 cup rye flour. Gradually add the remaining 1¾ cups all-purpose flour, thoroughly incorporating each batch before adding more flour. Knead at low speed for 5 minutes. Add the honey and continue kneading at low speed for another 5 minutes. Add any remaining or additional flour as necessary, and knead until the dough leaves the sides of the bowl, 1 to 2 minutes more. The dough will be wet and sticky because there is a high percentage of rye flour. (Exact proportions will vary according to temperature and humidity, as well as variations in flours.)

4. Transfer the dough to a lightly floured work surface, and knead it by hand for 1 minute. Form it into a ball and return it to the mixing bowl. Cover the bowl with plastic wrap or with a damp cloth, and let rest at least 40 minutes. The dough should rise slightly.

5. Return the dough to a lightly floured work surface and knead it again for 1 minute. Form the dough into a ball and place it on a lightly floured baking sheet or in a large shallow bowl lined with a cloth. Cover with a damp cloth and let rise at room temperature for at least 1 hour. The dough should rise slightly.

6. About 40 minutes before baking the bread, place a baking stone in the oven and preheat the oven to 475°F.

A TASTE OF HONEY

. . . .

Any sweetener, be it sugar, molasses, or honey, helps to make bread rise faster. In this bread, thick, rich honey and rye flour seem to have an affinity for each other. I love to change the kinds of honey I use (strong buckwheat honey is a favorite). Once the bread is baked and toasted, try spreading the toast with the same honey—the blending of flavors is incredible. When adding honey to dough, add it near the end of the kneading period, rather than in the beginning. In this way you'll retain the flavor of the honey while also boosting the dough's rising ability.

7. Transfer the dough to the baking stone. With a razor blade or a very sharp knife, make several long crisscross incisions in the top and sides of the dough so that it can expand evenly during baking. Bake for 20 minutes. Then reduce the oven heat to 375°F and bake until the bread is golden brown and the loaf sounds hollow when you tap the bottom, about 20 minutes more. Transfer the bread to a rack to cool—preferably one that allows air to circulate around the bread—to ensure a firm, crispy crust. Do not slice until the bread is thoroughly cooled; this will allow the crumb to firm up, making for a more attractive bread that is also easier to slice.

Yield: 1 LARGE LOAF

DOUGH HOOK VS. PADDLE

When preparing small quantities of bread, such as this *pain de campagne,* I prefer to knead with the paddle of an electric mixer rather than with a dough hook, for it works the dough better than a hook.

BAKING STONES

Baking stones or tiles placed on the lower shelf of the oven help transform an everyday oven into an old-fashioned brick bread oven. Stones or tiles also help distribute oven heat more evenly, and help absorb moisture from the dough, making for a thick, dense crust. Since oven temperatures (and performances) vary greatly, always keep a careful eye on what's in the oven, adjusting temperatures as needed. Baking stones can be found in many kitchenware shops.

MAYONNAISE

Mayonnaise

. . . .

This is tasty mayonnaise that's easy to make, with a nice slight tang to it. Chef Robuchon suggests using grape seed oil when preparing mayonnaise, because once it is chilled, the mayonnaise will not become too gelatinous, as happens with other oils. Be sure that all ingredients are at room temperature when you begin. The emulsion—the suspension of the particles of oil within the egg yolk—will not take if the oil or the egg yolks are too cold. For best results, rinse the mixing bowl with hot water, then dry it well before you begin.

1 cup grape seed oil (or substitute corn
   or safflower oil)
2 large egg yolks, at room temperature
1 tablespoon imported Dijon mustard,
   at room temperature

Sea salt and freshly ground white
   pepper to taste

1. Place the oil in a glass measuring cup with a pouring spout.

2. In a medium-size bowl, whisk the egg yolks until light and thick. Whisk in the mustard, salt, and pepper, and whisk until the mixture is thick and smooth.

3. Continue whisking and gradually add just a few drops of the oil, whisking until thoroughly incorporated. Do not add too much oil in the beginning, or the mixture will not emulsify. As soon as the mixture begins to thicken, add the remaining oil in a slow and steady stream, whisking constantly. Taste for seasoning. Transfer to a bowl, cover, and refrigerate for up to 5 days.

Yield: ABOUT 1¼ CUPS MAYONNAISE

CURRY SAUCE

Sauce au Curry

. . . .

A versatile sauce, this combination of curry, coconut milk, fruits, and vegetables may be prepared in advance. Serve it with roast chicken, or over rice or pasta. It is an essential ingredient in Jamin's popular appetizer *brochettes de poulet au curry* (page 35).

1 teaspoon unsalted butter
1 small onion, finely chopped
Sea salt to taste
3 tablespoons superfine flour, such as Wondra
2 plump fresh garlic cloves, minced
5 tablespoons curry powder
1 cup unsweetened coconut milk
1 Golden Delicious apple, cored, peeled, and cubed
1 Red Delicious apple, cored, peeled and cubed

1 banana, peeled and cubed
3 cups chicken stock (page 334)
Bouquet garni: several parsley stems, celery leaves, and sprigs of thyme, wrapped in the green part of a leek and securely fastened with cotton twine
1 teaspoon tomato paste
1 medium tomato, cored, peeled, seeded, and chopped

1. In a large saucepan, combine the butter, onion, and a pinch of salt over moderate heat. Cook until softened, about 2 minutes. Add the flour and stir to cook off the floury taste and to thicken, about 2 minutes. Add the garlic, curry powder, coconut milk, apples, banana, chicken stock, bouquet garni, tomato paste, and tomato. Cover, and simmer until the sauce thickens and the flavors have had time to mellow, about 1½ hours.

2. Transfer to a food processor and process until puréed. Pass through a fine-mesh sieve. Taste for seasoning. (The sauce may be prepared up to 3 days in advance. Cover securely and refrigerate.)

3. To serve, reheat gently in the top of a double boiler over simmering water.

Yield: 3 CUPS SAUCE

SEAFOOD VINAIGRETTE

Vinaigrette pour Poissons, Crustacés, et Coquillages

. . . .

A lively and unusual dressing, this vinaigrette adds a depth of flavor to any seafood salad. For best results, do not prepare it more than a few hours before serving.

6 tablespoons mayonnaise (page 323)
2 tablespoons best-quality red wine
   vinegar
¼ cup heavy cream

6 tablespoons aromatic shrimp bouillon
   (page 333)
Sea salt and freshly ground white
   pepper to taste

In a small bowl, whisk together the mayonnaise, vinegar, cream, and bouillon. Season with pepper, and salt if necessary.

Yield: ABOUT 1 CUP VINAIGRETTE

CLARIFIED BUTTER
Beurre Clarifié

. . . .

Since working with Chef Robuchon, who uses clarified butter with intelligence, I always keep a fresh jar of golden clarified butter in my refrigerator. It's particularly handy when you are sautéeing—pears or apples, for example—and don't want those little black bits that result when unclarified butter is heated to very high temperatures.

16 tablespoons (1 cup) unsalted butter

1. Cut the butter into small pieces and place them in the top of a double boiler over low heat. When they have melted, increase the heat to moderate and allow the butter to simmer until it stops crackling, an indication that the butter is beginning to "fry." Remove the pan from the heat and allow the residue to settle to the bottom of the pan. There should be a layer of milk solids on the bottom and a layer of foam on top.

Alternatively, prepare in a microwave: Place the butter in a 1½-quart microwave-safe dish. (Do not use a smaller container, or the butter will splatter all over the oven.) Cover loosely with paper towels. Microwave at full power for 2½ minutes. Remove from the oven and allow the residue to settle to the bottom of the pan. There should be a layer of milk solids on the bottom and a layer of foam on top.

2. With a spoon, skim off and discard the layer of foam. Line a fine-mesh sieve with moistened cheesecloth, and slowly strain the melted butter, discarding the milky solids that remain. Clarified butter may be stored for up to 1 month, refrigerated, in a sealed container. It will solidify as it cools.

Yield: ABOUT ¾ CUP CLARIFIED BUTTER

ON CLARIFIED BUTTER

. . . .

 Clarified butter has a gently nutty aroma and a fine, grainy texture. When used with care, it can heighten the flavors of many dishes.

In its natural state, butter has a high water content (about 16 percent) and a certain percentage (about 2 percent) of nonfat content. It is the water in the butter that makes it spoil more quickly, and the combination of water and nonfatty substances that causes it to blacken when very hot. Clarified butter is, in essence, purified butter, because this process removes the water and nonfatty substances, leaving 100 percent pure butter, which may be stored much longer. The greatest advantage of clarified butter is that it can be heated to high temperatures without burning, and it is particularly welcome when you want clean, perfectly browned fruits, vegetables, or meats.

Clarified butter may be used wherever butter is called for in cooking, but with care. It is the water in unclarified butter that causes it to sputter and foam when heated, a warning signal to turn down the heat. When overheated, clarified butter reacts like overheated oil: It will only smoke.

VINAIGRETTE

Vinaigrette

. . . .

Shall it be one part vinegar to three parts oil, or one to four, for the best vinaigrette? Should you add garlic, mustard, lemon juice, herbs? The "right" solution depends on the greens you'll be dressing, your personal taste, and the quality of the ingredients you have on hand. The choice of fresh greens and fresh herbs—with as much variety as possible—is just as important as the dressing.

This is, essentially, the vinaigrette used to dress the famous tossed green salad served at Jamin. The truffles, of course, are optional, but what an elegant option!

Whenever you roast poultry or meats, toss a spoonful or two of the rich cooking juices into the vinaigrette for extra depth of flavor.

The vinaigrette may be made in batches and kept for several days, refrigerated, in a small jar. Be sure to shake the jar vigorously to reblend the ingredients before tossing the salad.

1 tablespoon best-quality red wine vinegar
1 tablespoon best-quality sherry wine vinegar
Sea salt to taste
½ cup extra-virgin olive oil

Freshly ground white pepper to taste
1 tablespoon minced black truffle (optional)
1 to 2 tablespoons poultry or meat cooking juices (optional)

In a small bowl, whisk together the vinegars and salt. Add the oil in a thin stream, whisking until well blended. Season with pepper to taste. If you are using them, add the truffle and the cooking juices, and stir to blend.

Yield: ABOUT ⅔ CUP VINAIGRETTE

WHISKING TRUC

. . . .

When whisking liquids in a mixing bowl, the bowl has a tendency to move around on a flat surface. A common trick of professionals is to place a towel beneath the bowl, so it stays put.

GINGER SHELLFISH COURT BOUILLON

Court Bouillon pour Crustacés

. . . .

Fragrant with ginger, fennel, anise, and orange, this is a marvelously aromatic court bouillon, ideal for cooking all fresh shellfish. The court bouillon may be prepared several hours in advance, then brought to a rolling boil at cooking time. If you are cooking several particularly large shellfish—such as lobsters—you may need to double the recipe.

EQUIPMENT: One 8-quart stockpot

1 large carrot, cut into thin rings
1 large onion, cut into thin rings
1 celery rib, thinly sliced
2 plump fresh garlic cloves
1 ounce peeled and trimmed fresh
    ginger
Bouquet garni: several parsley stems,
    celery leaves, and sprigs of thyme,
    wrapped in the green part of a leek
    and securely fastened with cotton
    twine

1 teaspoon fennel seeds
1 teaspoon white peppercorns
1 segment of star anise
3 tablespoons coarse sea salt
2 cups dry white wine, preferably a
    Chardonnay
2 teaspoons white vinegar
Grated zest (orange rind) of 1 orange

In a large stockpot, combine 4 quarts water with the carrot, onion, celery, garlic, ginger, bouquet garni, fennel seeds, peppercorns, anise, and salt. Cover, and bring to a boil over high heat. Reduce the heat and simmer gently for 20 minutes. Add the wine, vinegar, and orange zest, and simmer for 5 minutes more. To cook shellfish, bring to a rolling boil before immersing the shellfish. (Strained, the court bouillon may be refrigerated for up to 2 days. Do not freeze, for it could turn bitter.)

Yield: 4 QUARTS COURT BOUILLON

ADVICE ON COOKING

WITH WINE

. . . .

In recipes such as this, where vegetables and wine are combined, always add the wine at the end. If added at the beginning, the acidity of the wine would prevent the vegetables from cooking thoroughly.

RICH FISH STOCK

Fumet de Poisson, Façon Joël Robuchon

. . . .

Rich and multidimensional, this isn't your basic fish stock, which is generally a rather neutral liquid without much personality. What makes this stock different? The flavorful fish bones are seared lightly before the liquids are added, creating an additional layer of flavor. Use any nonoily fish bones, such as red snapper and sole. For a pure, well-flavored stock, thoroughly rinse the bones, heads, and trimmings.

2 pounds nonoily fish bones, heads,
    and trimmings (gills removed), cut
    up
2 tablespoons extra-virgin olive oil
1 shallot, chopped
1 medium onion, chopped
3 ounces mushrooms, trimmed,
    cleaned, and chopped

Sea salt to taste
6 tablespoons dry white wine,
    preferably a Chardonnay
5 cups water
Bouquet garni: several parsley stems,
    celery leaves, and sprigs of thyme,
    wrapped in the green part of a leek
    and securely fastened with cotton
    twine

1. Thoroughly rinse the fish bones, heads, and trimmings under cold running water, so that no blood remains and the water runs clear, about 5 minutes. Drain and set aside.

2. In a large saucepan, combine the oil, shallot, onion, and mushrooms over low heat. Cook until softened, about 5 minutes. Add the fish bones, heads, and trimmings, increase the heat to high, and cook for 5 minutes more.

3. Season lightly. Add the wine, and boil for 15 seconds to remove the wine's acidity. Add the 5 cups water and the bouquet garni, and simmer, uncovered, for 20 minutes.

4. Remove the pan from the heat and set aside for 10 minutes, to allow impurities to settle to the bottom.

5. Line a sieve with moistened cheesecloth, set the sieve over a large bowl, and ladle—do not pour—the stock into the prepared sieve. Rinse out the saucepan and

return the strained stock to the pan. Boil until reduced to 3¼ cups, about 5 minutes. Cool at room temperature. Once cooled, transfer the stock to a sealed container. The stock may be refrigerated for 2 to 3 days, or frozen for up to 1 month.

Yield: 3¼ CUPS FISH STOCK

NOTES ON STRAINING

. . . .

When straining stock, never pour the liquid from the vessel through the strainer, or you are likely to pass unwanted impurities through the strainer. Rather, set the stock aside for at least 10 minutes, to allow the impurities to settle to the bottom. Then ladle the liquid into a sieve lined with moistened cheesecloth.

AROMATIC SHRIMP BOUILLON

Bouillon de Crevettes

. . . .

T his shrimp bouillon is an amazing idea, and after you try this you'll ask yourself, who needs fish stock! The flavors are complex and intense, and you'll find this will serve as an easy, elegant, and deliciously subtle stock for all sorts of seafood dishes.

1 pound raw small or medium shrimp
  (about 35)
Bouquet garni: several parsley stems,
  celery leaves, and sprigs of thyme,
  wrapped in the green part of a leek and
  securely fastened with cotton twine
1 quart water

1. In a medium saucepan, combine the shrimp, bouquet garni, and 1 quart water over moderately high heat. Bring to a boil and skim any impurities that may rise to the surface. Reduce the heat to low and simmer for 20 minutes, skimming occasionally.

2. Remove the pan from the heat, cover, and set aside to infuse for 15 minutes.

3. Line a sieve with moistened cheesecloth, place the sieve over a large bowl, and ladle—do not pour—the bouillon into the prepared sieve. The bouillon may be refrigerated in a sealed container for 2 to 3 days, or frozen for up to 1 month.

Yield: ABOUT 3 CUPS SHRIMP BOUILLON

BOILED CHICKEN AND VEGETABLES/CHICKEN STOCK

Poule au Pot/Bouillon de Volaille

. . . .

This is a great way to make a rich and full-flavored chicken stock while you're making dinner at the same time. Serve the boiled chicken and vegetables with cornichons, mustard, and coarsely ground salt and pepper, or save it to prepare chicken salad sandwiches. The bouillon is strained and reserved for later use.

EQUIPMENT: One 10-quart stockpot

4 pounds chicken trimmings (necks, wingtips, backs), rinsed and patted dry

Sea salt to taste

2 large onions, halved

2 whole cloves

1 chicken (3 to 4 pounds), well rinsed, patted dry, and trussed

3 plump fresh garlic cloves

Bouquet garni: several parsley stems, celery leaves, and sprigs of thyme, wrapped in the green part of a leek and securely fastened with cotton twine

4 large carrots, tied in a bundle with cotton twine

4 leeks, white and tender green parts, trimmed, well rinsed, and tied in a bundle with cotton twine

1 ounce trimmed and peeled fresh ginger

12 whole white peppercorns

1. Prepare the chicken trimmings: In a large stockpot, combine the trimmings, 1 tablespoon salt, and cold water to cover. Bring to a boil over high heat, skimming off any impurities that rise to the surface. With a slotted spoon, transfer the trimmings to a large sieve. Rinse, drain, and set aside. Discard the blanching liquid.

2. Prepare the onions: Spear the onion halves with a long-handled two-pronged fork,

and hold them directly over a gas flame (or directly on an electric burner) until scorched. Stick the cloves in 2 of the onion halves, and set aside. (Scorching the onions will give the broth a richer flavor.)

3. Rinse out the stockpot and add the blanched trimmings and all the remaining ingredients, including the scorched onions. Add cold water to cover, and bring to a boil over high heat. Skim off the impurities that rise to the surface. Reduce the heat and simmer very gently for 3 hours, skimming as necessary.

4. To serve: Remove the chicken and set it aside to drain. With a slotted spoon, remove the vegetables. Discard the bouquet garni, garlic, and ginger. Untie the chicken, carrots, and leeks. Carve the chicken and place the pieces on a large warmed platter. Surround the chicken with the vegetables. Serve immediately, with cornichons, mustard, coarsely ground pepper, and coarse sea salt for seasoning.

5. Finish the stock: Line a fine-mesh sieve with moistened cheesecloth and set it over a large bowl. Ladle—do not pour—the liquid into the sieve. Measure. If it exceeds 3½ quarts, return to moderate heat and reduce.

Yield: ABOUT 6 SERVINGS OF CHICKEN, AND 3½ QUARTS STOCK

LET'S CELEBRATE SPRING

....

It may be too early in the season to dine outdoors, but not to be thinking of it. This menu reminds me of springtime, daffodils, and the season's first strawberries. Uncork a bottle of chilled Champagne for the cheese puffs while you chill a bottle of Rhône Valley Condrieu. With the strawberries, return to Champagne.

....

TINY CHEESE PUFFS
GOUGÈRES

LOBSTER WITH GINGER AND SPRING VEGETABLES
NAGE DE LANGOUSTES AUX AROMATES

THE ULTIMATE STRAWBERRY SHORTCAKE
LE FRAISALIA

BASIC PASTRY

RECIPES

. . . .

Préparations de Base Pâtisserie

CRÈME FRAÎCHE

Crème Fraîche

. . . .

*C*rème fraîche is mature and tangy cream. It resembles sour cream but has better flavor and texture. *Crème fraîche* may be substituted for heavy cream any time you desire a bit of tang. It's excellent in sauces or salad dressings, and it can be whipped, to serve with fruit salad or when preparing *crème Chantilly*.

1 cup heavy cream
1 cup sour cream

1. In a medium-size bowl, whisk the heavy cream and sour cream. Cover, and set aside at room temperature until thickened, about 24 hours.

2. Transfer the mixture to the refrigerator and chill until thick, about 4 hours more. *Crème fraîche* may be stored up to 1 week, refrigerated, in a sealed container.

Yield: 2 CUPS

VANILLA CUSTARD SAUCE
Crème Anglaise à la Vanille

. . . .

Crème anglaise is a delicate egg-thickened custard sauce. This vanilla-rich version is a perfect accompaniment to a variety of desserts.

1 cup whole milk	3 large egg yolks
1 plump moist vanilla bean, split lengthwise	¼ cup sugar

1. In a large saucepan, combine the milk and vanilla bean over high heat. Bring to a boil and remove from the heat. Cover, and set aside to infuse for 15 minutes.

2. Place a large bowl in the refrigerator, and fill a larger bowl with ice. Set aside.

3. In the bowl of an electric mixer, whisk the egg yolks and sugar until thick and lemon-colored, 2 to 3 minutes. When you lift the whisk, the mixture should form a trail, or ribbon, on the surface. Set aside.

4. Return the milk mixture to high heat, and bring to a boil. Pour a little of the simmering milk into the egg yolk mixture, whisking constantly as the milk is added. Return the milk and egg yolk mixture to the milk in the saucepan. Place over low heat and cook, stirring constantly with a wooden spoon, until the mixture thickens, about 1 minute. Do not boil. To test for doneness, run your finger down the back of the spoon: If the mixture is sufficiently cooked, the mark will hold. The sauce should be the consistency of thick cream.

5. Strain the sauce through a fine-mesh sieve into the chilled bowl. Discard the vanilla bean. Place the bowl on the ice to stop the cooking. Stir occasionally to speed up the cooling process. (The sauce may be prepared to this point up to 1 day in advance. Once cooled, cover securely and refrigerate.)

Yield: 1 CUP SAUCE

VARIATION: For coffee-flavored custard sauce, add 2 teaspoons ground espresso coffee beans along with the vanilla beans when infusing. Strain through a fine-mesh sieve lined with moistened cheesecloth, and return to the saucepan.

VANILLA SUGAR

Sucre Vanillé

. . . .

This simple flavoring is a snap to prepare when you are making vanilla ice cream (page 308) or any other vanilla-flavored dishes. Note that the pods of the vanilla bean do not have much flavor on their own. Nonetheless, they infuse the sugar with a rich vanilla scent and flavor.

4 plump moist vanilla beans
4 cups sugar

1. Flatten the beans and cut them in half lengthwise. With a small spoon, scrape out the seeds and place them in a small bowl. Reserve the seeds for another use. Combine the pods and sugar in a jar.

2. Cover securely, and store for several weeks to scent and flavor the sugar. Use in place of regular sugar when preparing desserts.

Yield: 4 CUPS VANILLA SUGAR

SPONGE CAKE

Génoise

. . . .

*G**énoise,* or the classic sponge cake, is one of the few batters that need to be heated slightly before baking. The heat actually begins cooking the batter, making for a moist, homogeneous cake. A perfect *génoise* is not difficult to make, but the directions should be followed to the letter. The trickiest part is folding in the flour so that it is distributed evenly throughout the cake without excessively deflating the batter. For this procedure, I personally find that a balloon whisk, rather than the traditional spatula, is ideal. Be sure to use a cake pan deep enough to allow for the batter to rise as it bakes. I like to use a springform pan. Note that these instructions are for a heavy-duty mixer: If you are using a hand-held mixer, you will need to increase mixing times to attain the volume necessary for a light and airy sponge cake.

EQUIPMENT: One 8-inch springform pan

Unsalted butter, melted, and all-
    purpose flour, for the pan
4 large eggs
⅔ cup sugar

1½ tablespoons clarified butter
    (page 326)
1 cup all-purpose flour, sifted

1. Preheat the oven to 375°F.

2. With a brush, generously coat the bottom and sides of the cake pan with butter. Dust the pan with flour, and tap the sides to distribute it evenly. Shake out the excess and set aside.

3. Prepare a pot of boiling water large enough to support the bottom of a mixing bowl.

4. Place the eggs in the bowl of an electric mixer fitted with a whisk attachment, and whisk until fluffy. Continue whisking and slowly add the sugar in a steady stream, whisking until the sugar has dissolved, 2 to 3 minutes.

5. Place the bowl over the pot of boiling water. With a balloon whisk or hand-held mixer, beat continuously until the mixture is just warm, about 1 minute. (Test the warmth with your knuckle.)

6. Remove the bowl from the heat and return it to the electric mixer. Whisk until the mixture is cool, 2 to 3 minutes more, or until the batter has doubled in volume. The batter should be thick and lemon-colored, and should form a ribbon when the beaters are lifted. (With a hand-held mixer, this will take longer, up to 15 minutes total, depending upon the power of the mixer.)

7. Add the butter, stirring gently to just combine. With a balloon whisk, fold in the flour in several batches, whisking just until thoroughly incorporated. Be sure to lift the batter up well from the bottom of the bowl so that no hidden pockets of flour remain. The batter should be homogeneous, but overmixing at this point will undo all the airiness that was beaten into the eggs at the beginning.

8. Pour the batter into the prepared pan, and smooth the surface with a spatula. Place in the center of the oven and bake until a toothpick inserted in the center comes out clean, 18 to 20 minutes. Remove the cake from the oven and cool in the pan before unmolding.

Yield: ONE 8-INCH CAKE

VARIATION: For a chocolate sponge cake, replace 2 tablespoons of the flour with 1 tablespoon sifted unsweetened cocoa, preferably Dutch processed.

PUFF PASTRY

Pâte Feuilletée

. . . .

Puff pastry consists, essentially, of thin alternating layers of butter and dough, one on top of the other. The process of folding and rolling out serves to create these layers. In the oven, the heat melts the butter, which in turn "fries," and it is this frying that lifts and separates the layers of dough. The pockets that form between the layers are created by the evaporation of the water in both the dough and the butter.

5 tablespoons unsalted butter, melted and cooled	1½ cups all-purpose flour, sifted
½ teaspoon fine sea salt	10 tablespoons unsalted butter, chilled
6 tablespoons water	Several tablespoons all-purpose flour, sifted, for the turns

1. In a small bowl combine the melted butter, the salt, and the water. Stir to blend.

2. Place the flour in the bowl of a food processor. With the motor running, slowly pour the melted butter mixture into the feed tube, and process just until the dough begins to form a ball. The dough should be quite soft but not sticky. (Do not work the dough too much, or it will become elastic and thus difficult to use.) Remove the dough from the bowl and press it together to form a 5-inch square. With a knife, lightly mark an X in the top of the dough (to make it easier to form in step 4). Wrap in waxed paper and refrigerate for at least 30 minutes.

3. Just before removing the dough from the refrigerator, cut the chilled butter into 2 pieces and place on a piece of waxed paper. With a rolling pin, slowly pound the butter to flatten it into a 4-inch square. Use the paper to help even the edges. The pounded butter should have the same consistency as the dough.

4. Lightly dust the work surface with flour. Unwrap the dough and place it on the work surface. With a knife, lightly re-mark the X in the center of the dough. With the heel of your hand, press out 4 corners from the center of the dough, leaving in the center a slight mound just a bit larger than the 4-inch square of butter. Roll the rolling pin over the 4 corners to thin them. The center mound should be slightly thicker than the 4 corners. Place the pounded butter on top of the center mound. (If necessary,

adjust the butter to fit the dough by shrinking the square of butter.) Fold the dough flaps, one over the other, to cover the butter, as if forming an envelope, creating an even square. With a rolling pin, press down on the edges to seal, making sure that the butter is securely enclosed. Seal thoroughly, especially in the corners, but do not deform the square. Dust lightly with flour.

5. The first double turn: Roll the square out to form a rectangle three times as long as the original square. For a 5-inch square, the rectangle should be 15 inches long. The width will change only slightly. Apply even pressure as you roll, to ensure that the edges remain straight and that the dough does not widen. Dust off the excess flour with a brush. Fold the dough into thirds by bringing the end closest to you two thirds of the way to the other end, and then folding the remaining third over that. This should form a 3-layered 5-inch square. Turn the square to the left, making a 90° turn, so that the "open" end of the fold is on the right and the "closed" side is on the left, as for a book. Roll out to form a 15 × 5-inch rectangle, and fold in thirds again. The first double turn is complete. Gently poke two fingers into the center of the dough to mark the first double turn. Wrap in waxed paper, and refrigerate for at least 30 minutes.

6. The second double turn: Unwrap the dough. On a lightly floured surface, place the "open" side of the dough to the right, and evenly roll out to form a 15 × 5-inch rectangle. Dust off any excess flour. Fold the dough. Rotate the dough again with the "open" end to the right, and repeat the rolling and folding operation one more time. The second double turn is complete. Gently poke the tips of four fingers into the center of the dough to mark the second turn, wrap in waxed paper, and refrigerate for 30 minutes. (The dough may be prepared up to 1 day in advance. Cover securely and refrigerate. It may also be frozen, securely wrapped, for several weeks. Defrost thoroughly—overnight in the refrigerator—before continuing with the third double turn.)

7. The third double turn: Repeat step 6 exactly. Wrap the dough in waxed paper and refrigerate for at least 30 minutes. The puff pastry is now ready to be rolled out and baked as desired.

8. For a partially prebaked flat rimless shell: Divide the pastry into 4 equal parts, each about 4 ounces. Reserve 3 of these portions for another use. Butter the removable bottom of a 10½-inch tart pan. (The rim will not be used here.) Set aside. On a lightly floured surface, carefully roll the dough out to form an 11-inch circle. Place the removable tart bottom on top of the pastry, gently marking the dough lightly with a knife. (This will make it easier to cut, once the pastry is baked.) Slide the tart bottom beneath

the pastry and place it on a baking sheet, so the baked pastry will be easier to transfer. Generously prick the dough and refrigerate for at least 30 minutes.

9. Preheat the oven to 450°F.

10. Remove the prepared pan from the refrigerator. Place another heavy-duty baking sheet on top of the dough, to keep it from rising too much. Place in the center of the oven and immediately reduce the heat to 425°F.

11. Bake just until the pastry begins to firm up, about 10 minutes. Remove it from the oven and with a large sharp knife, carefully trim off and discard the excess pastry. Return the pastry to the oven and bake until it is brown around the edges, about 5 minutes more. Cool for at least 10 minutes (or up to several hours) before filling.

Yield: 1 POUND PASTRY, ENOUGH FOR 4 AVERAGE TARTS

POINTERS FOR SUCCESSFUL

PUFF PASTRY

THE WORK SURFACE. It should be smooth and cool, and more than large enough to roll out the dough. The ideal material is marble, which stays cool. If the surface is unusually warm, place a roasting pan full of ice cubes on top to chill it, but be sure to dry it thoroughly before rolling out the dough. The work surface should be free of all humidity.

BUTTER. Buy the best-quality, freshest butter you can find. High-quality butter has a lower proportion of water, which is desirable. When puff pastry bakes, the water in the butter forms the steam that makes it rise. Too much steam, however, will make for soggy pastry.

TIME. Puff pastry cannot be rushed, and the 30-minute rest period between turns must be respected. Each time you work the dough, you activate the gluten, making the dough more elastic. Rolling and handling the dough also warms the butter, increasing the chances of butter seeping out the sides when it bakes. The resting time allows the gluten to relax and also keeps the butter at the proper temperature.

EQUAL CONSISTENCY. The original dough and the pounded butter should have the exact same consistency. This is why it is important to pound the butter with a rolling pin, which makes it more supple and more like the dough into which it will be incorporated. Be sure to work quickly with the butter, so it stays cold and later does not bleed into the dough.

ROLLING. Before the square is rolled into a rectangle, press down on the top and bottom with the rolling pin. This helps to "set" the shape of the dough and keep the edges straight. Also, when rolling, keep the pressure evenly in the center: Too much strength on one side or the other will result in unevenly rolled dough, and the resulting pastry will rise unevenly. Do not press so strongly that the butter is forced out the sides. Do not pierce any air bubbles; they will disappear of their own accord. Use flour as generously as you like while rolling; just be sure to always dust off the flour once the dough is shaped.

"TURNS." When folding, make sure that all the edges are as even as possible, and that the 3 layers are equally distributed throughout. An uneven edge will cause a gap in the layers when they are folded, and the pastry will not rise properly.

BAKING. When preparing puff pastry for the tarts used in this book, roll the dough, then allow the flat sheet of dough to relax for at least 30 minutes in the refrigerator so that the gluten in the flour will relax and the pastry will not shrink while baking. Prick the pastry carefully so that it will not rise too much while baking.

FLAKY PASTRY

Pâte Brisée

. . . .

Light and flaky, this is a quick, easy all-purpose dough for all occasions, for both sweet and savory pastries. As with all pastry, you must work quickly so the gluten in the flour has little chance to develop.

EQUIPMENT: One 9-inch black tin tart pan with removable bottom

9 tablespoons unsalted butter, softened
1 small egg, lightly beaten, at room
  temperature
3 to 4 tablespoons water, at room
  temperature

Pinch of salt
2 cups all-purpose flour, sifted
1 teaspoon unsalted butter, softened,
  for the pan

1. In a food processor, process the butter until very light and smooth. Add the egg and process to blend. Add the water and process to blend. Add the salt and all but 2 tablespoons of the flour, and process just until the flour is incorporated. If the dough is exceptionally sticky, add the remaining 2 tablespoons flour and quickly process again. The dough should not form a ball. Do not overprocess.

2. With a pastry scraper, transfer the dough to a sheet of waxed paper. With your hands, gently form the dough into a ball, and then flatten it into a circle. Wrap in the waxed paper and refrigerate for at least 1 hour or up to 24 hours.

3. Meanwhile, butter the bottom and sides of the tart pan. Set aside.

4. On a lightly floured surface, carefully roll the dough out to form an 11-inch circle. Transfer the dough to the prepared tart pan. Without stretching the dough, lift it up at the edges so it naturally falls into the rim of the pan. With your fingertips, very delicately coax the dough into the rim. There should be a generous 1-inch overhang; allow it to drape naturally over the edge of the pan. Generously prick the dough lining the bottom of the tart pan, and refrigerate for at least 1 hour, or wrap loosely in foil and refrigerate for up to 24 hours.

5. Preheat the oven to 375°F.

6. Remove the prepared pan from the refrigerator. Place it, unwrapped, on a baking sheet. (Do not ignore this step, or you will end up with burnt bits of pastry on your oven floor.) Place the baking sheet in the center of the oven.

7. For a partially baked shell: Bake just until the pastry begins to firm up, about 5 minutes. Remove it from the oven, and with a large sharp knife, carefully trim off and discard the overhanging pastry to create a smooth, well-trimmed shell. Return it to the oven and bake until the pastry is brown around the edges, 8 to 10 minutes more. Cool for at least 10 minutes (or up to several hours) before filling.

For a fully baked shell: Bake 20 minutes more, for a total of about 35 minutes. Watch the pastry carefully. Ovens vary tremendously and the pastry may brown both unevenly and quickly. Cool for at least 10 minutes (or up to several hours) before filling.

Yield: ONE 9-INCH PASTRY SHELL

SWEET PASTRY

Pâte Sucrée

. . . .

At Jamin, this dough is generally prepared in batches five times this size, in a large electric mixer such as a KitchenAid or Kenwood. Chef Robuchon prefers to make it 1 day in advance, so it has time to mellow. The dough for a single pastry shell can easily be prepared in a food processor. If you are in a hurry, chill the pastry in the freezer for 20 minutes rather than in the refrigerator for the allotted hour's time.

EQUIPMENT: One 9-inch black tin tart pan with removable bottom

1 plump moist vanilla bean
4 tablespoons unsalted butter, softened
½ cup confectioners' sugar, sifted
2 large egg yolks, at room temperature

1 cup plus 2 tablespoons all-purpose
　flour, sifted
Pinch of fine sea salt
Unsalted butter, softened, for the pan

1. Flatten the vanilla bean and cut it in half lengthwise. With a small spoon, scrape out the seeds and place them in the bowl of a food processor. (The pod may be used to prepare vanilla sugar, page 341.)

2. Add the butter to the food processor and mix until very light, smooth, and well aerated. Add the sugar and process until thoroughly blended. The mixture should have the consistency of a thick frosting. Add the egg yolks and process to blend. Add 1 cup of the flour and the salt, and process just until the flour is incorporated. If the dough is exceptionally sticky, add the remaining 2 tablespoons flour and quickly process again. The dough should not form a ball. Do not overprocess.

3. With a pastry scraper, transfer the dough to a sheet of waxed paper. With your hands, gently form the dough into a ball and flatten it into a circle. Wrap and refrigerate for at least 1 hour, or up to 24 hours.

4. To line a tart pan or ring: Butter the bottom and sides of the tart pan, and set aside. Place a large piece of waxed paper on a flat surface. Place the dough on the waxed paper, and carefully roll it out to form an 11-inch circle. Invert the dough (dough side down, paper side up) into the prepared tart pan. Peel away and discard the waxed

paper. Without stretching the dough, lift it up at the edges so that it naturally falls into the rim of the pan. With your fingertips, very delicately coax the dough into the rim. There should be a generous 1-inch overhang; allow it to drape naturally over the edge of the pan. Generously prick the dough lining the bottom of the tart pan, and refrigerate for at least 1 hour, or wrap loosely in aluminum foil and refrigerate for up to 24 hours.

To prepare a hand-trimmed shell: Butter the bottom of the tart pan and set aside. On a lightly floured surface, carefully roll out the dough to form a 9-inch circle, setting aside the excess dough. Transfer the circle of dough to the prepared pan.

Form the trimming, or tart edge: Take a bit of the excess dough and roll it in your hands to form a small ball. Place the dough ball on a lightly floured work surface. With your fingers fully extended, roll the ball out to form a long, thin strip about the thickness of a chopstick. Apply even pressure while rolling. With a brush dipped in water, dampen the edge of the tart bottom. Gently transfer the dough band to the moistened edge of the tart. (This will ensure that the pieces do not separate during cooking.) Repeat as necessary to form the entire tart edge, moistening the ends of the bands so that they hold together.

Crimp the tart edge: With the small round end of a chopstick, press down on the edge at an angle. Repeat at evenly spaced intervals until the entire edge is crimped.

The keys to successful pastry are simple. All ingredients should be at the same temperature, preferably room temperature, so that one ingredient does not shock another, and so that they interact together to best advantage.

The butter should be well aerated (the food processor is ideal for this), so that the resulting pastry is very crusty. Pastry will be tough—and risks shrinkage—if the dough is overworked after the flour has been added.

If pastry dough is properly made—that is, made with ingredients at the proper temperature, not overworked, and thoroughly pricked after being placed in the tart tin—you should not need a filling of beans or rice for prebaking, for there should be no shrinkage or puffing. Rather, when it is transferred to a tart tin, allow the dough to hang over the edges of the tin a bit. Set the filled tart tin on a baking sheet in the oven, and once the dough is set—after about 5 minutes' baking—trim the pastry with a knife to form a neat, attractive shell.

Generously prick the dough lining the bottom of the pan, and refrigerate for at least 1 hour, or wrap loosely and refrigerate for up to 24 hours.

5. Preheat the oven to 375°F.

6. Remove the tart shell from the refrigerator. Unwrap and place it on a baking sheet. (For tart pans and rings, do not ignore this step, or you will end up with burnt bits of pastry on your oven floor.) Place the baking sheet in the center of the oven.

For a partially baked shell: Bake just until the pastry begins to firm up, about 5 minutes. Remove the shell from the oven and with a large sharp knife, carefully trim off and discard the overhanging pastry to create a smooth, well-trimmed shell. Return it to the oven and bake until the pastry is brown around the edges, about 15 minutes more. Cool for at least 10 minutes (or up to several hours) before filling.

For a fully baked shell: Bake 15 minutes more, for a total of about 35 minutes. Watch the pastry carefully: Ovens vary tremendously and the pastry may brown both unevenly and quickly. Cool for at least 10 minutes (or up to several hours) before filling.

Yield: ONE 9-INCH PASTRY SHELL

SHORTBREAD PASTRY

Pâte Sablée

. . . .

Shortbread pastry is one of my favorites, and this recipe—flecked with vanilla seeds and enriched with egg and almonds—is particularly delicious. The same dough may be used to prepare shortbread cookies: Simply roll out the dough, shape with cookie cutters, and bake. This is exceptional as a base for Chef Robuchon's extraordinary bittersweet chocolate tart (page 279), making a marvelous alliance of "bread and chocolate."

EQUIPMENT: One 9-inch black tin tart pan with removable bottom

1 plump moist vanilla bean
1 large egg yolk, at room temperature
2 tablespoons finely ground blanched almonds
½ cup confectioners' sugar, sifted

¾ cup all-purpose flour, sifted
Pinch of fine sea salt
5 tablespoons unsalted butter, softened
Unsalted butter, softened, for the pan

1. Flatten the vanilla bean and cut it in half lengthwise. With a small spoon, scrape out the seeds and place them in a small bowl. (The pod may be used to prepare vanilla sugar, page 341.) Add the egg yolk, and stir to blend. Set aside.

2. In a food processor, combine the almonds and confectioners' sugar and process until blended. Add the flour and salt and process to blend. Add the butter and process just until the mixture resembles coarse crumbs, about 10 seconds. Add the egg yolk and vanilla seeds, and turn the machine on and off just until the dough begins to hold together, about 10 times. Do not overprocess. The dough should not form a ball.

3. With a pastry scraper, transfer the dough to a sheet of waxed paper. With your hands, gently form the dough into a ball, and flatten it into a circle. Wrap and refrigerate for at least 1 hour, or up to 24 hours.

4. Meanwhile, butter the bottom and sides of the tart pan. Set aside.

5. On a lightly floured surface, carefully roll the dough out to form an 11-inch circle. Transfer it to the prepared tart pan. Without stretching the dough, lift it up at the edges so that it naturally falls into the rim of the pan. With your fingertips, very

delicately coax the dough into the rim. There should be a generous 1-inch overhang; allow it to drape naturally over the edge of the pan. Generously prick the dough lining the bottom of the tart pan, and refrigerate for at least 1 hour, or wrap loosely in foil and refrigerate for up to 24 hours.

6. Preheat the oven to 375°F.

7. Remove the tart shell from the refrigerator. Unwrap and place it on a baking sheet. (Do not ignore this step, or you will end up with burnt bits of pastry on your oven floor.) Place the baking sheet in the center of the oven.

8. For a partially baked shell: Bake just until the pastry begins to firm up, about 5 minutes. Remove the shell from the oven and with a large sharp knife, carefully trim off and discard the overhanging pastry to create a smooth, well-trimmed shell. Return it to the oven and bake until the pastry is brown around the edges, 8 to 10 minutes more. Cool for at least 10 minutes (or up to several hours) before filling.

For a fully baked shell: Bake 20 minutes more, for a total of about 35 minutes. Watch the pastry carefully: Ovens vary tremendously and the pastry may brown both unevenly and quickly. Cool for at least 10 minutes (or up to several hours) before filling.

Yield: ONE 9-INCH PASTRY SHELL

INDEX

. . . .

Basic recipes (*cont.*)
  boiled chicken and
      vegetables/chicken
      stock, 334–335
  clarified butter, 326
  curry sauce, 324
  ginger shellfish court
      bouillon, 329
  individual dinner rolls,
      318–319
  mayonnaise, 323
  rich fish stock, 331–332
  rustic wheat and rye bread,
      320–322
  seafood vinaigrette, 325
  vinaigrette, 328
Basil:
  garnishes, fried, 225
  and tomato tarts, savory,
      73–75
*Basilic, tarte friande aux tomates,
    poivrons, et,* 73–75
Bay scallops, *see* scallop(s), bay
Bean(s):
  green, salad with tomatoes,
      garlic, and shallots,
      66–67
  see also fava bean(s)
Beef, 198, 199
  tenderloin roasted in an
      herb-infused salt crust,
      197–199
Beets:
  with creamy horseradish
      dressing, 57
  and walnuts with walnut oil
      dressing, 69
Betteraves:
  et noix à l'huile de noix, 69
  sauce crème au raifort, 57
Beurre:
  clarifié, 326
  crevettes sautées au, 33
  marinière de pétoncles, 89–90
  rouge, saumon grillé au,
      125–126
  de vanille, ananas caramélisé,
      257–259
Blender, hand, 39
*Boeuf, rôti de filet de, en croûte
    de sel aux herbes,*
    197–199

Bouillon:
  aromatic shrimp, 333
  court, ginger shellfish, 329
  see also stock
Bouillon:
  court, pour crustacés, 329
  de crevettes, 333
  de volaille/poule au pot,
      334–335
Bouquet garni, 75
Bread:
  browning vs. broiling of, 37
  individual dinner rolls,
      318–319
  kneading of, 322
  rustic wheat and rye,
      320–322
  sweeteners in, 321
Butter, 41
  clarified, 326, 327
  fresh shrimp sautéed in, 33
  lemon, bay scallops with
      thyme and, 89–90
  vanilla sauce, warm
      caramelized pineapple
      with, 257–259
  whole grilled salmon fillet
      with red shallot sauce,
      125–126

C

Cabbage:
  creamy, salmon on a bed of,
      127–128
  red, salad with anchovy
      dressing, 55–56
Cakes:
  chocolate almond,
      individual, 285–286
  lemon, with double
      chocolate icing,
      298–299
  sponge, 342–343
*Canette rôtie aux pommes poêlées,
    sauce au miel, et au
    vinaigre,* 154–156
Cannelle:
  glace à la, 306
  *mousse au chocolat à la,
      feuillantines au chocolat,*
      295–297

  turbans de pommes à la,
      303–305
Carottes:
  *carré de porc rôti aux tomates,
      ail, oignons et,* 171–173
  râpées au citron et à l'ail,
      62–63
Carrot(s):
  boneless roast loin of pork
      with aromatic
      vegetables, 171–173
  grated, salad with lemon,
      62–63
Caviar:
  bay scallop bundles with
      oysters and, 141–142
  salad of sea scallops, wild
      mushrooms and,
      103–104
  sea scallops with, 137–138
Caviar:
  *étuvée de noix de Saint-Jacques
      au,* 137–138
  huîtres et noix de pétoncles au,
      141–142
  *salade de noix de Saint-
      Jacques aux girolles et
      au,* 103–104
"Caviar," fresh salmon,
    smoked salmon rolls
    with, 107–108
Céleri:
  *-branche, salade de, au
      Roquefort,* 61
  salade "bonne femme," 70
Celery:
  leaf garnishes, fried, 225
  root and apples in creamy
      mustard dressing, 70
  and Roquefort salad, 61
Cerises:
  clafoutis aux, 273–274
  soupe de, à la menthe, 315
Champignons:
  *côte de veau poêlée aux
      asperges et,* 175–177
  *fricassée de langoustines aux
      courgettes et,* 129–130
  *légumes, et raisins marinés à la
      coriandre,* 93–94
  mouclade façon Joël Robuchon,
      143–144

A NOTE
ABOUT THE AUTHORS

....

PATRICIA WELLS, an American journalist and former reporter for *The New York Times*, has lived and worked in Paris since 1980. Restaurant critic for the *International Herald Tribune*, Patricia is the author of several books, including the award-winning *Bistro Cooking* (winner IACP, 1989). She lives in Paris and Provence with her husband, Walter, news editor of the *International Herald Tribune*.

French chef JOËL ROBUCHON is considered the top chef working in France today. French critics and fellow chefs unanimously agree that his carefully considered cuisine—filled with intense, unmasked flavors—sets a new standard for modern French cooking. He is chef-proprietor of Jamin, a small Paris restaurant that has held Michelin's highest three-star rating since 1984. He lives in Paris with his wife, Janine, and their two children, Eric and Sophie.